4.94

Empowering Parents, Families, Schools, and Communities During the Early Childhood Years

Second Edition

Kevin J. Swick
University of South Carolina – Columbia

Copyright @ 2004, 2009
Stipes Publising, L.L.C.
ISBN 1-58874-854-5

Published by

Stipes Publishing L.L.C.
204 W. University Ave.
Champaign, Illinois 61820

About the Author

Kevin J. Swick is a Professor of Early Childhood Education at the University of South Carolina, Columbia, South Carolina. Dr. Swick has worked with parents, families, schools, and communities for many years. He has published over 100 journal articles and over 20 books and monographs on parent and family issues in early childhood education. He is currently involved in working with several early childhood family programs in South Carolina and throughout the U.S.. He teaches family involvement and parent/family dynamics courses in the Early Childhood Education Program at the University of South Carolina – Columbia. He received his Ph.D. in Education from the University of Connecticut in 1970.

TABLE OF CONTENTS

LIST OF FIGURES

INTRODUCTION

Traditional ideas about parent and family involvement are no longer adequate to creating strong parent-family and community involvement in schools and in the lives of children. Our ever changing society includes many new challenges and problems (Skolnick, 1991; Pipher, 1996; Swick, 2007): AIDS, drug abuse, threats from crime, global terrorism, illiteracy, excessive work-family stress, loss of traditional family supports, and increased mental health problems. In addition, chronic poverty, homelessness, and lack of basic resources strain the fiber of many families (Edin & Lein, 1997; The Annie E. Casey Foundation 2008 Kids Count Data Book, 2008).). These stressors have changed the dynamics of parenting, family life, and family-school-community relations (Swick, 2004).

The concept of family itself is broader and more encompassing of the many forms and structures of which it is comprised. In contrast to the narrowly conceived "nuclear family," today's family is more diverse. Families come in many forms: single parent, stepparent, two parents, intergenerational, foster parent, and in other structures. Indeed Rankin (2002) cites Elkind's concept of the "vital family" as more symbolic of family dynamics. The vital family is more focused on human relationships and on helping each other develop as caring and loving persons. This is the concept of family that is explored in this book.

It is also important to note that parents, families and communities are showing more skills, talents, and possibilities for strengthening children's learning and development (Swick, 2001). Indeed, many parents and families are using new ways to address these stressors: full time part-time work, extended family leave, stay-at-home dads, increased use of preschool early learning programs, acquisition of higher levels of education, and increased individual involvement in community enhancement (File, 2001; Gonzalez-Mena, 2009). Parents and schools are creating new elements in their partnership such as after-school care, summer programs, creative "serve and learn" projects, and more effective transition to school strategies. Communities are also getting into the act through more shared training, business/industry involvement, and other leadership activities (Amatea, 2009).

An Empowerment Approach

Early childhood educators need to craft and use responsive concepts and strategies in involving parents, families, and communities in strengthening children's early learning and development. Constructs that are integral to this process: empowerment, partnership, ecological framework, at-risk, and special needs. *Empowerment* aims to enable parents, families, and communities to gain more control over the settings in which all human beings grow and develop. At an individual level, empowerment refers to the skills and dispositions that enable parents and citizens to use education and schools as means for strengthening their position in nurturing and supporting children's learning and development (Bronfenbrenner, 1979, 1986, 2005). For example, Comer (1997) notes that his parents returned from school conferences with increased confidence in their efforts to guide their children in achieving success in school. At a group level such as in a family, empowerment refers to the process where people gain competence in sharing and helping each other become stronger as individuals and as a community (Beck-Gernsheim, 2002). For example, family-friendly work place practices such as allowing time off to care for a sick child increase parental competence in family and work functions (Schorr, 1997; Gonzalez-Mena, 2009). It is this concept of empowerment that is used throughout the book.

The Ecological Framework

The *ecological framework* refers to the totality of the environment in which families function (Bronfenbrenner, 1979, 2005). It attempts to convey that what happens to any person in the family impacts the total family dynamics. It is also conveying the reality that families are part of larger systems such as neighborhoods, schools, communities, and indeed of the powerful ecology of public policy making. Thus, throughout the book the reference to an ecological framework or ecological perspectives refers to the realities of how family members and surrounding environments impact families.

Bronfenbrenner's bio-ecological approach to understanding families is helpful because it is inclusive of all of the systems in which families are enmeshed and because it reflects the dynamic nature of actual family relations. It is also based on the idea of empowering families through understanding their strengths and needs. Each system (micro, exo, meso, macro, and chrono) interacts with the other systems and thus this dynamic process involves families in ever changing contexts and experiences (Swick & Williams, 2006). Indeed, each system depends on the contextual nature of the person's life and offers an evergrowing diversity of options and sources of growth. For example, because we potentially have access to these "systems" we are able to have more social knowledge, an increased set of possibilities for learning problem solving, and access to new dimensions of self-exploration.

2

Two additional constructs used in the book are: at-risk and special needs (Swick, 2004). *At-risk* is used to convey the kinds of situations that may cause harm to families. The use of this term does not suggest that families in these situations are less capable than other families. Likewise, *special needs* is used as a term that conveys the particular stressful contexts that all families experience over the life span. This is different in that in some cases special needs are also used to refer to particular challenges a child may face. Thus, wherever possible when the term is used it is clarified as related to the family or to the child or both, depending on the situation. The use of these terms is done so in a dynamic way, showing how families respond to situations that often impede their functioning. Empowerment is used as a construct to show how these situations can be changed by families and by early childhood professionals.

A Partnership Focus

Partnership is about the process of sharing goals, strategies, resources, and ownership of the education and support of children (Swick, 1991). It implies that each of the parties (families, schools, and communities) have shared interest in and ownership of the education and nurturance of children and themselves. Partnership strategies are integral to the success of early childhood education programs. It is a construct, however, that has yet to be fully realized. Too often teachers see partnerships with families as where parents and other family "assist teachers" with tasks they need accomplished for the school and classroom. And parents are often guilty of seeing partnership in relation to what teachers can do specifically for their child. We need to see the broader implications of partnerships for enhancing and enriching the education of all the people involved in the family-school-community relationship system (Swick, 1991; Lawrence-Lightfoot, 2003; Berger, 2008).

Overview of Chapters

Eight aspects of the empowerment and partnership approach to parent, family, and community involvement are presented and examined in this book: understanding and relating to the key needs of children, understanding parents and families, relating and responding to families, parenting/parent education/family strengthening, building strong partnerships, communication, community involvement, and organizing and using learning resources. Each of these areas is examined in relation to how early childhood educators can strengthen the role and involvement of parents, families and communities in young children's learning and development. The emphasis is on the entire span of the early childhood years (birth through 8 years of age).

Understanding and relating to the needs of children (Chapter One) is the foundation upon which early childhood education is based. Understanding these needs in relation to the concepts of empowerment and partnership as they are enacted within family-school-community is vital to children's well being (Bronfenbrenner, 1979). Three facets of this process are presented and discussed in this book: 1) identification of the key needs of children, 2) explication of how these needs emerge within the context of family-school-community, and 3) discussion of recent challenges families and schools face in trying to meet child needs in effective and appropriate ways.

Initially, Maslow's (1959) hierarchy of needs is described and used as a foundation for understanding children's emerging needs. Then Erikson's stages of psycho-social development are presented. Bronfenbrenner's (1979) ecological perspective is used to contextualize these needs in relation to how children grow and learn. Brazelton and Greenspan (2000) identify key "irreducible needs" of children. These needs are explored in relation to the ecology of human growth and learning. Possible ways for families, schools, and communities to support children in meeting these needs is also examined.

Understanding parents, families and communities is key to building and sustaining strong partnerships (Chapter Two) Early childhood educators need to pursue their development of attitudes, skills, and perspectives that focus on truly empathizing with the situations that families and communities face. Further, early childhood educators need to understand their own perspectives in this regard. A key to understanding families is in our self-renewal in developing and enhancing our perspectives of families and children. Thus, we need to explore how parent and family empowerment can emerge within family-school-community partnerships (Swick, 1991, 2004).

Four questions guide the presentation in this chapter of the book:

1) What are some useful tools and strategies we can use to strengthen our understanding of the needs of parents, families, and communities?

2) What are some viable theoretical and research perspectives for helping us gain better insights into the needs of parents, families, and communities?

3) What are some of the key conceptual and practical issues in understanding how parents, families, and communities deal with the challenges they experience in supporting children?

4) How can we better conceive the links between parents, families, communities and early childhood professionals as related to creating a stronger learning system for children and adults?

Relating and responding to families diverse strengths and needs is essential for positive relations with all families (Schorr, 1997). (Chapter Three) Through our interactions with families and communities, early childhood educators gain insights into the dynamics of family differences, how these are influenced by community life, and how these factors influence children's own growth and development. Through this learning process we come to understand that families seek health, desire goodness, and yet must negotiate the continuing stressors of their lives (Garbarino, 1992; Elkind, 1994). This chapter of the book explicates the key elements of a "framework" to use in understanding and then relating to family differences. This framework is rooted in the empowerment and partnership constructs and emphasizes the dynamics of a continuum of family types that are ever changing such as: healthy, special needs, at risk, and dysfunctional. The framework embraces and explains the value of a strengths approach while also recognizing the value of using diagnostic strategies in an empathic way. Families are indeed the key to any learning and development model, and this chapter offers insights and ideas on how to carry out this empowerment process.

In particular, *cultural differences and the different learning styles that accompany family differences are discussed and related to the partnership development process.* For example, early childhood educators may use parent leadership teams to promote better understanding and use of parent and family talents and skills. Additional strategies such as parent networking offer excellent growth opportunities.

The continuing learning and growth of parents is central to having strong family/school/community partnerships (Swick, 2004). (Chapter Four) Early childhood educators often refer to parents as the "child's first and most powerful teacher." The parents' sense of efficacy and growth is interrelated with their parenting and family leadership dispositions and activities (Powell, 1989). The explication of the key elements of parental integrity (which is a major facet of this chapter) enables educators and citizens to realize how powerful parenting is in strengthening families and communities (Pipher, 1996; Evans, 2004). A major support is the "education and growth" of parents in relation to their personal, parental, and community/work and career roles. This chapter explores various parent education and family literacy/strengthening concepts and strategies with the aim being to engage professionals, parents, and citizens in activities and processes that further strengthen their position as family leaders and helpers. In particular, the needs of high-risk parents and families are explored in relation to strategies and supports that make a difference in their functioning. The uses of parent networking, family strengthening strategies, and community empowerment efforts for strengthening families in difficult and often debilitating situations are especially emphasized and discussed.

A key construct in this chapter of the book is that parent education and family literacy can be early intervention and prevention factors in the lives of families. For example, engaging parents in appropriate and enjoyable literacy activities with their children is a powerful school readiness process for everyone in the family.

What are the important elements of strong parent/family/school/ community partnership and how do we pursue this process? These are two questions explored in Chapter Five of the book with particular emphasis on looking at parents and teachers as the real leadership team in the child's life (Comer, 1997). In addition, the components of a framework for building such partnerships is discussed, strategies and resources presented, and some ideas on how to continually refine this process is also explicated.

In particular, the elements of successful partnerships are presented and related to program practices that make a positive difference in the lives of children and families. In addition, examples of how these elements can be integrated into programs are discussed. This chapter presents several strategies that have proven effective in the partnership effort. For example, the use of conferences to help parents and teachers develop the needed understandings for their collaboration is reviewed. Other such strategies are also examined in relation to partnership development and renewal.

Communication is key to having and sustaining long-term partnerships (Swick, 1991). (Chapter Six) The processes of communication provide the means for parents, teachers, and citizens to share goals, concerns, and to eventually craft their vision for having effective learning environments. The core elements of this process are examined in this chapter of the book, with a focus on how to empower parent-teacher and family-school-community partnerships with meaningful and effective communication. Teacher and parent attitudes and skills as linked to communication are related to various aspects of the partnership construct. Cultural, nonverbal, and other particular aspects of communication are linked to some of the barriers and issues that professionals and parents face when trying to craft useful and effective strategies for nurturing children's learning and development. Further, strategies for achieving positive communication are explored relative to parents and families who typically do not participate in these aspects of their children's education.

Important relationship functions that communication can impact are validation and feedback-refinement. Critical to individual and partnership growth is the realization that one is important to the human processes that help to make life meaningful. Likewise, parents and professionals need each other's feedback to further empower themselves. These aspects of the communication process are examined in relation to how they can strengthen partnerships.

Families and schools can only achieve what communities value and support (Bronfenbrenner, 1979; Pipher, 1996). (Chapter Seven) Early childhood educators are seeking to strengthen community development and involvement. This chapter examines the following aspects of the "community" dimension of the family-school-community partnership:

1) How can communities become a more significant part of the lives of children and families? (Couchenour & Chrisman, 2000)

2) What collaboration success stories in real communities provide insights into creating more empowering family-centered early childhood practices? (Swick, 2004)

3) How can early childhood educators equip parents and families with skills and dispositions for effectively using and contributing to the community? (Pipher, 1996)

4) What key strategies can communities use to promote school readiness and thus strengthen entire communities for the long-term? (Comer, 1997)

5) How can communities be activated to become more like "learning centers" where children and families have multiple educational opportunities? (Thornton, 2001)

In the final chapter of the book, *a variety of strategies professionals and parents/citizens can use to sharpen their partnership building skills are presented*. (Chapter Eight) The realization of a "learning community" where early childhood educators, parents, and citizens learn and grow through continuing education is key to both the empowerment and partnership constructs (Swick, 2001). In addition to describing these resources for strengthening and renewing parent/family-school-community partnerships, several examples of how these resources might be deployed are presented. For example, the manner in which parents and teachers can use professional early childhood resources to be more effective in advocating for stronger community participation is explored.

Recurring features in each chapter in the book include "capsules" that open each chapter with a brief overview of key ideas; specific objectives for each chapter; case application activities that invite the reader to apply concepts presented; summative discussions, and listings of relevant web sites and references.

References

Amatea, E. (2009). Building culturally responsive family-school relations. Columbus, OH: Pearson.

Beck-Gernsheim, E. (2002). Reinventing the family: In search of new lifestyles. Malden, MA: Blackwell (Polity).

Berger, E. (2008). <u>Parents as partners in education: Families and schools working together</u>. Seventh Edition. Columbus, OH: Pearson.

Brazelton, T., & Greenspan, S. (2000). <u>The irreducible needs of children</u>. Cambridge, MA: Perseus.

Bronfenbrenner, U. (1979). <u>The ecology of human development</u>. Cambridge, MA: Harvard University Press.

Bronfenbrenner, U. (1986). Alienation and the four worlds of childhood. <u>Phi Delta Kappan 67</u> 6: 430-436.

Bronfenbrenner, U. (2005). <u>Making human beings human: Bioecological perspectives on human development</u>. Thousand Oaks, CA: Sage.

Comer, J. (1997). <u>Waiting for a miracle: Why schools can't solve our problems – and how we can</u>. New York: Dutton.

Couchenour, D., & Chrisman, K. (2000). <u>Families, schools, and communities: Together for young children</u>. New York: Delmar.

Edin, K., & Lein, L. (1997). <u>Making ends meet: How single mothers survive welfare and low-wage work</u>. New York: Russell Sage Foundation.

Elkind, D. (1994). <u>Ties that stress: The new family imbalance</u>. Cambridge, MA: Harvard University Press.

Evans, R. (2004). <u>Family matters: How schools can cope with the crisis in childrearing</u>. San Francisco, CA: Jossey-Bass.

File, N. (2001). Family-professional partnerships: Practice that matches philosophy. <u>Childhood Education 56</u> 4: 70-74.

Garbarino, J. (1992). <u>Children and families in the social environment. Second Edition</u>. New York: Aldine de Gruyter.

Gonzalez-Mena, J. (2009). <u>Child, family, and community: Family-centered early care and education</u>. Fifth Edition. Columbus, OH: Pearson.

Greenspan, S. (2000). <u>Building healthy minds</u>. Cambridge, MA: Perseus.

Lawrence-Lightfoot, S. (2003). <u>The essential conversation: What parents and teachers can learn from each other</u>. New York: Random House.

Maslow, A. (1959). <u>New knowledge in human values</u>. New York: Harper & Row.

Pipher, M. (1996). <u>The shelter of each other: Rebuilding our families</u>. New York: G.P. Putnam's Sons.

Powell, D. (1989). <u>Families and early childhood programs</u>. Washington, DC: National Association for the Education of Young Children.

Rankin, N. (2002). Introduction. In S. Hewlett, N. Rankin, & C. West. (Eds.). <u>Taking parenting public: The case for a new social movement</u>. New York: Rowman and Littlefield.

Schorr, L. (1997). <u>Common purpose: Strengthening families and neighbor-hoods to rebuild American</u>. New York: Anchor Books/Doubleday.

Skolnick, A. (1991). <u>Embattled paradise: The American family in an age of uncertainty</u>. New York: Basic Books.

Swick, K. (1991). <u>Teacher-parent partnerships to enhance school success in early childhood education</u>. Washington, DC: National Education Association.

Swick, K. (1994). Family involvement: An empowerment perspective. <u>Dimensions of Early Childhood 22</u>: 10-14.

Swick, K. (2001). Nurturing decency through caring and serving during the early childhood years. <u>Early Childhood Education Journal 29</u> 2: 131-137.

Swick, K. (2004). <u>Empowering parents, families, schools and communities during the early childhood years</u>. Champaign, IL: Stipes.

Swick, K. (2007). The dynamics of families who are homeless. In K. Paciorek. <u>Annual Editions: Early Childhood Education 06/07</u> (48-53). Dubuque, IA: McGraw Hill.

Swick, K., & Williams, R. (2006). An analysis of Bronfenbrenner's bio-ecological perspective for early childhood educators: Implications for working with families experiencing stress. <u>Early Childhood Education Journal</u>, *33 (5),* 371-378.

<u>The Annie E. Casey Foundation 2008 Kids Count Data Book: State Profiles of Child Well-Being</u>. Baltimore, MD: The Foundation.

Thornton, A. (Ed.). (2001). <u>The well-being of children and families: Research and data needs</u>. Ann Arbor, MI: The University of Michigan Press.

10

Chapter One

Understanding and Relating to the Needs of Children

CAPSULE: Early childhood professionals and parents gain tremendous power to be caring adults when they learn about children's needs and the growth process. Knowledge is indeed power as adults become skilled in relating and responding effectively to children's needs.

Chapter One Objectives:

1) Enhance your knowledge and understanding of children's essential needs, especially as portrayed in Maslow's hierarchy and in Erikson's stages of psycho-social development.

2) Strengthen your understanding of children's needs through gaining insights from the "irreducible needs" framework presented by Brazelton and Greenspan.

3) Increase your knowledge and insight into children's important learning needs, especially their development of a positive attitude toward learning and their skills in becoming life long learners.

4) Enhance your understanding and skills in developing family-school-community caring environments for children.

5) Strengthen your understanding of the various challenges we face in developing and sustaining caring environments for children.

6) Increase your knowledge and insight into how Bronfenbrenner's bio-ecological systems perspective can be used to provide children with more caring and nurturing environments.

7) Enhance your understanding of children's contexts and resources and how these sources can be used to strengthen children's learning.

The aim of strong early childhood family-school-community partnerships is to enhance and enrich children's development and learning. The focus of this chapter is on helping early childhood educators review and reflect upon the needs of children and how we can support children in reaching their full potential. This chapter emphasizes the formative years (birth to 8 years of age) through a discussion of important concepts and ideas about children's needs as interrelated with their development and learning.

To be responsive to parent and family needs we must fully understand children's growth and functioning. Seven topical themes comprise the focus: 1) Maslow's hierarchy of needs (with special focus on the 0 – 8 years age range); 2) Erikson's stages of psycho-social development; 3) Bronfenbrenner's ecological system for relating children's needs to their various contexts; 4) The irreducible needs of children as presented by Brazelton and Greenspan; 5) Key growth and learning experiences that are essential to children's optimal development; 6) Family-school-community as caring environments for children; and 7) Challenges families, schools, and communities face in creating a caring learning arrangement. Each of these topics is reviewed with special emphasis on how this information can be integrated into strong early childhood family-school-community partnerships that value and support children and families from diverse cultural and social contexts.

Maslow's Hierarchy of Needs

To Abraham Maslow (1968) the most important aspect of children's lives was their engagement in continual growth and learning. He saw "growth" as the most essential facet of all human life. But to be able to interact in the world effectively Maslow (1959, 1968) noted that our human needs must be adequately met. He outlined five levels of a "Hierarchy of physical, emotional, and intellectual needs" he used to help people guide their understanding of development and learning. Each level (Figure 1.1) depicts needs that are vital to the person's continuing growth.

Figure 1.1
Maslow's Hierarchical Levels of Human Needs

---

*Level 1 – Essential physical/body needs

*Level 2 – Essential safety, security, protection needs

*Level 3 – Essential love, affection, care needs

*Level 4 – Essential esteem and self-esteem needs

*Level 5 – Self-actualization needs

12

✱ Level 1 – Essential physical/body needs: This is the "basic needs" level where infants, toddlers, and children need food, water, and interactions that allow them to develop their physical and body skills. For example, it is known that chronic, severe malnutrition can cause serious damage to the child's developing brain – which in turn may limit the child's functioning (Eliot, 1999; Restak, 2003). Likewise, we know that primary grade children need nutritious lunches and a balance between work and play to be effective learners.

✱ Level 2 – Essential safety, security, and protection needs: To grow and be engaged in learning, children must be safe and feel secure in their relations with people and the environment. As Gonzalez-Mena and Eyer (2001) note, Maslow valued children's learning to manage their lives through appropriate interactions with the ecology. For example, children need protection from toxins in the home. We need to make sure our home and child care environments are clear of any poisons or other toxic substances (Gonzalez-Mena, 2006). Children also need safe schools where they feel secure in their daily lives. This protective function also offers us the opportunity to teach children about ways they can begin to self-manage and care for themselves (Thornton, 2001).

✱ Level 3 – Essential love, affection, and care needs: Perhaps more than any other learning that happens from birth through eight years of age, Maslow felt that children need to know they are loved and cared for by nurturing adults. Honig's (2002) advice in this regard is that children need the daily love and care of important adults. A third grade teacher noted that her children respond warmly to her love and care. "They love to be affirmed as they learn new skills and become a part of a learning community."

✱ Level 4 – Essential esteem and self-esteem needs: Maslow (1959) believed that people who have high self esteem sense their value to others and experience mutuality in their social relations. The suggestions of Honig (2002) help us realize how we can actively strengthen the esteem and self-esteem needs in children's growth efforts:

* Lovingly interact with infants, toddlers, and children many times throughout the day.
* Model the social and emotional behaviors you wish for children to learn.
* Establish an environment that supports and nurtures caring and loving relations among children and adults.
* Recognize and support the caring and empathic behaviors of children.

For example, in the primary grades it is important to recognize children's feelings as they attempt to negotiate the stressors of childhood. Their sensitivity to peer pressure and to new learning demands are

13

opportunities to help them gain confidence and new skills (Morrison, 2008).

Level 5 – Self-actualization: These are the needs that relate to children's development of a sense of achievement. Maslow cautions us to realize the development of achievement is ongoing and that our skills for "growing" are the keys to managing our move toward self-actualization.

CASE APPLICATION: Using the hierarchy of needs described, list and briefly explain what you believe are the most important care-giving behaviors early childhood professionals should emphasize during the birth – 3 years of life. Write up an example of one such behavior that shows how that care-giver can meet the needs Maslow describes. Also, show two ways you would apply these behaviors with primary grade children.

Erikson's Stages of Psycho-Social Development

Erik H. Erikson (1982) developed a "stages" construct to represent the major benchmarks in our development as human beings. The eight stages of psycho-social development as put forth by Erikson are briefly described in Figure 1.2.

Erikson is clear that these are dynamic stages of growth where each stage influences the other stages. While Erikson realized the early years were the formative years, he also felt that we can revisit different stages and redress particular issues to make our lives more meaningful. The process of renewal is very important in our lives.

At each stage of development Erikson noted specific actions that could strengthen the person's actualization of a particular stage. An example of how the process might be enhanced by adult involvement during the early years is shared for the first four stages.

Trust vs. Mistrust: Mooney (2000) notes that "parent-child attachment" enhances the infant's development of trust. She (Mooney, 2000, p. 44) states:

> Erikson stressed how important it is for babies to have significant relationships with a few key adults in order to accomplish the task of developing basic trust.

Further, as Gonzalez-Mena (2009) suggests, the attachment process is the very core of our emerging personality development. During the attachment process infants and toddlers develop a sense of hope and faith in their relations with important others.

Figure 1.2
Erikson's Stages of Psycho-Social Development

Age	Stage	Focus
0-1	Trust vs. Mistrust	Infant learns to trust significant adults and develop initial sense of healthy self esteem.
2-3	Autonomy vs. Shameand Doubt	Toddler learns to acquire a sense of autonomy and yet maintain healthy interpersonal relations.
4-5	Initiative vs. Guilt	Preschool children begin to develop a sense of purpose. The child is becoming more focused.
6-12	Industry vs. Inferiority	The growing child acquires a sense of being productive as a contributor to family and community.
Adolescence	Identity vs. Role Confusion	The adolescent begins the development of a sense of healthy and growing sense of identity.
Young Adulthood	Intimacy vs. Isolation	The young adult seeks to achieve authentic, caring relations with a significant other.
Middle Age	Generativity vs. Stagnation	The maturing person attains a sense of making a lasting impact on the lives of others.
Old Age	Ego Integration vs. Despair	The ageing adult attains a sense of meaning in their life that relates to their total goodness as a person.

Autonomy vs. Shame and Doubt: When adults provide toddlers with opportunities to assert themselves within safe and supportive settings they can realize their self-development in healthy ways. Learning to become independent while being accepted and valued by significant adults is critical to young children's sense of competence (Brazelton & Greenspan, 2000).

Initiative vs. Guilt: Helping children gain confidence in their self-directed learning efforts is a primary goal of this stage of development. Mooney (2000) tells about Susan's (a first grade teacher) efforts to help children handle this process.

> Susan, who often said to the children she taught, "Life is a work in progress!" She understood that sometimes children need a place to set a project for a while until they decide to come back to it. She encouraged the children to write stories, and her five-year-old students knew what an editor was. They were not afraid to make mistakes. (p. 54)

Children in this stage need adults like Susan who help them develop confidence in their emerging skills.

Industry vs. Inferiority: Ann Susting, a student teacher in a second grade classroom, used service-learning as the core of her unit to help the children see themselves as capable community members. She says "the children were really proud of how their work in the food pantry would help many people less fortunate than them. The pantry manager let them know how important they were to the work of the program." Indeed, Erikson warns that when children are unable to establish their sense of competence they may become very insecure and act out in anger or withdraw into isolation. Thus, strong community service programs can and should become a part of a caring curriculum that fosters a sense of worthiness and value in children (Freeman & Swick, 2003).

CASE APPLICATION: Using the insights gained from Erikson's s stages of psycho-social development, design activities that might help parents and family be more effective helpers of children during the first four stages of development. The big question you are trying to help parents with is: What is really important for parents to do to support children's personal and social development?

Bronfenbrenner's Bio-Ecological System for Relating to Children's Needs

Clearly, children can best meet their essential needs through supportive relations with caring adults. As Garbarino (1992) states:

> The developing infant's basic reality lies in the relationship he or she has to primary care givers – particularly the mother, in most families in most societies. It is impossible for individuals to exist independently of other people. Indeed, that which makes us human is our relatedness –

linguistic, intellectual, economic, political, and religious.
(pp. 11-12)

Children grow and develop within an interrelated set of systems such as the family, neighborhood, church, school, community, work place, and larger society. Very importantly, a culture's beliefs about children and families are influential factors in this bio-ecological perspective (Bronfenbrenner, 2005). To show how children's needs are impacted by the systems in which they live and grow, ***critical applications of Bronfenbrenner's bio-ecological perspective to children's growth needs are highlighted.***

✦ Application to meeting children's essential physical needs: Healthy development and learning require that children's physical needs be met in an adequate manner. While the primary system (the child's family) is the logical place for these needs to be met, as Garbarino (1992) notes, *if indeed the family lacks educational competence and/or needed economic and related resources,* then these needs are not likely to be met. For example, if government policy fails to include nutritional education and needed prenatal care for mothers, children's physical well being is jeopardized (Bronfenbrenner, 2005). Inadequate school food programs also put children at risk. Every facet of the child's environment is a potential influence on that child's healthy physical development. Three points (Presented in Figure 1.3) are noteworthy (Garbarino, 1992; Heymann, 2000; Folbre, 2001).):

Figure 1.3
✗ Three Applications of Ecological Systems
Approach to Children's Lives

---

1) Educate all parents during the prenatal period or prior to about essential nutritional and physical needs of the child and how to meet these needs.

2) Strengthen programs like Women, Infants, and Children (WIC) to provide parents and family with needed food, vitamins, and related education on physical well being.

3) Increase emphasis on strengthening the food and nutrition programs in early childhood centers and schools.

✗ Application to meeting children's essential safety and health needs: Poor health and violence are two interacting forces that have a powerful negative influence on children's well being (Miller, 2001; Noddings, 2002). For example, Garbarino (1992) explicates that in U.S. society, *many harmful behaviors are accepted as discipline* and not recognized as violent even though they often bring harm to the child or spouse. Peaceful problem-solving skills, non-violent behavior, and peace education need attention in the earliest years of life (Swick, 2005). Alice

17

Miller (2001) notes the extreme problems we face in protecting children from violence:

> Today the problem of child abuse looms large in our public awareness. What is less well known is that what we consider a proper upbringing frequently includes severe humiliations thathave far-reaching consequences – humiliations we do not consciously recognize because we have been rendered incapable of perceiving them at the very beginning of our lives. (p. xiv)

It is imperative that early childhood educators advocate for more humane ways of assuring children's safety and health. We need to seek the healthiest environmental conditions in homes, schools, and communities (Brazelton & Greenspan, 2000). This focus on assuring the well-being of children must be a global effort – reaching out to the children and families of all nations (Bellamy, 2002).

★Applications to children's need for love and caring: Beyond all else that happens to children in their life, *love and care* stand out as the most essential needs for their growth (Garbarino, 1992). Three caring elements of children's environments deserve our close attention and are presented in Figure 1.4 (Honig, 2002):

Figure 1.4
★ Three Important Caring Elements for Children

---

1) Parents realize and then carry out attachment and nurturance behaviors that help children feel securely attached and loved.

2) Other adult early childhood care givers also provide children with loving and nurturing relations on a regular basis.

3) Communities learn about and integrate into their ecologies the attributes of love, care, and nurturance. Children need to see and feel love from all parts of the community.

★ Applications to the child's esteem and self-esteem needs: Children have a need to value and hold others in esteem as well as to be recognized as valuable by others (high self-esteem). This process is about the development of trust and mutuality in ourselves as a part of our daily relations with others (Noddings, 2002; Greenspan, 2007). Three applications for parents and early childhood educators are (Sears & Sears, 2002):

1) Provide children with warm, nurturing, and responsive interactions throughout the early childhood years.

2) Support children in developing a positive and growing sense of self esteem.

3) Engage children in experiences that nurture in them caring attitudes and behaviors with others. Learning to care extends children's esteem skills toward valuing and nurturing others.

✗ Applications to children's self-acutalization needs: One of the most insightful principles of Bronfenbrenner's theory is that children need ever-evolving, more complex, rich experiences with many adults that encourage them to be life long learners (Bronfenbrenner, 1979). In effect, our goal as early childhood educators should be to facilitate parent, family, and child in becoming life long learners. In support of children's self-actualization needs, Vygotsky's (1978) sociocultural theory provides a working model for assisting children in using achievement as one means to further grow and learn.

This theory correctly notes that parents and other significant adults can play a major role in children's actualization by engaging in supportive, nurturing, and teaching roles with them (Bransford, Brown, & Cocking, 2000). Three applications to supporting children in self-actualizing ways are noted in Figure 1.5 (Berk, 2001; Sears & Sears, 2002):

Figure 1.5
Supporting Children's Self-Actualization

---

1) Arrange and continually renew interesting and challenging learning environments where children can experience hands-on, people rich learning.

2) Observe and interact with children in supportive and challenging ways related to their learning and use of their new knowledge in productive and satisfying ways.

3) Pay special attention to children's social and emotional learning; our affect toward people and ideas is the most powerful predictor of how we actualize our learning.

Helping children "self actualize" their emotional understanding of relating to others is vital to their total growth and learning.

CASE APPLICATION: Select one facet of the ecology of children's development of caring and show how their early interactions with adults in their lives does indeed influence their eventual development of caring. Develop one example of how an infant or toddler shows the early signals of becoming a caring person. What factors in the environment seem most influential in children's learning about caring?

The Irreducible Needs of Children

Interrelated with Maslow's hierarchy of needs for human growth and learning are the "irreducible needs" of all children as delineated by Brazelton and Greenspan (2000). These needs reflect some of the seminal work of Maslow and provide an important view of how needs take shape in contemporary society. In the rationale for the "irreducible needs" of children, Brazelton and Greenspan (2000) speak to the urgency for our attention to these needs:

> In essence, behind the competitive advantage in evolution, lies nurturing care. The long period of dependency of human beings provides an opportunity for human beings to develop emotionally-based psychological capacities during a long childhood of protection and care.

The nurturance of children toward human competence is essential for the health and well-being of society.

The first "irreducible need" discussed by Brazelton and Greenspan (2000) is *the need for ongoing nurturing relationships.* This is a need area noted by Erickson, Freud, Maslow, and others as it speaks to the very foundation of our being. This need area, when fully developed, energizes us in the sense of our believing that we are significant people in the world, and that we are surrounded by caring and loving people (Honig, 2002). It is also noteworthy that recent research on children's early brain development strongly suggests that a lack of caring and nurturing relationships with adults can actually impede the parts of the brain that helps us manage and express our emotions (Bransford, Brown, & Cocking, 2000; Zigler et al, 2002). Chronic stress because of threats in the ecology, abusive relations with others, malnutrition, or consistent exposure to violence are risk factors that eventually destroy the emotional fabric of children and contribute to their lack of trust in the world around them (Garbarino, 1992; Greenough et al, 2001; Nelson et al, 2008).

Meeting this need of ongoing nurturing relationships with parents, family, caregivers, and other significant adults, provides children with a context and direct experiences for learning how to care (Noddings, 2002). As Brazelton and Greenspan point out:

> Supportive, warm, nurturing emotional interactions with infants and young children help the central nervous system grow appropriately. Listening to the human voice, for example, helps babies learn to distinguish sounds and develop language. (p. 1)

All of children's emerging talents are based in their early development of trust (Berk, 2001). This development of trust and mutuality occur throughout the early childhood years when children themselves feel loved and have models of love and care in their parents, family, and caregivers. When children experience this love and see it in many aspects of their daily lives, they develop real strength in being caring and loving persons themselves (Brooks & Goldstein, 2001; Swick & Williams, 2008).

Three areas of adult involvement with children are emphasized in Figure 1.6 as noted by Brazelton and Greenspan (2000):

Figure 1.6
Applications to Adult Nurturance of Children

---

1) During the early childhood years, every child should have at least one or two primary caregivers who spend large amounts of loving, caring, nurturing, enriching, and mutually rewarding time with the child.

2) Throughout the early childhood years parents and caregivers should emphasize children's emotional growth and ability to communicate emotions in healthy and proactive ways.

3) Parents and other early childhood caregivers should show appreciation, validation, and positive regard for the prosocial skills that children develop.

Another "irreducible need" of children is for *physical protection, safety, and regulation* (Brazelton & Greenspan, 2000). While this need-area may seem obvious to many people, it is not being met in the lives of many children in the U.S. and globally (Garbarino & Bedard, 2001). For example in the 1996, 1997 and 2000 issues of The State of America's Children, the Children's Defense Fund noted that:

* One in three victims of physical abuse is a baby less than twelve months old. Every day a baby dies of abuse or neglect at the hand of some caregiver.

* Twenty five percent of U.S. children live below the poverty level.

* Only 8.4 percent of infant and toddler care in U.S. child care centers is considered developmentally appropriate.

* Close to 40 percent of infants and toddlers experience some form of neglect prior to their first birthday.

Globally, children are experiencing chronic neglect and abuse, especially in war zones and areas where illiteracy and poverty are high (Bellamy, 2002).

Clearly, many parents who neglect and/or abuse their children are themselves under severe stress and have often lacked positive nurturing role models in their lives (Miller, 1998; Swick & Williams, 2008). Stressed parents are more likely to commit abuse and fail to nurture and protect children (Peled, Jaffe, & Edleson, 1995). Communities and the larger society have important protective roles to play: making sure the environment is toxin free, that crime and violence are contained and hopefully transformed, and that children have ample opportunities to learn how to effectively interact with others (Schubert & Little, 1998; Bronfenbrenner, 2005).

An especially important role for parents, families, communities and society is to better monitor and guide the vast influential arena of media environments (Garbarino & Bedard, 2001). We now know that today's children spend about 40 percent less time with their parents and about twice as much time watching television or playing video games (Brazelton & Greenspan, 2000).

We need for parents and early childhood educators as well as all citizens to address the protective factors that allow for children to become decent and caring citizens – as presented in Figure 1.7.

Figure 1.7
Protective Factors That Nurture Decency in Children

* Develop caring and supportive practices for parents so that they can be optimally involved in protecting and nurturing their children.

* Aim to create toxin free environments in homes, neighborhoods, and communities so that children can grow up in healthy ways.

* Develop prosocial and socially positive neighborhoods where children and families can interact freely and without constant concern for their safety.

* Monitor and address child and family abuse issues, and foster healthier family life in all communities – thus creating safe, secure, and loving environments for children.

* Develop societal standards and accompanying monitoring schemes to address the violent and unhealthy media programs and games that many children experience.

Important to the child's healthy development is *being understood and nurtured as a unique person* (Brazelton & Greenspan, 2000). This process of "differentiation" as a person begins prior to birth where biology and environment begin the inter-play of development and learning (Nathanielsz, 2001).

Throughout the early childhood years a major task of parents and caregivers is their nurturance of the child's learning strengths and needs. Each child needs to be seen and related to as a very special individual. Brazelton and Greenspan (2000, pp. 87-92) note the following as helpful guidelines in this regard:

* *Respect and value the child's learning system:* Each child is unique in biology, environment, and personality. Using their

22

talents and strengths as a beginning point in learning is very important to their long-term growth needs (Small, 2001).

* *Work jointly with families in knowing and responding to the child's needs*: Parents, family, and early childhood educators should observe, interact with, and relate to the child's needs in a partnership manner (Eldridge, 2001; Patrikakou et al, 2005).

* *Empower children through emotionally rich and positive learning experiences:* Learning to be empathetic, to care, and to express our emotions in positive and meaningful ways is essential to our development of our caring and competence (Bowman, Donovan, & Burns, 2000; Mann & Carney, 2008).

* *Help every child find success:* The early years provide professionals and families with an opportunity to support the child in a success approach to learning. While each child will have different potential, all can be successful at appropriate goals and tasks tailored to their unique skills and abilities (Rushton, 2001).

* *Use small learning groups:* In small groups, children not only have more learning opportunities, but also often receive more attention to their concerns and needs (Bransford, Brown, & Cocking, 2000; Morrison, 2008).

* *Set aside "foundation building" time each day:* Help children develop and sharpen their auditory processing, visual-spatial processing, sensory modulation, motor planning and sequencing, and emotional learning on a daily basis (Brazelton & Greenspan, 2000; Greenspan, 2007).

Providing children with developmentally appropriate and culturally responsive experiences enhances their growth as learners (Brazelton & Greenspan, 2000). Far too often children are treated as miniature adults or ignored in relation to experiences that enhance their growth. As Berk (2001) indicates, children benefit from nurturing and challenging learning experiences. For example, when new knowledge is linked to the child's cultural context, it is more readily internalized (Hilliard, 2002).

Children also need limits, structure, and adults who have appropriate and supportive expectations for their growth and learning (Brazelton & Greenspan, 2000). For example, infants thrive when they have nurturing relations with adults who provide structure and continuity to their lives. They seek limits so they can process all of the richness of this new environment. In the wisdom of the classic message of Selma Fraiberg (1959):

The protective function of the parent is so vital in early childhood that even children who are exposed to abnormal dangers may not develop acute anxiety if the parents are present. It is now well known that in war-time Britain the children who remained with their parents even during bombing attacks were able to tolerate anxiety better than the children who were separated from their parents and evacuated to protected zones. (p. 13)

Children's wellness requires stable, supportive communities and cultural continuity (Brazelton & Greenspan, 2000). For example, we know that war, chronically violent environments, and related abusive situations can traumatize the child and negatively influence their perspectives and feelings about themselves and about others (Garbarino & Bedard, 2001; Magid & McKelvey, 1987). On the other hand, recent research indicates that safe and nurturing environments where children experience relations with several loving adults and have multiple opportunities to safely explore their community, show positive gains socially and academically (Berk, 2001).

Likewise, healthy communities provide families with needed resources and supports so that parents and other family can nurture and engage children in meaningful learning (Schubert & Little, 1998; Swick, 2004). A significant part of this context is educating children for cultural continuity. In societies like ours, where change is the norm – continuity is the "security blanket" each of us needs in order to put all of the change into a workable schema (Montgomery, 2001). A strengths model is important where early childhood educators help families use the positive features of their cultural system to enhance their parenting and family dynamics (Garbarino, 1992; Bronfenbrenner, 2005). In terms of specific actions we can take in all communities, Brazelton and Greenspan (2000) suggest the following:

*   Nurture the development of strong neighborhoods where people learn about each other and become each other's helpers.

*   Support and renew the health of schools, churches, civic groups and other agencies and groups so they form a web of continuity and security for families and those who support families.

*   Capitalize on federal and state resources in ways that help families in your local community.

*   Develop comprehensive family resource and support centers that help multi-problem families address their stressors early in the family's life.

*   Nurture strong and high-quality child development programs and early education programs.

Children's development and learning is interrelated with their fulfillment of these "irreducible needs" in ways that support their empowerment. We need to provide the supports, resources, care, and education that will assure that these important needs are met for all children.

CASE APPLICATION: Using your context (school, center, teaching activity) as a basis, develop a plan for engaging families, schools, and communities in activities that address the "irreducible needs" of children. Share your plan in ways that advocate to improve the well being of all children and families – such as in a newspaper article or in other advocacy venues.

Key Growth and Learning Experiences for Children

A significant part of children's development is their acquisition of growth processes that support their ability to learn effectively (Berk, 2001).

The early learning of children must positively reinforce and support their active inquiry efforts (Bransford, Brown, & Cocking, 2000). From birth infants seek to know how to relate and gain some response from others in their environment. They interact intentionally to meet needs and to gain a sense of participation in the world around them. As noted by Bransford, Brown, & Cocking (2000), three learning areas stand out in relation to children's early growth:

1) They attempt to secure the physical resources (food, warmth, protection) needed for their survival.

2) They experiment with various "strategies" to obtain the resources and information they need.

3) They seek "theoretical schemas" on how things work in the world.

Children continue their learning in these areas throughout the early childhood years.

A significant part of children's inquiry is the assistance they receive from responsive adults (Greenspan, 1999; Conrad, 2008). Active learning must be supported through adult guidance that provides children with the right mix of encouragement and assistance. Vygotsky called this process that of scaffolding – where adults provide the right information and experience so children can enhance their learning (Berk, 2001).

One very powerful strategy children use to learn and grow is play. Adults can use children's play behavior as a context to nurture in them the scaffolding process, using the non-threatening situations of play to add to one's possible ideas for solving various puzzles (Berk, 2001).

The *content of children's early play* is especially significant because it represents another part *of their need to learn about their value and role in the lives of important others* such as parents, family, and other caregivers (Berk, 2001)).

Children's active learning needs to be directed toward their conceptualizing themselves as lovable and worthy persons. This can only be learned through loving relations with caring adults. Honig (2002) says it well:

> The infant's perception of the caregiver's love and nurturance has a second dimension: how the child perceives his own worthiness and lovability. A baby who has been neglected or abused may grow into a child who deems himself unlovable or a child victim who acts fearful in many situations. Or as described earlier, the child may behave in ways that exasperate and stress a teacher or caregiver to the point of responding sharply or showing strong disapproval. (p. 8)

In effect, active learning during these early years of life should be guided by loving parents and caregivers who model and engage children in learning empathy, caring, and decency behaviors (Bowman, Donovan, & Burns, 2000).

The kindergarten / primary school years offer many opportunities to help children expand and enrich their caring skills. For example, as children learn to take care of their environment they also see the important role their caring plays in the lives of others. Noddings (2002) suggests that family and school can help children most by engaging them in community service learning where they see how their caring impacts others including senior citizens, the sick and poor, and others who have needs.

Emotional learning is rooted in the early attachment experiences of children (Honig, 2002). Learning how to manage, develop, and refine our emotional skills is clearly connected to all aspects of our lives. Goelman (1995) labels this process as our "emotional intelligence" and sees it as the most important learning we do. Our emotional intelligence includes our understanding of our feelings, motivations, and how we use and express these thoughts, actions, and feelings (Goelman, 1995). He (Goelman) suggests that we use increasing sophisticated activities to engage children in sharpening their emotional intelligence during the primary school years. For example, as children learn to apply their social skills to self-management they should articulate how this improves their learning.

For children, learning self-respect, self-control, empathy and compassion for others, and how to use these perspectives and actions is significant

cant to their total well-being (Hoffman, 2000). For example, as Hoffman notes – children need three skills to guide their social and emotional learning: 1) a sense of self growth (recognizing they are unique from but connected to other people), 2) an understanding of and skills for using the knowledge that the feelings of others are important and are connected to them, and 3) a mental schema of what is right and wrong and how to apply this knowledge in their social and emotional growth. Children need adult guidance in developing their emotional learning. Sears and Sears (2002, p. 117) list caregiver strategies for helping children learn to be empathic and compassionate (See Figure 1.8):

Figure 1.8
Caregiver Strategies for Helping Children
Learn Empathy and Compassion

---

*   Respond to your child's cries with loving attention.

*   Read your child's cues and respond to them appropriately.

*   Respond to each child's unique personality and temperament.

*   Use play to help children learn and further develop various life skills.

*   Help your child learn that others have feelings too and help him or her learn to be sensitive to the feelings of others.

*   Encourage your children to be fair and to be responsive to situations where someone is treated unfairly.

*   Model empathy and compassion in your daily life so that you further enhance your capacity for love and care.

*   Teach your child about cultural diversity by introducing them to people and situations different from them.

*   Show children how we have many things in common with people of all cultures.

*   Involve everyone in the family in service to others in the community and use these service experiences as opportunities for learning.

Children must also *learn to problem-solve* various situations. Learning to solve problems involves our using existing knowledge, processing a new and unfamiliar situation, and integrating our knowledge in new ways and in new contexts in an attempt to resolve a disparate dilemma (Berk, 2001). The process requires children to learn to use four steps (Bransford, Brown, & Cocking, 2000):

1) Initial learning (both what children learn and how they learn it is important to their later use of this information in solving new dilemmas.)

2) Learning to apply knowledge to "abstract" contexts (this is

key to seeing how one's knowledge relates to unfamiliar or unknown situations.)

3) Developing an experimental mindset (learning that solving problems involves various combinations of our existing knowledge and experimentation with new issues and situations is vital to becoming a long-term problem-solver.)

4) Continually expanding and enriching one's knowledge base (what we know is very interrelated with what we can learn about new situations.)

Clearly, these steps are dynamic and impact each other as we learn to solve various dilemmas and stressors. Brooks and Goldstein (2001, Chapter 10) offer the following strategies (Presented in Figure 1.9) as ways that parents and other early childhood caregivers can help children with this important learning process.

Figure 1.9
Parent and Teacher Strategies for Helping Children Learn

---

* Model positive and reasoned problem solving for your children.

* Provide children with appropriate choices at an early age where they are challenged to use their knowledge to solve various problems.

* Help children to use a problem-solving sequence such as the following.

  - Articulate the problem as an authentic situation.

  - Explore the situation and consider at least two or three alternatives as potential solutions.

  - Develop a plan for follow through and a scheme by which to remind each other if people are not following through.

  - Review the plan to see if it is working.

  - Discuss the results and make desired changes.

One of the reasons children learn more effectively to solve problems when they are using such a logical sequence is related to another important aspect of their learning: *language learning* (Berk, 2001). Language provides children with the critical tool for articulating problems, shaping an image of how it might be solved, organizing processes to solve it, and then to "talk back" to themselves to see how their plan worked (Greenspan, 1999).

Newborns are already passionately engaged in language learning. Monastersky (2001) explains:

And newborns are born listeners, with an ability to hear differences between sounds that adults can't hope to match, says Patricia Kuhl, a professor of speech and hearing sciences at the University of Washington. She calls them "citizens of the world," because they can perceive phonemes from all languages. (p. A-15)

As Greenspan (1999) explains, infants use nonverbal gestures as a means of beginning their dialogue with parents and family. This process is very critical in that it either encourages the infant to continue and enrich their dialogue through language development or it discourages and possibly impedes their efforts (Honig, 2002).

As children grow they develop their initial language and language skills – thus empowering them to become more intense explorers of their world. Their acquisition of language is linked to three forces: 1) becoming proficient in meeting their needs (without language one is continually dependent on others for meeting needs); 2) gaining an understanding of what is happening so they can be a part of it (language opens up many avenues for social and emotional contacts); and 3) sharing with others what we think and how we feel about our ever changing situation (Bransford, Brown, & Cocking, 2000).

Beyond the obvious "survival value" of language is how children use language to deepen their own understanding of themselves (Greenspan, 1999). Indeed, children and adults use their own personal issues and concerns to advance their symbolic growth as well as to enhance their social status in this very challenging world. Berk (2001) says that our acquisition of language and self-growth skills is as Vygotsky observed – very interrelated. Berk notes

> In Vygotsky's sociocultural theory, this "communication with the self" becomes an indispensable tool for *self-regulation* the central means through which children take over the support provided by others, turn it toward the self and use it to guide and control their own thinking and behavior. Notice how self-talk induces a delay in responding, during which the child can think about past and present events, speculate about their possible consequences, discuss those alternatives with the self, formulate plans, and use that information to guide impending action. (p. 77)

Language learning is best nurtured through strategies such as those presented in Figure 1.10 (Greenspan, 1999).

Figure 1.10
Parent and Teacher Strategies for Nurturing Children's
Language Development

---

* Model the use of language in ways that show children it is a peaceful, functional, and enjoyable learning and communication tool.

* Support children's early communication and language use by engaging in interactions with them that: encourage, enrich, extend, and enhance their language growth.

* Create and renew learning environments that provide a rich set of materials and experiences – thus promoting and supporting children's experiential growth – which is essential to their language growth.

* Respond and engage with children in using language in fun and enjoyable ways; such as in playing games, literacy activities, and doing family or classroom plays.

* Observe, take note of, and attend to any impediments to the child's full and rich language development. For example, have the child "checked" at regularly scheduled well-care medical appointments.

* Create "language scaffolds" by taking note of where the child is at (what is his zone of proximal development), and then developing learning situations that support the child's learning of new language.

* Read to and share books and stories with your child every day and have fun and enjoyment in the process.

Play is so important to children's language learning as well as all facets of their learning (Berk, 2001; Greenspan, 2007). Part of children's vitality, imagination, and overall cognitive, social, and emotional growth is their ability to PLAY.

Children learn to be effective at play through five situational supports (Bransford, Brown, & Cocking, 2000; Greenspan, 1999, 2007):

1) Adults provide rich play environments stocked with interesting, open-ended, and rich materials and resources.

2) Children are "expected" to play and are positively reinforced when they engage in various forms of play as appropriate to their development and growth.

3) Where appropriate, adults interact with children in playful situations and yet allow children their own space to use play in their own inventive ways.

4) Adults ask children about their play, comment supportively on children's observations about their play, and encourage

children to use their reflections on play to advance their understanding of various concepts and ideas.

5) Children are given multiple opportunities to explore new dimensions of play, thus encouraging their development of creativity and imagination.

Linked to and extending from children's play and other early learning is the *skill of being a continuing learner* (Montgomery, 2001). In the early childhood years children observe adults for cues on how to interact in the environment and in relation to other people. By the nature of their inquisitive stance, children are open to acquiring the life skills needed for becoming life long learners. As human beings, our brains are programmed to take in and process experience in relation to our growth. Yet, when children are taught in their early years to fear new events or activities, to withdraw from problematic situations, or to "shut down" their brains when confronted with fearful or anxiety producing events – they learn not to explore or seek growth in their development. <u>Our brains are "wired" to seek information about our environment unless we are precluded from this exploration process.</u>

For example, in learning how to use our emotions in positive and caring ways – we seek out adults who are caring and nurturing. This model of emotional learning provides us with a schema for continued learning, which is a major part of our ability to grow through our emotional experiences with self and others.

How can we facilitate children's efforts to become engaged and responsive life long learners? Bergen and Coscia (2001) suggest the following ideas:

* Provide children with adult role models who themselves are continuous learners.

* Provide children with a multiplicity of learning opportunities.

* Help children master particular activities they are engaged in, thus promoting benchmarks of success in their lives.

* Encourage, involve, and support children's learning how to function in many different ways.

* Organize and provide literacy rich environments where children observe and participate in learning to use literacy.

* Foster risk-free play environments where young children can experiment with different ideas on solving stressors and issues and are supported in this difficult and challenging process.

* Be sure that children are always "emotionally safe" in their sense of the learning ecology.

*   Support and promote continued language learning in children as it opens doors to further growth.

Life long learners value the various "intelligences" that Gardner (1993) explicates as providing us with the tools we need to reach our potential. It is vital that children experience all of the domains of learning and growth: music, art, poetry, physical motor activities, drama, logico-mathematical relations, literacy, leadership, intra-personal perspectives and skills, and the many other intelligences (Bergen & Coscia, 2001).

Within our many dimensions of learning, children have access to *learning about their culture and that of others* (Montgomery, 2001). Culture provides children with a context for understanding who they are as well as gaining a sense of who others are and how they became a part of their lives. Cultural continuity is important to helping children develop an authentic sense of self, experience meaning in their daily activities, and develop trust and belief in themselves as capable of contributing to and being an important part of this cultural group (Rogoff, 2003).

Three elements of cultural learning are vital to children's growth in becoming caring and competent persons (Garbarino, 1992; Bronfenbrenner, 2005):

1)   Learning about their own culture and their part in helping it grow and develop as well as having this culture nurture their learning and growth.

2)   Learning about the cultures of others and how they can play a role in supporting and nurturing the value of having strength in all cultures.

3)   Gaining insights into how they can use their culture to strengthen their identity and that of others.

Strategies for supporting children's cultural learning are noted by Montgomery (2001) and by Swick, Boutte, & Van Scoy (1995-96):

*   Help children to develop a positive sense of self within their cultural context.

*   Engage children in learning about their cultural identity through exposure to important aspects of the culture, participation in family and cultural activities, and hearing stories and other narratives about important facets of their culture.

*   Involve children in taking part in culture making activities such as special holidays, celebrations, and other important cultural events.

*   Help children use their literacy efforts to enhance their cultural understanding. Have them keep journals on their cultural ideas and experiences.

* Participate with children in cultural enhancement by visiting people and places that represent other cultures.

* Model positive and culturally sensitive behaviors and attitudes when discussing people of other cultures. Combat cultural stereotypes by presenting to children more accurate and healthy symbols of people and experiences in other cultures.

* Involve children (and yourself) in becoming culturally insightful through the use of self-assessments about your cultural knowledge and behavior.

Culture is all that happens to us in our lives. We can help children truly become global citizens by modeling how to live with others and learn through compassionate sharing and support (Rogoff, 2003).

CASE APPLICATION: After reading this section, identify and discuss three ways that parents and early childhood educators can effectively help children become successful and develop skills and behaviors that will assure they will be life long learners.

Family-School-Community as Caring Environment for Children

Perhaps the most significant learning children experience is that their family, school, and community are caring places to live. But for many children the reality is poverty, a lack of skilled and loving adults, and unsafe and insecure neighborhoods and communities. To explicate the key learning and growth experiences children need without addressing the need for empowered families, schools, and communities would be a futile process. While the remaining chapters of this book address these ecological issues, we turn in this part of the chapter to articulating needed attributes of care in family, school, and community.

The three most important care attributes needed in the *family environment* are noted in Figure 1.11 (Swick, 2001, 2004):

Figure 1.11
Most Important Care Attributes Needed in Family

---

1) Caring, loving, and involved parents and/or other adult family in the lives of children.

2) Opportunities for everyone in the family to share, care, and learn from and with each other.

3) Involvement in using each other's talents to help others in the community.

Caring school environments speak louder to children than anything teachers and caregivers might say (Comer, 1997). Here are some examples of caring attributes that every school can achieve (Bransford, Brown, & Cocking, 2000):

*   Develop and continually renew in all staff the need for courteous, kind, and inviting relations with children and families.

*   Let children know they are "known and valued" by doing things like posting their work in hallways, writing positive notes home about their achievements, guiding their behavior in nurturing ways, and other important prosocial rituals.

*   Use "talk and listen" time where teachers and children set aside time to simply enjoy each other through interesting and caring dialogue.

*   Create multiple points in the school day and program for children to be the initiators and leaders of the teaching and learning process.

*   Develop and use "service time" where teachers, parents, and children jointly serve others in need such as helping out in various community improvement projects.

*   Use teacher-child advisory times to take stock of the school's caring quotient. How are we doing type questions can lead to a renewal of school as a caring place to live.

Community caring is all about people taking care of each other and empowering each other to be nurturers in all aspects of their lives (Brazelton & Greenspan, 2000). People form "community" to create symbolic boundaries that support their efforts to achieve both individual and communal growth. During the early childhood years, families are in need of community security, support, and resources that strengthen their position to be effective parents and caregivers as well as contributing members of the community (Garbarino, 1992).

Communities can develop caring patterns of functioning by seeking to make sure the following protection, security, services, and opportunities exist and are affordable and accessible to families.

*   Create health and safety measures that provide all families with needed health care, protection, and a sense of security in their daily lives.

*   Determine and then seek to provide services that support parents and family in developing meaningful and productive lives. Especially important in this effort is to help families address high-risk situations early in their lives, thus possibly precluding these stressors from becoming life long issues.

* Develop and then access high-quality child care programs for all families with young children.

* Encourage business and industry to use family-friendly workplace practices and to engage their workers in determining critical needs for carrying out effective parenting.

* Provide a variety of recreational and cultural activities throughout the community that invite parents and children to become members of the community.

* Continually develop and renew quality educational centers and resources in the community that are open and affordable to all people.

* Encourage and support community service learning as a foundation of life for everyone in the community and begin this effort during the early childhood years.

CASE APPLICATION: Survey your friends and colleagues about their list of qualities we should nurture in children to help them become caring and nurturing persons.

How can communities begin to integrate these things into the family and school as well as in the community?

Challenges Families, Schools, and Communities Face in Creating Caring Environments

Ultimately, the partnership between families, schools, and communities makes quality living possible for young children. Research is very clear that families in isolation are unable to nurture children very well and that highly stressed communities also are lacking in the needed strength to help families and schools do a quality job for children and parents. Five challenges faced by families, schools, and communities in trying to create high-quality environments for children are noted as we close this chapter. These challenges will appear in various forms throughout this book.

1) *Continuous renewal and re-commitment to the mission of creating and sustaining high-quality environments for the children we claim to value.* In far too many cases, our verbal affirmation of children as our societal priority is not matched by our actions. Often during economic down-turns education and family strengthening projects are the first to be cut and mental health programs are typically treated even worse (Sawhill, 2003).

2) *Development and use of continuing education of the family-school-community partners toward realizing respectful and*

nurturing forms of adult-child relationships (Greenspan, 1999; Honig, 2002). Many adults are simply mis-informed with regards to how to relate to children appropriately and in loving ways. Because of their abusive or neglectful childhoods they had no role models or simply lack insights on the importance of nurturing and loving adult-child relations (Honig, 2002) Thus, every community needs a continuing education of citizens about quality early childhood practices that emphasize the role of adults in nurturing children toward care and competence. This might occur through media presentations, faith-based initiatives, civic group programs, and school sponsored activities. The important point is to promote high-quality adult-child relations. The goal must be to educate each other in peaceful and prosocial ways to empower ourselves so that we can be emotionally and socially literate role models for our children.

3) *Development of a system for making collaborative family-school-community partnerships workable and of value to all who support children* (Garbarino, 1992). Many communities purport to have partnerships for children and yet these structures lack systemic means for articulating, pursuing, and achieving desired goals. Effective systems have five attributes (Morse, 1998):

   a) <u>A system and process for decision making</u>: If communities are to organize needed child and family resources better then they need an identified group, process, and structure for making this happen.

   b) <u>A system for creating needed resources and then getting the job done</u>: Emerging from the decision making team must be structures that make the resources visible and available in the sense that child and family helpers can deliver these resources to those in need.

   c) <u>Strategies for families being able to access resources</u>: Many parents and their helpers know the frustration of available resources they cannot access because of a lack of transportation or other impediments. Important to the success of any early childhood partnership is indeed putting in place the family-access strategies like transportation, child care, and other support strategies.

   d) <u>Development of leadership renewal and expansion strategies</u>: Successful early childhood family-school-community partnerships have in place leadership training and sustaining efforts so that each generation can connect to the mission of high-quality services for children and families.

e) <u>Sustaining the future through wise actions now</u>: Forward thinking communities craft actions that insure a healthy and vital quality of living for future generations. For example, high quality child care can indeed establish a sense of decency in the future generation. Environmental policies such as eliminating lead from the environment are certainly a move toward a healthier future generation.

4) *Crafting collaborative strategies that help the partners optimize their resources and strategies for strengthening families* (Forest, 2003). Four steps are noted and discussed throughout the book relative to enhancing the partnership's ability to deliver needed resources.

a) <u>Assess the key needs through strong stakeholder inputs</u>: Prior to investing energy into optimal service delivery we need to know what the real needs are; what do parents and citizens feel about these issues?

b) <u>Identify all of the available resources/strategies existent in the partnership</u>: An important role for the partnership is to articulate all of the resources each has to offer in strengthening families. Once available resources are known additional issues can then be addressed: cost, funding support, access, delivery, quality points, and other related topics. In addition, "gaps" in existing and needed resources can then be established.

c) <u>Organizing resources for effective delivery to families is vital to the mission of such partnerships</u>. There are important aspects of this process: How can the resources be most effectively delivered? In what ways can we improve quality? How can we share resources and funding to enhance and enrich our family resources? In what ways can we help each other strengthen our individual and collaborative work?

d) <u>Continuous refinement and enhancement of partnership services for families</u>: A major benefit of coming together in working partnerships is the review of: How we are impacting families? How can we strengthen what we do? Where do we need to change? and How can we achieve these processes?

5) *Develop and use an empowerment evaluation system that supports continuous improvement in the partnership* (Schorr, 1997; Amatea2009). In so many cases, partnership between

families, schools, and communities lack a responsive and helpful evaluation system. Efforts to meet children's needs require an empowerment evaluation scheme that engage the partners in reviewing the what, how, who, when, and where issues that greatly influence their potential to be truly helpful to children. Wandersman (1999) explains:

> The goal of empowerment evaluation is to improve program success. By providing program developers with tools for assessing the planning, implementation, evaluation of programs, program practitioners have the opportunity to improve planning, implement with quality, evaluate outcomes and develop a continuous quality improvement system." (p. 96)

Questions that probe the substance and value of services for children provide an important means for program development. Consider these three questions:

a) What long-term indicators suggest that the partnership efforts are positively influencing children's growth and well-being? For example, is the number of low-birth weight babies declining due to better maternal care and nutrition during pregnancy?

b) What collaborative activities can the partnership point to as effective in strengthening the quality of children's lives?

c) How can the partnership be strengthened to thus provide better services. For example, would a "one-stop shop" system increase the access and use of services for children and families in the community?

Families, schools, and communities will always face challenges in creating high quality environments and services for children. Strong and functional evaluation and refinement schemes are one means for empowering this effort to more likely achieve its goals.

SUMMATIVE DISCUSSION OF APPLICATION POINTS

Understanding children's needs and the manner in which they learn how to respond to their needs and the needs of others is the rationale for having strong early childhood family-school-community partnerships. Maslow, Bronfenbrenner, and other early childhood thinkers have delineated the processes children use to learn how to be learners, thus enabling them to grow and develop throughout their lives. Yet we also see that children often experience abuse and other degrading situations that impede their learning and growth. Clearly, families, schools, and communities are the ecologies in which children develop and learn. Thus the following application points should promote much discussion and action in our use of various early childhood education interventions:

1) Children must have their "basic" needs of love, security, safety, nurturance, and related support needs met if they are to reach their optimal growth and development.

2) As professionals and citizens we need to advocate for safer communities, more family strengthening, and higher quality early childhood care if we are to nurture children toward being effective learners,

3) Parents and teachers should use every opportunity to help children learn "how to learn" and to use their skills in empowering themselves to be healthy and contributive people.

4) All citizens need to be engaged in caring for the nation's greatest resource – its children!

Helpful Web Sites

Connect for Kids; <http://<www.connectforkids.org>

National Institute on Early Child Development and Education (EC): <http://<www.ed.gov/offices/OER/ECI/>

Early Childhood Care and Developmenr: <http://<www.ecdgroup.com>

I am your child: <http://<www.iamyourchild.orfg>

The National Academy for Child Development: <http://<www.nacd.org>

References

Amatea, E. (2009). Building culturally responsive family-school relationships. Columbus, OH: Pearson.

Bellamy, C. (2002). The State of the World's Children. New York: United Nation's Children's Fund.

Bergen, D., & Coscia, J. (2001). Brain research and childhood education: Implications for educators. Olney, MD: Association for Childhood Education International.

Berk, L. (2001). Awakening children's minds: How parents and teachers can make a difference. New York: Oxford University Press.

Bowman, B., Donovan, M., & Burns, M. (2000). Eager to learn—Educating our preschoolers: Executive summary. Washington, DC: National Research Council.

Bransford, J., Brown, A., & Cocking, R. (Eds.). (2000). How people learn: Brain, mind, experience, and school. Washington, DC: National Academy Press.

Brazelton, T., & Greenspan, S. (2000). The irreducible needs of children. Cambridge, MA: Perseus.

Bronfenbrenner, U. (1979). The ecology of human development and learning. Cambridge, MA: Harvard University Press.

Bronfenbrenner, U. (2005). Making human beings human. Thousand Oaks, CA: Sage.

Brooks, R., & Goldstein, S. (2001). Raising resilient children. Chicago, IL: Contemporary Books.

Caldwell, B. (1989). A faltering trust. In D. Blazer (Ed.). Faith development in early childhood. Kansas City, MO: Sheed & Ward.

Carter, B., & McGoldrick, M. (Eds). (1999). The expanded life cycle: Individual, family, and social perspectives. Third Edition. Boston: Allyn and Bacon.

Chavkin, N. (1993). Families and schools in a pluralistic society. Albany, NY: State University of New York Press.

Children's Defense Fund. (1996). Status of America's Children – 1996. Washington, DC: Children's Defense Fund.

Children's Defense Fund. (1997). Status of America's Children – 1997. Washington, DC: Children's Defense Fund.

Children's Defense Fund. (2000). Status of America's Children – 2000. Washington, DC: Children's Defense Fund

Comer, J. (1997). Waiting for a miracle: Why schools can't solve our problems – and how we can. New York: Dutton.

Conrad, N. (2008). Fostering emergent literacy through parent/child reading relationships. In M. Jalongo. (Ed.), Enduring bonds: The significance of interpersonal relationships in young children's lives. (pp. 107-128). New York, NY: Springer.

Couchenour, D., & Chrisman, K. (2000). Families, schools, and communities: Together for our children. New York: Delmar.

Eldridge, D. (2001). Parent involvement: It's worth the effort. Young Children, July, 65-69.

Elkind, D. (1994). Ties that stress: The new family imbalance. Cambridge, MA: Harvard University Press.

Eliot, L. (1999). What's going on in there? How the brain and mind develop in the first five years of life. New York: Bantam.

Erikson, E. (1982). The life cycle completed: A review. New York: W.W. Norton.

Folbre, N. (2001). The invisible heart: Economics and family values. New York: The New Press.

Forest, C. (2003). <u>Empowerment skills for family workers</u>. Ithaca, NY: Cornell University, Family Development Press.

Fraiberg, S. (1959). <u>The magic years: Understanding and handling the problems of early childhood</u>. New York: Simon and Schuster.

Freeman, N., & Swick, K. (2003). Pre-service teaching interns strengthen the fabric of their communities. <u>Generator</u>, 21 (4), 15-16.

Garbarino, J. (1992). <u>Children and families in the social environment. Second Edition</u>. New York: Aldine de Gruyter.

Garbarino, J., & Bedard, C. (2001). <u>Parents under siege: Why you are the solution, not the problem in your child's life</u>. New York: The Free Press.

Gardner, H. (1993). <u>Multiple intelligences: The theory in practice</u>. New York: Basic Books.

Goleman, D. (1995). <u>Emotional intelligence: Why it can matter more than IQ</u>. New York: Bantam Books.

Gonzalez-Mena, J., & Eyer, D. (2001). <u>Infants, toddlers, and caregivers. Fifth Edition</u>. Mountain View, CA: Mayfield.

Gonzalez-Mena, J. (2006). <u>The young child in the family and the community. Fourth Edition</u>. Columbus, OH: Pearson.

Gonzalez-Mena, J. (2009<u>). Child, family, and community: Family-centered early care and education. Fifth Edition.</u> Columbus, OH: Pearson.

Greenough, W., Emde, R., Gunnar, M., Massinga, R., & Shonkoff, J. (2001). The impact of the caregiving environment on young children's development: Different ways of knowing. <u>Zero To Three</u>, 21 (5), 16-23.

Greenspan, S. (1999). <u>Building healthy minds: The six experiences that create intelligence and emotional growth in babies and young children</u>. Cambridge, MA: Perseus.

Greenspan, S. (2007). <u>Great kids</u>. Philadelphia, PA: DeCapo Press Books.

Heymann, J. (2000). <u>The widening gap: Why America's working families are in jeopardy and what can be done about it</u>. New York: Basic Books.

Hilliard, A. (2002). Language, culture, and the assessment of African American children. In L. Delpit & J. Dowdy. (Eds.). <u>The skin that we speak</u>. New York: The New Press.

Hoffman, M. (2000). <u>Empathy and moral development: Implications for caring and justice</u>. New York: Cambridge University Press.

Honig, A. (2002). <u>Secure relationships: Nurturing infant/toddler attachment in early care settings</u>. Washington, DC: National Association for the Education of Young Children.

Magid, K., & McKelvey, C. (1987). <u>High risk: Children without a conscience</u>. New York: Bantam Books.

Mann, M., & Carney, R. (2008). Building positive relationships in the lives of infants and toddlers in child care. In M. Jalongo. (Ed.), <u>Enduring bonds: The significance of interpersonal relationships in young children's lives.</u> (pp. 147-158). New York, NY: Springer.

Maslow, A. (1959). <u>New knowledge in human values</u>. New York: Harper & Row.

Maslow, A. (1968). <u>Toward a psychology of being</u>. New York: D. Van Nostrand.

Miller, A. (1998). <u>Paths of life: Seven scenarios</u>. New York: Pantheon Books.

Miller, A. (2001). <u>The truth will set you free</u>. New York: Basic Books.

Mills, L. (2003). <u>Insult to injury: Rethinking our responses to intimate abuse</u>. Princeton, NJ: Princeton University Press.

Monastersky, R. (2001). Look who's listening. <u>The Chronicle of Higher Education</u>, July 6, A14-A16.

Montgomery, W. (2001). Creating culturally responsive, inclusive classrooms. <u>Teaching Exceptional Children</u>, March/April, 4-9.

Mooney, C. (2000). <u>An introduction to Dewey, Montessori, Erikson, Piaget, and Vygotsky</u>. St Paul, MN: Redleaf Press.

Morrison, G. (2008). <u>Fundamentals of early childhood education. Fifth Edition</u>. Columbus, OH: Pearson.

Morse, S. (1998). Five building blocks for successful communities. In F. Hesselbein, M. Goldsmith, R. Beckhard, & R. Schubert. (Eds.). <u>The community of the future</u>. San Francisco, CA: Jossey-Bass.

Nathanielsz, P. (2001). <u>The prenatal prescription</u>. New York: HarperCollins Publishers.

Nelson, C., Levitt, P., & Gunnar, M. (2008, June 27). The impact of early adversity on brain development. A paper presented at the National Symposium on Early Childhood Science and Policy, Harvard University.

Noddings, N. (2002). <u>Starting at home: Caring and social policy</u>. Berkeley, CA: University of California Press.

Patrikakou, E., Weissberg, R., Redding, S., & Walberg, H. (Eds.). (2005). <u>School-family partnerships for children's success</u>. New York: Teachers College Press.

Peled, E., Jaffe, P., & Edleson, J. (Eds.). (1995). <u>Ending the cycle of violence: Community responses to children of battered women</u>. Thousand Oaks, CA: Sage.

Restak, R. (2003). <u>The new brain</u>. New York: Rodale.

Rogoff, B. (2003). <u>The cultural nature of human development</u>. New York: Oxford University Press.

Roseman, M. (2008). Early language development and adult/child relationships: An intricate connection. In M. Jalongo. (Ed.), <u>Enduring bonds: The significance of interpersonal relationships in young children's lives</u>. (39-56). New York, NY: Springer.

Rushton, S. (2001). Applying brain research to create developmentally appropriate learning environments. <u>Young Children</u>, September, 76-82.

Sawhill, I. (Ed.). (2003). <u>One percent for the kids</u>. Washington, DC: Brookings Institution Press.

Sears, W., & Sears, M. (2002). <u>The successful child: What parents can do to help kids turn out well</u>. Boston: Little, Brown and Company.

Schorr, L/ (1997). <u>Common purpose: Strengthening families and neighborhoods to rebuild America</u>. New York, NY: Anchor Books.

Schubert, R., & Little, R. (1998). Our children are the community of the future. In F. Hesselbein, M. Goldsmith, R. Beckhard, & R. Schubert. (Eds.). <u>The community of the future</u>. San Francisco, CA: Jossey-Bass.

Small, M (2001). <u>Kids: How biology and culture shape the way we raise our children</u>. New York: Doubleday.

Swick, K. (2001). Nurturing decency through caring and serving during the early childhood years. <u>Early Childhood Education Journal</u>, 29 (2), 131-137.

Swick, K. (2004). <u>Empowering parents, families, schools, and communities during the early childhood years</u>. Champaign, IL: Stipes.

Swick, K. (2005). Promoting caring in children and families as prevention of violence strategy. <u>Early Childhood Education Journal</u>, *32 (5)*, 341-347.

Swick, K., Boutte, G., & Van Scoy, I. (1995/96). Families and schools: Building multicultural values together. <u>Childhood Education</u>, Winter, 75-79.

Swick, K., & Williams, R. (2008). How attention to family stress dynamics can prevent homelessness among very young families. In M. Jalongo. (Ed.), <u>Enduring bonds: The significance of interpersonal relationships in young children's lives</u>. New York: Springer.

Thornton, A. (Eds.). (2001). <u>The well-being of children and families: Research and data needs</u>. Ann Arbor, MI: The University of Michigan Press.

Vygotsky, L. (1978). <u>Mind in society: The development of higher mental processes</u>. Cambridge, MA: Harvard University Press.

Wandersman, A. (1999). Framing the evaluation of health and human service programs in community settings: Assessing progress. <u>New Directions for Evaluation</u>, 83, 95-102.

Zigler, E., Fin-Stevenson, M., & Hall, N. (2002). <u>The first three years and beyond: Brain development and social policy</u>. New Haven, CT: Yale University Press.

Chapter Two

Understanding Parents, Families and Communities: Key to Building Strong Partnerships

---

CAPSULE: Gaining insight into the ways that parents, families, and communities function is linked to our ability to be effective early childhood educators. Understanding provides us with the perspectives and tools to reach out and serve families with empathy and compassion. Understanding also gives us the power to help others become empowered.

Chapter Two Objectives:

1) Gain skills and insight into how to learn about parents, families, and communities and enable your interactions with people to be reasoned, sensitive, and responsive.

2) Strengthen your theoretical and research knowledge about families so that you can bring essential perspectives and support resources to the partnership.

3) Increase your understanding of the issues and challenges that parents, families, and communities experience so that your help and support is grounded within the realities being faced.

4) Broaden your knowledge and understanding of how the family learning system works in relation to the many stressors families experience.

Fostering nurturing relationships with parents, families, and communities requires that we first understand the dynamics, issues, and patterns of functioning of our partners. We must learn about parents, families, and communities so that we truly have knowledge and perspectives that help us to design and carry out early childhood practices (Barbour & Barbour,

2001). Parents and families report that "informed" teachers of young children know the parents and other family members and involve them in various ways (Swick, 1997; Lawrence-Lightfoot, 2003).

How do we come to know and value the lives of parents, families, and community members? There are at least four key elements in this endeavor: 1) tools and strategies for learning about parents, families, and communities; 2) theoretical and research perspectives that strengthen our understanding of parents, families, and communities; 3) a close analysis of critical conceptual and practical issues impacting the parents and families we serve; and 4) developing important insights relative to the construct of the family as a "learning system" (Swick, 2004).

Gaining knowledge and skills in using appropriate tools for learning about parents, families, and communities strengthens our inquiry practices (Pipher, 1996; Gonzalez-Mena, 2006). If we are to be responsive to and supportive of parents, children, and families, we need to be aware of their strengths and needs, as well as the dynamics of community and family issues they experience in their lives. There are a variety of "tools" we can use in this learning process as listed in Figure 2.1 (Swick, 2004):

Figure 2.1
Tools to Use in Learning about Families

---

* Action research
* Systemic observation strategies
* Demographics
* Surveys and questionnaires
* Telephone and other technologies
* Child and family interviews
* Focus groups
* School orientation programs
* Related advocacy/educational activities

These tools and processes are reviewed in relation to supporting our professional growth in becoming informed helpers.

Theoretical and research perspectives about families help us to contextualize the information we gain through our inquiry process (Fishel, 1991; Swick, 2004). For example, three people can read the same demographic data on families who comprise the school's population and arrive at very different conclusions as to the meaning of that data. We need to know how our personal perspectives influence our interpretation of different events and experiences. Learning about the different theoretical and research-informed perspectives on families strengthens our knowledge and skill in seeing what is truly happening in families.

Knowledge about parents, families and communities needs to be contextualized in relation to the diversity of family needs and strengths. The importance of diversity is interrelated with the development of parents and families from the perspective of a dynamic continuum. Thus, both a community systems view and a family systems construct are explored.

The review of complex perspectives of family issues is also examined from other points of view. For example, how do parents and families see different issues such as the work/family stressors that professionals often refer to in their analyses? How is an empowerment process best supported in families? What are the characteristics of early childhood professionals that are most nurturing of a positive family-school-community relationship system?

In a synthesis manner we then look at how the family is indeed a learning system and how the community should be supportive of this process (Swick, 1991, 2004) We ask two important questions in this regard:

1) How do healthy families in diverse cultural settings use their learning system to advance and strengthen each other and the family itself?

2) What do supportive communities do to foster positive and meaningful learning and growth in families?

Tools and Strategies for Learning about Families

Using a variety of tools and strategies in our learning strengthens the insights we develop and enriches our sensitivities to the talents, needs, and skills of the parents and families we serve.

Action research related to specific inquiries about parents, families and/or communities can provide valuable insights (Cochran, 1988; Hatch, 1995). For example, one teacher does case studies with several families of children in her classroom to become more sensitive to their skills and needs. Another teacher studies families to see how their learning approaches impact children's literacy interests and skills. She surveys families on their reading habits with children and uses this information to develop programs to help parents and children strengthen their literacy skills.

Systemic observation of parents and families is also invaluable in learning about their strengths and needs (Leavitt, 1994; Hanson & Lynch, 2004). One set of observation questions posed by Swick (1993) revolves around families' interests and involvement:

1) What are family interests?

2) How do families spend time when they are together?

3) How are families involved in the community?

4) What school activities do parents attend and participate?

Another area of interest to early childhood educators might be that of *parental talents and strengths* as shown in Figure 2.2.

Figure 2.2
Gaining Insights about Parental Talents and Strengths

---

1) What talents appear in the parents' work with their children and the school?

2) What strengths seem evident in your observation of parents?

3) How do parents use their talents and skills to support their children's learning and growth?

4) In what ways can you help parents enhance their talents and skills?

5) How might you be more effective in using parents' skills and talents in your early childhood program?

Relevant demographic data about parents, families, and the community offer another perspective on our relations with families. Sources of such data vary, with the United State Census Bureau as a rich resource in this regards. The Children's Defense Fund and Kids Count are also excellent sources of data as well as local Chamber of Commerce and local government agencies (Couchenour & Chrisman, 2000; Hanson & Lynch, 2004). Three values of local demographic data are:

1) We can learn about changing patterns of living and family dynamics.

2) Particular risk factors for families, children, and the community may surface in our data analysis.

3) Specific parent, child and family strengths may be observed.

Surveys and questionnaires provide an ongoing means for gaining parent and family insights on a variety of topics. Many early childhood professionals use the survey technique to gain information on parent, child, and family talents and skills. From this information they often develop resource programs where parents and children put their skills to work in teaching others (Diss & Buckley, 2005). Other survey emphases may be to collect data on parent education topics, parent concerns, level of parent and family interest in special projects, and to gain the parental perspective. Leavitt (1994) notes that a lack of insight into the real values and strengths of child and family often lead to an imbalance of power in parent-professional relations.

Questionnaires can be used to assess parental support of various school or center projects, parent willingness to be a part of particular activities, and parent and family valuing of different educational and social activities. In setting up a parent program design for her preschool center, one teacher used the following questions:

1) What topics are you as a parent most interested in learning about?

2) What days and times best suit your family schedule for coming to the school for programs and activities?

3) Are you willing to serve in calling other parents to remind them of upcoming programs?

4) Would you be willing to serve on a committee?

5) Do you like family meal nights here at the center and would you come to these events?

Other early childhood teachers have used questionnaires to gain parental assessment of specific parts of their educational and support program. For example, do parents find the monthly conferences useful and helpful? Some teachers have even used *Focus Groups* where parents in small groups assess and help re-design specific activities. One Children's Center uses parent focus groups to support their development of new Parent – Teacher – Association projects for the upcoming year. These discussions reveal the various ideas of parents and their willingness to commit to helping with specific activities (Swick, 2004).

Various technologies can strengthen the parent/family-teacher relationship and thus enhance the early childhood educator's understanding of parent and family needs (Swick, 1991; 2004). For example, many teachers comment that having regular telephone contact with parents increases their empathy and understanding of child, parent, and family situations (Epstein, 1995). Email, teacher and family Web sites, and other computer uses have provided an innovative way for parents, families and schools to learn about each other in ongoing ways. Particular strengths that these means provide include:

1) Early childhood educators have continuing access to parent concerns and thus are learning about families as they grow and change.

2) Parents and family feel invited to be a part of the educational and school life of their child. Teacher invitations are the strongest means for parents to feel comfortable about sharing their lives and their efforts.

3) Teachers and parents can more easily develop a knowledge base of each other through these interactive uses of technology.

We learn more about families through our *interactions with children* than any other medium – if we are indeed listening and responding to their individual needs and situations (Comer, 2001; Keyser, 2006). For example, Mrs. Chestnut uses "family profiles" that the children develop as a part of their literacy work in second grade. These profiles involve everyone in the family-school team in highlighting the strengths of children and families and are an annual celebration event for everyone. Family profiles include the stories, artifacts, special achievements, and issues and challenges experienced by the family. Another possibility is for teachers to have children interview their parents about what the parents want the teacher to know about the child, the parent and the family. Then there are multiple *informal learning moments* where children's work, behavior, and perspective reflect a set of family dynamics that are so informative and helpful to teachers. We must be sensitive though to the confidentiality of teacher-child relationships as well as parent-teacher relationships. Our ethics must inform how we relate to child, family, and community situations, with the strengthening of everyone our main goal and the protection and enhancement of their integrity indeed a key to this process (Feeney & Freeman, 1999)

Families are the richest context of information (Pipher, 1996) on children and yet this source is often ignored. What happens in families is in every sense more revealing than any survey or focus group outcomes. For example, here is a list that an early childhood teacher of twenty years compiled about what she learns from home visits and other family contact events like "family night" at the early childhood center:

* How parents relate to their children.
* What parents really want for their children.
* What talents, strengths, and needs are prevalent in the child's life.
* The talents and needs of parents and how these can be interrelated with the early childhood program.
* How parents are most willing to help out in their child's school.
* The unique features and needs of the child to which parents want teachers to be really sensitive to.

Orientation, open house, and related information and social support programs also provide important opportunities for learning about parents and families. These events provide a venue for meeting parents, introducing them to the life of the school, asking them for their help, distributing surveys and sign up sheets, providing parenting materials, and very importantly, simply having the needed dialogue with parents and family that help us to better support each other (File, 2001; Diss & Buckley, 2005).

Within the community and society we also learn a great deal about the children, parents, and families we serve (Swick, 1991). As Bronfenbrenner

(1986, 2005) suggests, when the community ignores the needs of families we can be sure that parents and children suffer this loss in the form of poor health care, lack of quality child care, and other important human development supports. Thus, our involvement in awareness and advocacy education in the community can instruct our knowledge of the dynamics and challenges faced by parents and families. For example, Garbarino and Bedard (2001) list the following as challenges faced by many parents and families in our society:

1) Chronic poverty that erodes the very fabric of family life.

2) Child neglect and abuse that emanates from illiteracy and a history of abuse in the family of origin.

3) Television violence that is present in practically every half-hour of programming in the child's life.

4) Lack of needed job skills which in turn often impact parenting in negative ways.

5) High job stress that typically reduces the time parents have for being with their children and family.

In addition to these ways of learning about parents, families and communities, various strategies are integrated with the content of the different parts of this book.

CASE APPLICATION: Using your current early childhood context, explain how you might gain knowledge about the families you will be or are serving. What tools seem most useful to you? How might you use these tools and in what ways do you plan to involve families in this action research process? How can you best use the information gained to further involve families?

Theoretical and Research Perspectives Help us Better Understand Families and Communities

Theoretical and research perspectives inform our perceptions of family dynamics and potentially strengthen our skills for better supporting parents, families, and communities (Comer, 1997; Swick, 2004).

Bronfenbrenner's (1979) *ecological framework* views the family as a system in which members develop their socio-emotional selves, their identity is thus actualized within several inter-locking relations with other systems. In a very real sense, the family is the micro-system of the larger society. A basic premise of the ecological systems framework is that each person in the family is impacted by whatever happens to other family members (Bronfenbrenner, 1979). For example, Fishel (1991) notes that a crisis for the mother of two young children reverberates through their lives too! Likewise, the success of a parent in achieving new work or professional goals can positively influence other family. But we are not passive members of this ecological system; rather, we are active players (Kotre, 1999). Five ecological principles (Figure 2.3) help us to be more responsive to parents, families and communities (Bronfenbrenner, 1979, 2005; Garbarino, 1995).

Figure 2.3
Five Ecological Principles for Understanding Families

---

1) Our individual identity emerges within the dynamics of the family as a learning system.

2) Whatever happens to any particular family member influences all members in some ways.

3) Distortion or dysfunction in family dynamics can negatively impact the behavior and learning of all family.

4) Family interactions in other systems (such as church, school, work, neighborhood) are powerful in influencing family relations.

5) Supportive "other systems" like child care or work can empower families in critical ways such as increasing their ability to acquire more education or increase their economic viability.

Families are linked to all of the human development systems. What families do impacts society and of course, societal events influence families. Mary Pipher (1996) notes that the Sioux word *tiospaye* conveys the power of having a safe and nurturing ecology for parents and children to grow and learn. She (Pipher, 1996) states:

> The tiospaye gives children multiple parents, aunts, uncles and grandparents. It offers children a corrective factor for problems in their nuclear families. If parents are difficult, there are other adults around to soften and diffuse the situation.

Systems beyond the family but interacting with it (exo-systems) are also important in the lives of parents and children. Bronfenbrenner (1979) noted that systems like the work place, while not visible to family who do not participate directly in them, are very influential. For example, Galinsky (1999) interviewed children on their perceptions of their parent's work involvement and found that children are very cognizant of the positive and negative facets of this system. They cited their parents' overload from work as the most negative factor and their parents' achievements in the work place as the most positive feature.

Likewise, the various processes and activities that connect families with other important systems (meso-systems) are key to their involvement in helpful support services and relationships (Swick, 1991, 2004). These connecting, nurturing meso-systems become especially important in the lives of families whose cultural life system is different from that of the prevailing community system. For example, child care centers and schools have found it especially helpful to have bilingual staff, culturally knowledgeable parent and community leaders, and interpreters to support the development of positive and family supportive relationships (Powell, Zambrann, & Silva-Palcios, 1990). Regular parent-teacher contacts during the primary school years increase children's potential for school success (Lawrence-Lightfoot, 2003).

The policies evident in the societal practices of government and the overall culture (macro-system) have important roles in how families function (Garbarino, 1995). For example, when rules and regulations isolate a significant part of society's families from needed medical and health care, the welfare of all families is ultimately negatively impacted (Swick & Graves, 1993; Schorr, 1997; Bronfenbrenner, 2005).

The interplay of the different social systems is critical to the healthy growth and development of parents, children, and families (Pence, 1988; Pipher, 1996). When parents and children suffer from a lack of needed resources (housing, food, clothing, medicine, and other basics), the lives of these parents and children are in jeopardy. We need broader and more responsive concepts of care and support for families. The ecology of the community must respond to the changing needs of families. As Folbre (2001) notes:

> Policies designed to promote care for other people appear unproductive only to those who define economic efficiency in cramped terms, such as increases in GDP. The weakening of family and social solidarity can impose enormous costs, reflected in educational failures, poor health, environmental degradation, high crime rates, and a natural atmosphere of anxiety and resentment.

> The care and nurturance of human capabilities has always been difficult and expensive. In the past, a sexual division of labor based upon the subordination of women helped minimize both the difficulties and the expense. Today, however, the costs of providing care need to be explicitly confronted and fairly distributed. (p. 230)

Thus, the interactive nature of family support systems must be re-thought to account for the changing dynamics of our entire social system. Early childhood educators need to see the realities that families confront.

CASE APPLICATION: Explain how the ecological perspective of family dynamics might help you better relate to the needs and strengths of families. Give at least two examples of how ecological situations impact families in either strengthening their lives or impeding their efforts.

The empowerment perspective of relating and responding to parent, family, and community needs during the early childhood years is oriented toward realizing parent, child, family, and community strengths and nurturing these strengths. It requires early childhood professionals to see parents, children, and families in positive and supportive ways (Swick, 2004). The following are noted as important ways to frame our work with families (Swick, Da, Ros, & Kovach, 2001):

*   View each child, parent, and family as unique, and as having special talents and needs, strengths, and challenges in their lives.

*   Recognize that the source of "power" in each person's life is caring! Learning to care first for our selves, then for others and the environment needs to be a part of parent and family education for empowerment.

*   Our work with parents, children, and families must be based in mutual respect.

*   All parents, children, and families have cultural and social contexts in which they live and grow.

*   Understanding and nurturance are key to achieving a caring relationship with families. Harsh judgment, delimiting stereotypes, and rigid mental frameworks have no place in this perspective.

Recognizing and acting on the diverse strengths and needs of families is also important for supporting parents, children, families, and communities (Comer, 1997). Parents and families have never matched the idealized "image" of family that is often put forth in media and other social system venues. By their very nature and design, families are dynamic and responsive systems for human growth and learning (Pipher, 1996). As noted by Barbour and Barbour (2001):

> Family structure is never permanent; members form a particular configuration for only a brief time and then change comes about. For example, when Jana was in eighth grade, her teacher asked her to draw and label two pictures: one of her family when she was in kindergarten and another of her family now.

Jana's explanation shows her grasp of family change. In her kindergarten picture, Jana drew and labeled, my real mom, my dad, my brother, and me. In her eighth-grade picture she drew herself in the center with other people in clusters around her. Closest to here were figures labeled "dad and my older brother," On the other side but distanced from her were four people labeled "my stepsister, my step-mom, my stepbrother, and my little sister. (p. 54)

Through events like death (Jana's "real mom" had died when she was in elementary school), job changes, and divorce, families change. Cultural and societal factors also impact families. Even "experiences" that parents and families have in their culture and in socio-cultural settings they move to have significant influences on them (McKenry & Price, 1994).

A starting point for early childhood educators is to recognize the strengths that exist in families of all types and structures. How we perceive and then act in relation to family dynamics is more powerful than any other message we might send to families. Three dimensions of family diversity (Figure 2.4) help us to gain better understanding of their strengths, needs, and challenges (Swick, 1987; Elkind, 1994; Hanson & Lynch, 2004).

Figure 2.4
Three Dimensions of Family Diversity

---

1) All families have a "culture" in which they have formulated beliefs and values that guide their daily lives.

2) Parents and families are especially interested in advancing and improving the status of the lives of their children.

3) Parents and families are eager to grow, change, and adapt their culture through nurturing relationships with various helping early childhood professionals.

This view of families is consistently supported by research that shows that high-quality early childhood parent education and family literacy programs are positively received and used by parents of various cultural and socio-economic contexts (Nunez & Collignon, 2000; Keyser, 2006).

Four guidelines provide early childhood educators with direction on using family diversity as a means for further strengthening families (Lawrence-Lightfoot, 2003):

1) Through many interactions, families come to understand important cultural and social factors that impact their lives and that offer opportunities for strengthening their lives.

2) Create inviting settings and human relations contexts where families of different cultures and social situations find some artifacts and people they can relate to comfortably. For example, having bilingual early childhood resource personnel and parent leaders can be a positive and supportive factor.

3) Engage all early childhood professionals in continuing education related to cultural and social diversity in parents and families. This education should capitalize on the talents of parents as well as those of authorities in the field of multicultural education. Joint staff and parent training programs have proven especially meaningful as they provide opportunities for parents and staff to share common interests and concerns.

4) Develop and use parent-teacher curriculum and program review teams to assess and refine learning resources and activities to better reflect and support the cultural understanding of everyone in the community.

As the diversity of family structures suggest, the development of parents and families is like a dynamic continuum (Carter & McGoldrick, 1999). It is like an ever evolving spiral, influenced by our family origins, refined as we develop "our" families, and renewed again as our children become adults and launch their families. Within this set of rich and ever-changing dynamics, families develop, grow, and respond to each others' needs and strengths while also becoming members of the larger community. The socio-psychological perspective of family life provides us with another construct for better understanding families.

The socio-psychological perspective emphasizes the nature of how families deal with change by trying to establish healthy relationships to support them in their interactions with the larger social systems (Kerr & Bowen, 1988; Walsh, 1998). The development of trusting and nurturing relations during the early childhood years helps families foster the needed faith, sustenance, and resilience needed for responding to the natural changes that occur in families. For example, the trust developed in parent-child relations serves as the foundation for then expanding the family's relations with other systems as church, school, and work (Caldwell, 1989). It is important for early childhood professionals to recognize and act on the principles of the socio-developmental perspective such as shown in Figure 2.5 (Erikson, 1982). After-school tutoring programs in the early school years offer children additional caring adults to interact with and learn from.

Figure 2.5
Principles of Socio-Developmental Perspective

---

1) During the early childhood years parents and children are trying to establish the socio-emotional fabric (trust, mutuality, faith, care

56

and other attributes of loving relations) needed for articulating their identities as loving and caring persons.

2) The early childhood years are indeed the most change-oriented of any period that families face with the possible exception of adolescence. Parents typically have recently married, formed a new family, are trying to establish careers and jobs, and are also challenged with new social roles in their new family.

3) Supportive extra-family systems (quality child care, family-friendly work places, preventive counseling) help parents and children to more positively respond to the challenges of the early years.

4) Strong and harmonious marital dyads (or similar adult friendship dyads) lay the foundation for nurturing and sustaining strong family dynamics.

5) Healthy family dynamics are based in three key interpersonal life processes: respect for the integrity of each other, role-flexibility in helping each other develop individual identities, and ongoing positive and mutually rewarding and meaningful communication.

Unfortunately, for many families the stressors they face and experience erode their integrity and reduce their ability to grow in caring and positive ways. Early childhood intervention and prevention programs aim to support in families the development of healthy life styles.

It is very important for early childhood professionals to recognize that families of diverse cultures use different ways to respond to stress and to nurture and care for their children and families (Comer, 2001, Rogoff, 2003). In some cultures "healthy" family functioning is based in an intergenerational system where parents often rely more on grandparents in their decision making than on professionals. In other cases, a more communal child care system is common. In the nuclear family system, parents may rely more on pediatricians and family professionals for advice. Regardless, the traits of healthy parent-child relations and related supportive and nurturing care should be emphasized. Early childhood professionals should respect these cultural differences (Gonzalez-Mena, 1994) and indeed capitalize on the strengths present in the varying family systems (Swick, 2004).

A macro-system or community perspective of families is also very instructive of both the health of families and the overall well-being of the community (Brazelton & Greenspan, 2000). Healthy families require community contexts that nurture their well-being. The community perspective should provide families with safety and protection from harm.

A review of the quality of life in neighborhoods surrounding the school or child care center is instructive regarding child and family experiences. Community provisions for health care, education, recreation, child care, and meaningful human involvement in work and play are vital to the

57

family's sense of growth and well-being (Swick, 1997). We must also take account of how the community handles cultural diversity. Are all families valued? What needs in the community suggest some families are being isolated from needed services and why? For example, are homeless children fully integrated into school and community activities? (Swick, 2000).

Likewise, communities need healthy families in order to sustain their growth as viable places to live. The decline of family well-being signals a very poor future for society (Sachs, 2005). We can use the following five questions to guide our use of the community perspective in enhancing our understanding of families and communities:

1) What is the community like in which our children and families live? Is it safe, secure, enjoyable, and caring? If not, what messages are parents and children receiving?

2) What kinds of supportive resources exist to help families in need or in crisis? Are there adequate housing supports, access and affordability in child care, health and medical care resources for all families, and related social, educational, and economic supports?

3) Do parents, children, and other family members have opportunities to learn, grow, contribute, and be nurturing citizens? What educational and job opportunities exist for teen parents, families with heavy work schedules, or unemployed and underemployed parents?

4) What venues exist for all parents to have input into the quality of life the community? Are there advisory groups that actually impact child care standards, school practices, and community improvement?

5) What is the status of child care and early education in the community? Are there adequate quality child care slots? Is the early education program responsive to the varying cultural, language, and social contexts needs of the children and families?

Families are like all dynamic learning systems in that they renew themselves best through healthy intra-and extra family relations (Kerr & Bowen, 1988). The family system perspective emphasizes the interaction of the family with each other and with its important and sustaining systems. As Swick (1987) notes:

> A systems view of development and learning recognizes the interactive nature of all systems. In this perspective, the family system is in continuous interaction with other systems such as the school or the neighborhood. Each hu-

man being is a system and is a part of many other systems: family, school, work place, and society. The outcome is a "nest" of interlocking systems comprised of individuals and groups. (p. 14)

Within the family system, role assignments, structural arrangements, and relationship patterns become critical to how people learn and grow. Thus, during any phase of family development such as the early childhood years, roles, structure, and relationships are used to negotiate the dynamics of individual and group continuity and change (Anderson & Carter, 1984). When adults in the family have clear and appropriate constructs of their roles, the needed stability-change dynamics are maintained in ways that foster individual growth while also promoting the family's overall well-being. Three important principles of the family systems perspective provide insights into how families learn and grow (Minuchin, 1984; Minuchin & Nichols, 1993):

1) Parental beliefs (often heavily influenced by family of origin experiences) about family roles and relationships strongly influence the way they organize all aspects of family functioning.

2) Parental locus of control and overall level of integrity impact marital dynamics, parent-child relations, and the ways parents structure role assignments within the family system.

3 Changes in any single aspect of the family influence all other elements of the family system. For example, divorce changes the way people relate to each other which also impacts how people then handle role and task assignments.

Cultural attributes influence the dynamics of the family system. Beliefs, values, and role expectations are three key attributes that have a powerful influence on the children and parents. For example, in many minority cultures sharing and cooperation are valued more than independence and competition (Garbarino, 1992). Another example of how cultural factors affect parent and family dynamics is seen in the respect that many Latino and Asian parents show for the wisdom of the their parents. Child rearing decisions are often the result of modeling the instructions and actions of grandparents. Thus, role expectations and values in these families will optimize intergenerational relations. Parent educators and other early childhood educators need to be cognizant of these cultural influences and respond to them in their planning of parent and family involvement and educational activities (Lynch & Hanson, 1998; Powell, 1989).

Each of the theoretical/research perspectives on families discussed in this section of the chapter provide important insights into understanding parents, families, and communities. Understanding some of the important

59

conceptual and practical issues involved in relating to families is also critical to our being effective helpers.

> **CASE APPLICATION**: Contrast two theoretical perspectives presented in relation to explaining how families relate to each other and as to how we as early childhood educators can better support their needs. In effect, how can we use these perspectives to strengthen our relations with families? Also, in small groups share reports on the work each of you did on comparison of two theoretical perspectives.

Understanding Families: Conceptual and Practical Issues

Learning about parents and families is enhanced when we become informed about the issues that prevail in their lives. We review issues such as what are parent views of their contexts, what is a family empowerment approach, how can we best facilitate an empowerment process in families, what are key dispositions in early childhood professionals that nurture this positive strengths perspective in families, and how can we better understand and use parental strengths as "educators" of their children.

Parent and family views of "understanding" in relation to their situations and contexts: Too often early childhood professionals dominate the construct and application of "understanding family needs" to the detriment of the development of meaningful parent/family-professional relations (Powell, 1989). The parent and family view is critical to having accurate and useful insights into family needs and strengths. It is important for professionals to know how parents see their behavior, their situations, and what resources and support they feel the strongest about (Keyser, 2006).

For example, in an early childhood home visit program evaluated by the author, several parents were asked to list the needs they felt most important to them. When home visitors saw the list many of them were surprised in that what parents saw as most important did not match their professional needs-assessment. Parents were more likely to list personal items (I need more time for myself to get my head straight to be a good parent) and professionals saw basic child (health or educational enrichment) and family needs. It was not that parents and professionals differed on the needs; rather, they saw things differently and their priorities were different. Thus when we take the parental perspective seriously and act on it, we increase the parents' sense of power in being a parent (Goodnow & Collins, 1990; Swick, 2004).

What is an empowerment approach: We have some key insights that are especially helpful in defining empowerment in relation to strengthening parents, families, schools, and communities. Maslow's (1968) construct that human beings self-actualize best when they have a proactive needs-meeting perspective and system is foundational to the empowerment paradigm. Our ability to be creative in negotiating the person-environment dynamics in favor of positive and growing strategies is indeed important. When people are mostly stymied in this regard, their growth is limited. Swick and Graves (1993) suggest:

> Major deficiencies in one's support context (malnutrition, detachment, abuse, poverty) threaten the growth process and weaken one's integrity. (p. 51)

An empowerment approach is also about helping people resolve psycho-social issues in ways that enhance their sense of self and self-other relations (Erikson, 1982). For example, helping parents develop their self-confidence through adult education and job skills training can positively influence how they view their relations with their children. As parents view their "self" as growing, their self-other relationships are likely to be strengthened (Garbarino, 1992).

It is also important to contextualize the parent and family issues that might contribute to or impede empowerment. Bronfenbrenner's (1979, 2005) ecological theory shows how power really emerges from the nature and structure of human relationships. Thus our sense of where parents are at within their extended family dynamics becomes very important in cultural contexts that value strong intergenerational relations (Lynch & Hanson, 1998). In addition, understanding how chronic poverty negatively impacts family interactions is key to constructing ways for parents and children to resolve some of the inevitable tensions that come from such a situation (Nunez, 1996).

Closely related to context is the manner in which parents and families perceive their ability to function in healthy and nurturing ways (Dunst, Trivette, & Deal, 1988). In many cases, parents and families have experienced continuing problems, failed attempts at resolving crises, and chronic depression that often result from this cycle of despair. From these experiences parents and families often develop perceptual orientations that are negative and self-defeating (Garbarino, 1992). Parent and family empowerment is about helping people develop more proactive mental schemes for problem solving and functioning healthy.

Facilitating an empowerment process in parents and families: In helping parents become empowered we need to be sensitive to involving them and ourselves in using five insights (See Figure 2.6) to guide our functioning (Baum & Swick, 2008).

Figure 2.6
Five Insights on Empowering Families

---

1) <u>Understanding context</u> is key to establishing a basis for family strengthening. Parents and families as well as helping profession-

als need to know what the important needs are, the strengths and resources that families can bring to the table, and how professionals and parents/families can jointly pursue a family-strengthening agenda (Powell, 1998).

2) Developing trusting relationships within the family and between family and professional helpers is essential to engaging families in empowering activities (Swick, 1991, 2004). A priority value of parents in the behavior of family helpers with whom they relate is that this person be trustworthy (Galinsky, 1990).

3) Nurture a sense of mutuality that parents, families, and early childhood professionals value in their helping relationships. Reciprocity is at the center of healthy relationships and it is key to any long term empowerment of parents and families (Garbarino, 1992).

4) Developing a sense of purpose and action in achieving success in parenting and family functioning (Spacapan & Oskamp, 1992). Life-skills education, involvement of and professionals in joint assessment and planning work, and on-going parental involvement in their children's growth and learning are some ways to promote this needed sense of control (Barbour & Barbour, 2001).

5) Support open and honest communication (Couchenour & Chrisman, 2000). Being good listeners, responsive to cultural differences, and nurturing in our relations with parents and families is key to creating the needed inviting atmosphere where families and professionals sense the authenticity of their partnership.

Across cultures, parents and families point to three important communication elements that empower them: respectful insights about their family situation, friendly and inviting interactions, and trusting relations with early childhood educators (Chavkin, 1993; Comer, 2001; Swick, 2004).

Key attributes of early childhood professionals that nurture a family strengthening approach: Unfortunately, research shows that without purposeful education and self-insight and corresponding behavioral change, many early childhood professionals inhibit if not impede the growth of many parents and families, especially those families that are culturally or socially different from themselves (Powell, 1989, 1998).

A key attribute of effective early childhood educators is empathy (Couchenour & Chrisman, 2000). In noting the real value of empathy in nurturing family growth, Swick and Graves (1993) state:

> Such understanding [as emerges in an empathetic relationships] suggests that the professional is able to relate to the other person's situation in a proactive manner, promoting the total well-being of the family members involved. In this sense, understanding connotes the skill of moving beyond traditional stereotypes that act to isolate professional helpers and families. Observations now become mutually

formulated insights that evolve from the family's ideas as
well as the professional's. (p. 53)

Interrelated with empathy, several facilitative attributes are noted in
the research (Swick, 1991; Swick & McKnight, 1989): positive teacher attitudes toward parents, listening and responding sensitively to parent and
family views, teacher leadership in initiating parent and family support
activities, continual teacher training on parent and family education and
involvement, high support from administrators, and a values system that
views parents and families as the child's key teachers. Interestingly, parents
note the following attributes of teachers as key: "trust, warmth, closeness,
positive self-image, effective classroom management, family-centeredness,
knowledge of subject matter, continuing interactions with parents, positive
discipline approach, and nurturance" (Swick, 1991, p. 40).

Understanding and valuing parents and family as the child's key
educators: Healthy growth in families occurs best when parents and other
adult family members act in the role of "educator" in the global sense of
that construct. Ruddick's (1995) point that "care and nurturance" are
central to this educational process. Early childhood educators (who often
function in the role of parent educators too!) need to be sensitive to nurturing in parents this value of their role as educators. As noted in Figure
2.7 it begins with parental self-care and develops through interactive
and growth experiences to include the care and nurturance parents give
to children, other family, and of course through their many roles in the
community (Small, 2001).

Figure 2.7
A Developmental-Interactive View
of Parental Growth in Caring

Caring in the Community

Caring for Child and Family

Marital / Friendship Caring

Caring for Self

Our very important role as early childhood educators includes facilitating in parents the recognition that the following beliefs and behaviors
can support their work in caring and nurturing for their children and
themselves (Noddings, 1992; Galinsky, 1987; Swick, Da Ros, & Kovach,
2001):

* We must value and respect the unique and special role and
  life of each person.

* Our ultimate goal in life is to become caring and nurturing
  people who positively influence the dynamics of self, self-other,
  self-environment, and self-idea.

* We need to be cognizant of our responsibility to empower others through respectful and caring relations.

* Our sensitivity to the values and interests of culturally different families helps everyone, nurturing in all the key reality that we are indeed able to grow and learn through our differences and commonalities.

CASE APPLICATION: Interview a parent about their perspectives on their own empowerment efforts. What do they see as most needed as they nurture and care for children? How do they feel you can be most helpful in your role as a early childhood education professional?

Families and Communities as Learning Systems

We are gaining new insights about how families and communities are interacting learning systems that impact human learning and development. A comprehensive understanding of families requires us to gain insight into these systems and how they influence parents, children, families, and communities.

The *family learning system* is comprised of three important elements: structure, roles, and relationships. The manner in which a family is structured (the number of adults and children, nuclear, intergenerational, step-family, who and how decisions are made, and various expectations that family have for each other) impacts how people behave, see themselves, relate to others, and indeed come to learn and share with others (Fishel, 1991). The structure of a family establishes "boundaries" (lines that speak to us about what, where, and how we can behave) in relation to how parents, children, and other family interact with others. Wide cultural variations in family structure require us to be cognizant of how cultural factors might influence children's approaches to learning and growth. Bi-lingual, multicultural families have rich experiences that emanate from their family system. We need to see these variations as strengths and as "sources of learning" for our classrooms, schools, and communities (Chavkin, 1993; Taylor & Whittaker, 2009).

The roles that parents, children, and family perform are the substance of their learning relationships (Swick, 1991). It is through role assignments that families achieve the needed services and activities to sustain and support their growth. Roles also provide us with schemas on how the human process of functioning works. Again, cultural variation tells us much on how families respond to varying social, spiritual, economic, and political influences in their lives. For example, in many first generation Hispanic migrant families it is expected that older males will leave school early to help sustain the larger family economically.

64

In more progressive American cultures this would be seen as truancy from school and is indeed illegal. But in migrant cultures that depend on working "adults" to optimize their survival this is viewed as essential and honorable. In doing a focus group with several English as a Second Language migrant parents, the author noted that parents complained that teachers and administrators often failed to see just how important it was for their older children (usually high school age) to be working.

<u>Relationships</u> are the heart and soul of family learning (Pipher, 1996). The ways in which parents, parents and children, and other family interact with each other regularly speak louder than any verbal exchanges that may occur in families. Our relationships (how we care and nurture each other) establish the value, the support, and the expectations we have of each other. The relationship patterns established in families during the early childhood years are especially significant. As Swick (1991) notes:

> The family's power is in its identity as that process evolves through the many interactions of family members during the early childhood years. Beginning with the parents' beliefs and actions, and extending outward through parent-child and then family-community transactions, a context is developed that serves as our most intense learning arena. (p. 121)

Significantly, in most cultures, warm, nurturing, and intimate family relations have an overwhelmingly positive influence on children and adults (Brooks & Goldstein, 2001).

Community learning systems help us to better understand families and their challenges and also offer us insights into ways that we might strengthen our communities as places where families can indeed be empowered (Barbour & Barbour, 2001). Indeed, research on healthy families show they are connected to supportive relatives, neighbors, churches, community groups, and other supportive resources (Pipher, 1996). We also have evidence that high-crime, chronic poverty, low-resource communities degrade and stress families as well as other citizens (Nunez & Collignon, 2000). Communities impact families in many ways but during the early childhood years seven key elements of this system are particularly powerful:

1) <u>Safety and security</u> are cornerstones of parent, child, and family well-being (Maslow, 1968). That is, families of diverse cultures, talents, and interests must be able to find the community at minimum as a safe place where they can freely learn, live, and contribute to others. As Brazelton and Greenspan (2000) note:

> Communities struggling with cohesion, safety and security, lack of communication among

members or polarized beliefs will generally not have the wherewithal or energy for reflective action. There are many examples of unsafe and chaotic communities that are fragmented into weary, isolated families or individuals or warring factions based on polarized beliefs. There are also many communities that have formed cohesive bonds that cross cultural divides and allow for reflective planned actions on behalf of education, health, open space, and other needs of children.

(pp. 162-163)

2) <u>Healthy development of self and family</u> is another benchmark of communities that truly care for their people (Schorr, 1997). We need to see "health" as inclusive of environmental factors (toxins like lead poisoning, for example) that might negatively impact child and family health as well as the preventive pediatric prenatal and post-natal health care procedures. And we must also see health and medical care as family affairs, opportunities to educate ourselves and families about proactive ways to living with meaning and in healthy ways. Emotional health thus becomes a priority as well as physical health. Early childhood professionals can have a major impact on the well-being of children, parents, and families when they advocate and act to achieve: prenatal health care for all women who are pregnant regardless of socio-economic or other status indicators; on-going health and wellness care checkups and corresponding services for all children; and continuing parent, family, and community education on toxins and other health dangers and how to act in preventable ways (Brazelton & Greenspan, (2000).

3) <u>High-quality child care and early education</u> is a key to communities that hope to empower parents, children, and families (Garbarino, 1992; Schorr, 1997). Parents and families during the early childhood years need out-of-home care that nurtures not only their children but them too! It is imperative that only highly skilled and caring staff interact with children while parents are at work or about other tasks. It is also key that caring communities advance the quality of child care issues to the top of city and community council agendas (Bronfenbrenner, 2005). We need new visions on how to craft, fund, and deploy high-quality infant, toddler, and early child care programs.

4) <u>Strong parent and family education and support efforts</u> are needed to help families acquire the needed skills and resources to truly enhance and enrich them and their children (Schorr,

1997). Communities should assess the "health and status" of their parents and families through identifying risk indicators that call for community involvement. For example, homelessness and chronic poverty among young families are major problems in many communities (Nunez, 1996). Family support efforts should include the basics (resources to meet immediate life needs) but also offer empowerment activities through education, job training, and parenting education (Swick, Da Ros, & Kovach, 2001).

5) <u>Adult education, job training, and family literacy strategies and resources</u> can serve to help parents and families create self-sustaining and productive habits early in the formation of family life (Darling, 1989). Communities that lack the empowerment infrastructure that education and job training produce often become places of failure, high crime, and human degradation (Schorr, 1997). In contrast, caring and strong communities produce the needed human capital to respond effectively to human growth and change.

6) <u>Opportunities for social and recreational involvement</u> enrich the lives of parents and families, particularly during the early years (Brazelton & Greenspan, 2000). Outdoor and indoor recreational/educational activities like zoos, museums, libraries, concerts, and other very stimulating and nurturing experiences, help parents and children gain new insights into themselves, each other, and their community (Pipher, 1996). Even in smaller communities, adults can organize stimulating and important identity-enhancing activities. School or church sponsored youth activities, family meals at school, and other activities like these are very important to child and family development.

7) <u>Chances to participate in community development and policy setting</u> establish a basis for every person to have ownership in the well-being of each other (Comer, 2001). Family-school-community partnerships offer the most viable means for nurturing a sense of ownership of the school and community in citizens who often feel isolated from the power structure. Beginning with parent leadership training for serving as school volunteers or as members of school decision making teams to include their involvement in city or county councils, such school-community activities can indeed empower all parents and families.

Ultimately, families and communities are learning systems where we gain our ideas about our identity and our place in the community. We need to attend to all of the perspectives and realities of the human learning systems that impact parents and families if we are to gain the needed insights for then supporting and partnering with them as we all grow and learn. In effect, as Swick (1991) suggests, communities must play their part if schools and families are to succeed.

> In particular, communities need to be in covenant with families and schools regarding the mission of creating learning environments where children can grow and succeed. Everyone in the community needs to see the education and well-being of children and families as their priority; schools they serve must not be challenged to handle this role in isolation from the very sources it serves. (pp. 157-158)

SUMMATIVE DISCUSSION OF APPLICATION POINTS

Parent-teacher and family-school-community relations are most powerful when early childhood professionals have insights into how families develop and function. Without a strong system for learning about families, early childhood professionals are likely to distort or limit the process of partnership development. The following application points offer many opportunities for helping family-school-community achieve positive and meaningful relations.

* Regardless of the difficult circumstances in which families may be living, *focus on their strengths*. Make a list of the attributes of the family that you value. Have the family do this same activity with each other to highlight their talents and appreciation of each other.

* Learn about families through many lenses. Do not use one-dimensional stereotypes to "judge" families; rather, use many perspectives and tools to gain an "understanding" of families.

* Get to know families through their perspectives by interviewing them, holding focus groups with them, and doing activities with them. Joint parent-professional activities strengthen the partnership and help parents see themselves as important people.

* Know the issues that families are experiencing and advocate for strategies that will strengthen families. Help families get involved in this process so they are leaders in the partnership.

Suggested Web Sites

Administration for Children and Families. <www.act.dhhs.gov>

National Parent Information Network/ERIC. <npin.org>

Zero to Three. <www.zerotothree.org>

National Network for Family Resiliency. <www.nnfr.org>

Future of Children. <www.futureofchildren.org>

Families and Work Institute. <www.familiesandwork.org>

National Center for Fathering. <www.fathers.com>

Family Village. <www.familyvillage.wisc.edu>

Federation for Children with Special Needs. <www.fcsn.org>

Stand for Children. <www.standorg/>

References

Anderson, R., & Carter, I. (1984). Human behavior in the social environment: A social systems approach. New York: Aldine Publishing.

Barbour, C., & Barbour, N. (2001). Families, schools, and communities: Building partnerships for educating children. Columbus, OH: Merrill Prentice Hall.

Baum, A., & Swick, K. (2008). Dispositions toward families and family involvement: Supporting preservice teacher development. Early Childhood Education Journal, 35 (6), 579-584.

Brazelton, T., & Greenspan, S. (2000). The irreducible needs of children. Cambridge, MA: Perseus.

Bronfenbrenner, U. (1979). The ecology of human development and learning. Cambridge, MA: Harvard University Press.

Bronfenbrenner, U (1986). Alienation and the four worlds of childhood. Phi Delta Kappan, 67 (6), 430-436.

Bronfenbrenner, U. (2005). Making human beings human: Bioecological perspectives on human development. Thousand Oaks, CA: Sage.

Brooks, R., & Goldstein, S. (2001). Raising resilient children. Chicago, IL: Contemporary Books.

Caldwell, B. (1989). A faltering trust. In D. Blazer (Ed.). Faith development in early childhood. Kansas City, MO: Sheed & Ward.

Carter, B., & McGoldrick, M. (Eds). (1999). The expanded life cycle: Individual, family, and social perspectives. Third Edition. Boston: Allyn and Bacon.

Chavkin, N. (1993). Families and schools in a pluralistic society. Albany, NY: State University of New York Press.

Children's Defense Fund. (1998). Child care challenge. Washington, DC: Children's Defense Fund.

Cochran, C. (1988). Parental empowerment in Family Matters: Lessons learned from a research program. In D. Powell (Ed.). <u>Parent education as early childhood intervention</u>. Norwood, NJ: Ablex.

Comer, J. (1997). <u>Waiting for a miracle: Why schools can't solve our problems – and how we can</u>. New York: Dutton.

Comer, J. (2001). Schools that develop children. <u>The American Prospect</u>, 12 (7), 3-12.

Couchenour, D., & Chrisman, K. (2000). <u>Families, schools, and communities: Together for young children</u>. New York: Delmar.

Darling, L. (1989). <u>Family literacy project</u>. Louisville, KY: Family Literacy Project.

Diss, R., & Buckley, P. (2005). <u>Developing family and community involvement skills through case studies and field experiences</u>. Columbus, OH: Pearson.

Dunst, C., Trivette, C., & Deal, A. (1988). <u>Enabling and empowering families: Principles and guidelines for practice</u>. Cambridge, MA: Brookline Books.

Edin, K., & Lein, L. (1997). <u>Making ends meet: How single mothers survive welfare and low-wage work</u>. New York: Russell Sage Foundation.

Elkind, D. (1994). <u>Ties that stress: The new family imbalance</u>. Cambridge, MA: Harvard University Press.

Epstein, J. (1995). School/Family/Community Partnerships: Caring for the children we share. <u>Phi Delta Kappan</u>, May, 701-712.

Erikson, E. (1982). <u>The life cycle completed</u>. New York: W.W. Norton.

Feeney, S., & Freeman, N. (1999). <u>Ethics in the early childhood educator: Using the NAEYC Code of Ethics</u>. Washington, DC: National Association for the Education of Young Children.

File, N. (2001). Family-professional partnerships: Practice that matches philosophy. <u>Young Children</u>, 56 (4), 70-74.

Fishel, E. (1991). <u>Family mirrors: What our children's lives reveal about ourselves</u>. Boston, MA: Houghton Mifflin.

Folbre, N. (2001). <u>The invisible heart: Economics and family values</u>. New York: The New Press.

Galinsky, E. (1987). <u>The six stages of parenthood</u>. Reading, MA: Addison-Wesley.

Galinsky, E. (1990). Why are some teacher-parent relationships clouded with difficulties? <u>Young Children</u>, 45 (5), 2-3 + 38-39.

Galinsky, E. (1999). <u>Ask the children: What America's children really think about working parents</u>. New York: Morrow.

Garbarino, J. (1992). <u>Children and families in the social environment</u>. New York: Aldine de Gruyter.

Garbarino, J. (1995). <u>Raising children in a socially toxic environment</u>. San Francisco, CA: Jossey-Bass.

Garbarino, J., & Bedard, C. (2001). <u>Parents under siege: Why you are the solution, not the problem in your child's life</u>. New York: The Free Press.

Gonzalez-Mena, J. (1994). <u>From a parent's perspective</u>. Salem, WI: Sheffield.

Gonzalez-Mena, J. (2006). <u>The young child in the family and the community</u>. Fourth Edition. Columbus, OH: Pearson.

Goodnow, J., & Collins, W. (1990). <u>Development according to parents: The nature, sources, and consequences of parents' ideas</u>. New York: Lawrence Erlbaum Associates, Publishers.

Hanson, M., & Lynch, E. (2004). <u>Understanding families: Approaches to diversity, disability, and risk</u>. Baltimore, MD: Paul H. Brookes.

Hatch, A. (1995). <u>Qualitative research in early childhood settings.</u> Westport, CT: Praeger.

Kerr, M., & Bowen, M. (1988). <u>Family evaluation</u>. New York: W.W. Norton.

Keyser, J. (2006). <u>From parents to partners: Building a family-centered early childhood program</u>. Washington, DC: National Association for the Education of Young Children.

Kotre, J. (1999). <u>Make it count</u>. New York: The Free Press.

Lawrence-Lightfoot, S. (2003). <u>The essential conversation: What parents and teachers can learn from each other</u>. New York: Random House.

Leavitt, R. (1994). <u>Power and emotion in infant-toddler day care</u>. Albany, NY: State University of New York Press.

Lynch, E., & Hanson, M. (1998). <u>Developing cross-cultural competence: A guide for working with children and their families</u>. Baltimore, MD: Paul Brookes.

Maslow, A. (1968). <u>Toward a psychology of being</u>. New York: D. Van Nostrand.

McKenry, P., & Price, S. (1994). <u>Families and change: Coping with stressful events</u>. Thousand Oaks, CA: Sage.

Minuchin, S. (1984). <u>Family kaleidoscope</u>. Cambridge, MA: Harvard University Press.

Minuchin, S., & Nichols, M. (1993). <u>Family healing</u>. New York: The Free Press.

Noddings, N. (1992). <u>The challenge to care in schools</u>. New York: Teachers College Press.

Nunez, R. (1996). The new poverty: Homeless families in America. New York: Insight Books (Plenum Press).

Nunez, R., & Collignon, K. (2000). Supporting family learning: Building a community of learners. In J. Stronge & E. Reed-Victor (Eds.). Educating homeless students: Promising practices. Larchmont, NY: Eye on Education.

Pence, A. (1988). Ecological research with children and families. New York: Teachers College Press.

Pipher, M. (1996). The shelter of each other: Rebuilding our families. New York: Ballentine.

Powell, D. (1989). Families in early childhood programs. Washington, DC: National Association for the Education of Young Children.

Powell, D. (1998). Reweaving parents into the fabric of early childhood programs. Young Children, 53 (5), 60-67.

Powell, D., Zambrann, R., & Silva-Palcios, V. (1990). Designing culturally responsive parent programs: A comparison of low-income Mexican and Mexican-American mothers' preferences. Family Relations, 309, 298-304.

Rogoff, B. (2003). The cultural nature of human development. New York: Oxford University Press.

Ruddick, S. (1995). Maternal thinking. Boston, MA: Beacon Press.

Sachs, J. (2005). The end of poverty. New York, NY: The Penguin Press.

Schorr, L. (1997). Common purpose: Strengthening families and neighborhoods to rebuild America. New York: Anchor Books/Doubleday.

Skolnick, A. (1991). Embattled paradise: The American family in an age of uncertainty. New York: Basic Books.

Small, M. (2001). Kids: How biology and culture raise our children. New York. Doubleday.

Spacapan, S., & Oskamp, S. (Eds.). (1992). Helping and being helped: Naturalistic studies. Newbury Park, CA: Sage.

Swick, K. (1987). Perspectives on understanding and working with families. Champaign, IL: Stipes.

Swick, K. (1991). Teacher-parent partnerships to enhance school success in early childhood education. Washington, DC: National Education Association.

Swick, K. (1993). Strengthening parents and families during the early childhood years. Champaign, IL: Stipes.

Swick, K. (1997) A family-school approach for nurturing caring in young children. Early Childhood Education Journal, 25 (2), 151-154.

Swick, K. (2000). Building effective awareness programs for homeless students among staff, peers, and community members. In J. Stronge & E. Reed-Victor. (Eds.). Educating homeless students: Promising practices. Larchmont, NY: Eye on Education.

Swick, K. (2001). Nurturing decency through caring and serving during the early childhood years. Early Childhood Education Journal, 29 (2), 131-138.

Swick, K. (2004). Empowering parents, families, schools and communities during the early childhood years. Champaign, IL: Stipes.

Swick, K., & McKnight, S. (1989). Characteristics of kindergarten teachers who promote parent involvement. Early Childhood Research Quaterly, 4 (1), 19-30.

Swick, K., & Graves, S. (1993). Empowering at-risk families during the early childhood years. Washington, DC: National Education Association.

Swick, K., Da Ros, D., & Pavia, L. (1999). Inquiry as key to early childhood teacher education. Childhood Education, 75, (2), 66-70.

Swick, K., Da Ros, D., & Kovach, B. (2001). Empowering parents and families through a caring inquiry approach. Early Childhood Education Journal, 29 (1), 65-71.

Taylor, L., & Whittaker, C. (2009). Bridging multiple worlds: Case studies of diverse educational communities. Columbus, OH: Pearson.

Walsh, F. (1998). Strengthening family resilience. New York, NY: Guilford.

Chapter Three

Relating and Responding to
the Needs and Strengths
of Diverse Families

CAPSULE: Understanding the dynamics of families is the starting point to supporting them in dealing with their stressors. Family differences help to highlight challenges, issues, and resources that families can use to resolve or at least to deal effectively with problems. Early childhood professionals need to use their insights on family differences to promote the family in their efforts to grow and learn.

Chapter Three Objectives:

1) Gain knowledge and insight into a framework for understanding and responding to family differences.

2) Explain how you might use this framework in your work with parents and families.

3) Strengthen your understanding of the role of culture in family functioning and how you can use cultural knowledge to enhance your relations with families.

4) Apply your knowledge of the family differences framework to relating to families living in different situations and contexts.

5) Outline and explain strategies you see as important to your work with families.

Many factors influence how families behave and function. Lynch and Hanson (1998) remind us of the need for early childhood educators and other helping professionals to be open to the breadth of these factors and of how individual families may respond to them:

Cultural practices as well as the individual characteristics of the person or family may influence the interactions between service providers or interventionists and the families receiving services. Similar to the plants in the garden, the individuals within a community all share basic needs, but they will differ as to their specific needs and the types of environments that support growth. The interventionist or service provider, similar to the gardener, must individualize interventions for each family to address families' concerns and priorities and tailor services to families' needs and resources. Being sensitive, knowledgeable, and understanding of the families' cultural practices enhances this process and relationship. (pp. 4-5)

The main purpose of this chapter is to engage the reader in gaining insight into better relating and responding to the needs and strengths of diverse families. In pursuing this purpose, an empowerment framework for conceptualizing positive and meaningful ways to understand family differences is presented and discussed. Additionally, the role of culture in influencing family life is examined as well as the role of various stressors in family dynamics. A family typology (healthy, special needs, at-risk, and dysfunctional) is used to help us improve our sensitivity to the complexity of family life and to fulfill our need to be in caring roles and relations with all families. Finally, we will explore some basic strategies for strengthening families.

A Framework for Dealing with Family Differences

The basis for relating and responding effectively to the needs of families is an empowerment paradigm. As noted in Chapter Two, the work of Bronfenbrenner (1979), Maslow (1968), Erikson (1959) and others provides the theoretical and research foundation to this construct. As opposed to past constructs in this regard, *the empowerment paradigm emphasizes an empathetic orientation to our work with families* (Dunst, Trivette, & Deal, 1998; Hanson & Lynch, 2004). The construct of empathy includes several elements of perceptual and interpersonal psychology as noted by Swick and Graves (1993):

It [empathy] implies that one has the ability to understand another person's situation (inclusive of that person's self-assessment) in an ecologically sensitive and comprehensive manner. Such understanding suggests that the professional is able to relate to the other person's situation in a proactive manner, promoting the total well-being of the family members involved. In this sense, understanding connotes the skill of moving beyond traditional stereotypes that act to isolate professional helpers and families. Ob-

servations now become mutually formulated insights that
evolve from the family's ideas as well as the professional's.
(pp. 52-53)

Central to the work of early childhood educators is developing an
empathetic approach in relating and responding to the needs of families.
The starting point is in developing self-perceptions that recognize our
strengths, limitations, and motivations to be truly caring people (Swick,
2006).

With a foundation of self-worth, early childhood professionals see
others as worthy and important. It is very important for the parent-
professional relationship to have a strong sense of mutuality. When
we have this sense of support for each other everyone is strengthened
(Spacapan & Oskamp, 1992). This process of being empathetic helpers
requires us as professionals to develop and refine partnership skills,
communication behaviors, and problem-solving strategies.

Partnership skills include listening, helping, responding in caring
ways, and many other attributes that foster caring relations. Likewise,
open and responsive communication is critical to having healthy and
meaningful relationships. For example, in cases where family culture
is distinct from that of the helping professional, it is essential that we
read more than just verbal responses, we need to be sensitive to what
they believe is most important in the lives of their family (Erickson &
Kurz-Riemer, 1999). Problem-solving is the process families and helping
professionals use to negotiate the needs-resources balancing act and to
solidify family well-being. But we must also recognize that "our ways" of
meeting needs may not honor the culture or interests of some families.
Lynch and Hanson (1998) share an example where both parents and
helping professionals agreed on the need for more nutritious food for the
child but differed greatly on how to do this.

In this instance the child's weight gain and nutrition were
of concern both to the parents and to the health care professionals. The nutritionists working in conjunction with
the primary care physician recommended a new diet for
the child. A visiting nurse later found that the family was
not following the recommended regimen because some
of the foods were considered to be "hot" foods or "cold"
foods in that culture and, therefore, were not appropriate
for the child's condition. (p. 507)

Powell (1989) tells about a similar cultural situation where parents
continued to "bottle prop" when feeding their infants in spite of their
verbally affirming that holding babies warmly during feeding was more
appropriate. When questioned about their behavior these parents noted
that while they agreed with the parent educator, their parents said that

bottle propping worked fine and thus they did not want to disagree with them. Indeed, we must work with the total family system in using problem solving in respectful ways (Bronfenbrenner, 2005).

As caring professionals who desire to support parent, child, and family growth during the early years, we need to gain insight into the families we work with and use this information to enact the empathic perspective. Swick and Graves (1993, pp. 56-57) identify six question areas that professionals can use to guide their work – see Figure 3.1.

Figure 3.1
Six Question Areas to Guide Early Childhood
Educators' Work with Families

---

1) Who are the families we serve? What do we know about these families that can strengthen us in being caring helpers?

2) What do we know about ourselves as early childhood helping professionals? How do we think about the families we serve?

3) What are the programs, services, and activities we offer families? Are they "enabling and empowering" in that they respond to family-perceived needs?

4) How do our program activities reflect family respect and family autonomy? Do we use parent input in the shaping of program activities?

5) How is the uniqueness of each family's integrity accounted for in our programs? Are there opportunities for helpers and families to learn about each other's needs and strengths?

6) What is the predominant view of our staff regarding families and our relationship with families? Is it one of positive, nurturing partnerships, or is it a cynical view?

These questions help us probe where we are at in relation to our images of the families we want to help.

To actualize this strengths-oriented approach we need to address the issues of mutuality, respect for family uniqueness, and the need to continually seek a partnership approach. The empowerment process is based in the idea that all of the people involved in the relationship process are valued and validated. The following points help guide our work in this regard (Chavkin, 1993; Comer, 2001; Kelly, 2006).

* Recognize the important role that "reciprocity" plays in parent/family-professional relationships.

* Recognize and review your "motivations" to be in a caring role with parents, children, and families.

* Make collaboration the benchmark of the way your family program works.

* Continually review and refine your "strengths" as a helper. List the traits you see as your real strengths, and then make a list of need areas you want to improve.

* Realize that helping situations are systemic in nature and that whatever happens in one part of that relationship system impacts all other aspects of it.

Five Case Application Strategies

1) TEAM WITH THE FAMILY: Work with the family on their concepts and perceptions of the type of involvement that best suits their needs. Individualized efforts meet with the most success in engaging parents and family in meaningful partnerships (Comer & Haynes, 1991). Your Task: Interview a family and design an individualized involvement plan with them.

2) USE A STRENGTHS VIEW OF THE FAMILY: Effective, caring helpers look for and promote the strengths of the family. In telling about one of her heroes, Jennifer (a women pediatrician), Sara Lawrence-Lightfoot (1999) says:

> This focus on empowerment is central to Jennifer's practice and shapes the rituals and policies at the center. "A women must feel…this is about *you*. *Your* body. *Your* baby. *You* are at the center. *You* are problem-solving, learning, asking questions. *You* can decide. I want to give knowledge – through classes groups, teaching, mentoring, reading – so that they can make good and informed choices." (pp. 23-24)

The use of close, intimate relationship building strategies by Jennifer, extend to all truly caring early childhood professionals. Here we are looking first for what is good about the parent and family. Of course, we also observe for needs but do so in a nurturing way.

Your Task: In your work with parents or families encourage them to keep a journal of their strengths and positive accomplishments.

3) DEVELOP AND USE A PROACTIVE STANCE: People who are positive and proactive invite more supportive and growing responses in others (Spacapan & Oskamp, 1992). Develop a working style that is characterized as using concrete and helpful activities and strategies. For example, making sure a parent has transportation to a medical appointment for her

child's well-care checkup is a positive step in gaining the entire family's confidence and support.

Your Task: List what you think parents and families will like most about you and your relationship style. How can you strengthen these positive features of your self?

4) USE FAMILY-CENTERED PROBLEM SOLVING: The key point here is to involve the family in the problem solving process. This can be most effectively achieved through using parent identified problems or issues they need to address (DeJong & McKinney, 2002). Once parents gain experience in positively influencing their own lives and their children's, their overall use of proactive strategies is likely to be enhanced (Powell, 1998; Diss & Buckley, 2005).

Your Task: Design an activity where families can simulate solving a problem they feel is common to most parents and children.

5) USE MENTORING AND OTHER PARENT LEADERSHIP: Early childhood professionals have long recognized that parents have the context, the motivation, and usually the skills to become effective helpers of other parents (Keyser, 2006). The mentoring and nurturing relations that parents achieve through helping each other provide children with a strong role model, reinforce in the parent a positive self image, expand the resources for parents and families to use, and provide the professional with a stronger base for creating the needed "culture" for empowerment (File, 2001). As Powell (1989) has noted, many parents respond better to the help of parents they know and respect because their context is often similar and because they have seen how hard each other works to deal with the daily issues of parenting and family life. But this strategy is not an answer in all cases. In some cultures, parents may resist the overtures of other parents because it may be seen as a sign of weakness by the parent (Chavkin, 1993). Thus we must be careful not to stereotype or over-generalize the value of any particular involvement or support strategy. It is also evidence to support the need for involving parents and families in the selection of resources and strategies to support their family vision.

Your Task: Organize various strategies for helping parents to become mentors and advocates for each other.

The framework used here to conceptualize some important aspects of family differences is presented with a positive focus in the forefront of our working relations with families (Swick, 1991, 2004). The framework

80

includes four types of family situations: Healthy, Special Needs, At-Risk, and Dysfunctional. Each type of "family situation" is interrelated with contextual factors in the various systems in which parents and family function. At this point in the chapter the following elements of this framework and its appropriate uses are presented: the meaning of the "types" of family situations, the concepts related to their use (health, risk, special needs, dysfunctional), further discussion of the concept of risk, how this framework should be used, viewing the framework as a dynamic continuum, and emphasizing the value of this framework for achieving needed feedback.

Meaning of the "types" of family situations: A continuum of four types of family situations is noted: healthy, special needs, at-risk, and dysfunctional. These situational categories should be used to gain an understanding of where families are at in their overall functioning. Appropriate cultural, social, and family-specific data should be used in relation to how families function within these various contexts. *Healthy* refers to families that predominantly are characterized by attributes such as love, spirituality, caring, sharing, teaming, good communication, respect, mutuality, supportiveness, and other indicators that suggest the family is strong in negotiating various stressors (Pipher, 1996; Stinnett, 1979).

Special needs refer to family responses to situations that call for more than the average coping efforts. These situational contexts will mean unique things to different families. Stress levels and indeed perceived-stress vary greatly from family to family. Typically, family illness, a death in the family, and even positive events such as the birth of a new infant call for special coping from family (Carter & McGoldrick, 1999; Coloroso, 2000). Various factors play a role in how families dealing with special needs manage particular stressors: perceived threat, impact of the stress events, available supports to help deal with the stress, chronicity of the stressor(s), developmental functioning of the family (early childhood, adolescence, etc.), and other factors that are related to cultural, economic, social, and educational attributes (Seligman & Darling, 1989; Hanson & Lynch, 2004). The important point here is that "special needs" represent family contexts where the family members perceive and are experiencing stressors that reach beyond "their" normal coping resources but within the realm of problem solving efforts (Small, 2001). "Special needs" may also reflect particular challenges faced by a child or adult in the family. For example, a child may confront severe learning problems thus increasing already difficult special needs family situations.

At-risk refers to family situations where the stress is impacting families in negative ways. The term "risk" implies possible danger or harm is likely unless some preventive or corrective action is taken (Garbarino, 1992; Bronfenbrenner, 2005). Risk factors may include individual, environmental, or more likely combinations of individual and environmental factors. For example, illiteracy combined with chemical dependency is indeed a high-risk, volatile combination of events and likely to cause great harm (Huston, 1991). At-risk also refers to experiential contexts. For example, has the parent had a history of being abused? Our contextual past is a marked influence on the risks we currently face.

Dysfunctional connotes a breakdown in the family's socio-emotional system for living. This type of family situation is characterized by contextual factors such as chaos, violence, isolation from reality, continuing swings in moods and behavior, and other identifiers that suggest the family is indeed over whelmed and unable (at least at the time in question) to cope (Burland, 1984; Swick & Graves, 1993; Swick, 2008).

Elaboration on the concepts of healthy, special needs, at-risk, and dysfunctional: These concepts of family functioning occur within very dynamic situations and in relation to ever changing family systems.

HEALTHY: The concept of "healthy families" is indeed dynamic. The processes parents, children and family use in their daily lives distinguish "healthy" patterns of relating to stress. Swick (1991, 2004) identifies eight relationship processes (See Figure 3.2) that support families in their attempts to develop healthy responses in various life situations.

Figure 3.2
Relationship Building Processes Healthy Families Use

---

* Role flexibility

* Trust development

* Help-exchange

* Responsive listening

* Individuation

* Group functioning skills

* Nurturance

* Problem-solving

Healthy families use these relationship-building processes to develop a positive environment. Of particular interest is that families who are nurturing show more proactive efforts to live in positive ways (Rohner, 1986; Hanft, Rush, & Shelden, 2004)).

> Healthy families have problems just like all families; it is the way they respond to these stressors that determines their health or dysfunction. Swick (1991) notes: Healthy families tend to anticipate what kinds of feedback different actions might instigate; that is, they ask the question *What*

If…? This enables them to visualize various scenarios with regard to different actions. (p. 45)

One of the key features of healthy family responses is to explore various possibilities. At the same time, healthy families seem to plan life patterns, making needed adjustments in response to developmental shifts or ecological changes (Swick, Da Ros, & Kovach, 2001). This healthy approach to life is shaped early in the family's development and parents play the key role in laying the foundation for overall healthy family living.

CASE APPLICATION: What do you think healthy families do that we can share with all families as a proactive attribute for nurturing our effective helping skills. How would you nurture these attribute in families?

SPECIAL NEEDS: All families experience special needs situations over the life span. In some cases there may be a child who has special needs. In other situations the family is experiencing some form of extreme stress. The inherent stressors of our developmental journey (illness, accidents, unemployment, natural disasters, and other events) assure that every family will eventually confront special needs situations (Garbarino, 1992; Bronfenbrenner, 2005). It is the intensity of these experiences and their duration in some cases that can create serious challenges for parents, children, and other family (Coloroso, 2000). Indeed, healthy families experience these stressors too; it is the way we respond and this is so unique to each family system. ***In the context of this book special needs refers to these very stressful situations (child-specific or family-specific) that challenge families beyond their normal functioning*** (Coloroso, 2000).

Families in these situations need support and help, often in the form of validation that things can and will work out, temporary assistance with basic needs, and social and psychological support in adjusting to new relationship boundaries (Coloroso, 2000; Galinsky, 1990).

Parent, child, and family overload is perhaps the most prevalent and growing stress in families today (Elkind, 1994; Carlsson-Paige, 2008). Several factors have influenced the development of this "special needs situation" (Elkind, 1994): an increase in longevity, the emergence of an information economy, changing parent and child roles, increased work and family demands, as well as confusion over the role of families in our society (Bond, et al. 2003). Cultural influences also are evident in that many parents and their children have conflict over what roles in the mainstream culture are appropriate and which are inappropriate. Intercultural education in this regard is now becoming a part of many early childhood education programs (Chavkin, 1993).

Other special needs stressors include situations like the economic displacement of workers. Most families will experience these type challenges; yet it is in their response that we see how families begin to shape life long patterns of problem solving. Severe and enduring stress that is a part of some special needs experiences occurs in families in unique ways and yet there is a pattern of responses we need to understand.

The "stages" or sequence of family responses to special needs include: a sense of rage and/or fear, a desire to be isolated, reality distortion, breakdown in communication, serious lack of communication, chronic high-stress, problems in daily functioning, and feelings of shame or despair (Coloroso, 2000; Garbarino, 1992). While each family reacts uniquely to special needs situations, a review of some of these response patterns is presented.

Often we are initially struck with <u>a sense of fear and/or rage</u> at our predicament. Klein (1985) shares that when he and his wife came to the realization that their child had spastic cerebral palsy they had a sense of rage at this invasion of the family's normal development. He noted that both he and his wife were fearful of typical things like going to the grocery store that had never bothered them prior to this experience.

Another response is <u>a sense of real isolation</u> from our prior life situation. After a bitter divorce one mother noted (Swick, 1991):

> I felt dead, like something had died in my life. The many fights were over. Now it seemed as if those fights had filled a need to cling to my life. But now everything seemed cloudy. My daughter felt the same way, like an awful sense of relief – death. Except for work or school neither of us left the house for over half of the year. (p. 71)

With support and understanding, most families ***respond in healthy ways to this initial need for aloneness***. Typically people do need a period of retreat to deal with the emotional stress and to have time for re-mapping their lives (Scarf, 1995). Yet, we eventually must return to live in the world. Seligman and Darling (1989) tell the story of the parent of a dwarf who found this return avenue through group meetings with other parents.

> At first we could not bring ourselves to go (to the meeting). Maybe we didn't want to see what she was going to look like. We did go to the next meeting…That was the turning point, because at that meeting we began talking to a number of dwarfs. That's when we found out it was going to be O.K.: that dwarfs live like other people – they married, they drove cars, they took vacations, they held jobs – they could be like other people. (p. 45)

84

The stress of special needs situations can also impact people toward distortion of their realities (Scarf, 1995). We may continue to dry-clean the clothes of a spouse or continue other habits to protect us from the grieving. Naturally, we must eventually return to a normal picture of reality. Support, empathy, and encouragement seem to strengthen us to renew our commitment to life (Pipher, 1996).

There are additional reaction patterns in families: communication breakdowns, withdrawal from regular communication, facing daily high stress, difficulty in doing daily rituals, and an overall sense of despair (Swick & Williams, 2008). Fortunately, most families respond in healthy ways to these situations. As early childhood professionals we can be a part of the family's healing and renewal team.

CASE APPLICATION: Take note of a special need situation your family faced or of another family you know faced. What did you learn from the situation that you could use to help families in similar situations? What other "special needs" situations have helped you become more effective in relating to families who experience very difficult circumstances?

AT-RISK: Risk factors, as noted previously, are likely to happen in all families. The term risk means that some danger or likely problem is about to happen or will happen unless some preventive or corrective action is taken (Swick, 2004). In relation to the lives of young families, the construct of risk is especially relevant to our empowerment focus. Drawing upon the work of Garbarino (1982, 1992), Schwartzman (1985) and Dimidjian (1989), Swick and Graves (1993) note:

> Through the study of children and families, it has been noted that certain conditions or attributes put individuals and groups at risk. Researchers have consistently noted that when certain conditions were present (such as extreme poverty or low-resource social contexts), the individual and/or family integrity was threatened (at risk). In this sense, risks function like "stressors" in that they often require an inordinate amount of attention in order to maintain a level of adequate functioning. Left unattended they erode the family and/or the person's system for carrying out development and learning. (pp. 16-17)

In an effort to strengthen our understanding of the at-risk construct, Swick and Graves (1993) delineate levels of "riskness" (See Figure 3.3).

Figure 3.3
Levels of Riskness in Family Functioning

* Low risk

* Moderate risk

* High risk

Low-risk is used to denote families with just one or two risks of little long-term impact if attended to and if placed within a supportive context. Moderate-risk implies that two or more serious risk conditions are present, pervasive, and do represent a distinct threat to the family. High-risk indicates that the family is experiencing very high stress from events that place the total family functioning in danger. Usually these are multiple, interacting risks that combine to create the need for very high support and intervention with the family.

As Garbarino (1992) and Bronfenbrenner (2005) point out, children and families in the highest risk situation usually are confronting multiple stressors. Risk conditions have various sources within the person-environment ecology: individual and family resilience, intergenerational factors (such as family histories and mental health patterns), constitutional attributes (for example, the physical health of family members), and socio-ecological factors such as the economic stability of the community (Swick & Williams, 2008).

The most alarming aspect of high-riskness in families is the "ecology of despair" (Caldwell, 1989) that it can foster. Once this negative cycle of behavior becomes entrenched in young families it can foster even more riskness. Poverty alone or severe unemployment in the household, or possible combinations of these risks can be addressed effectively through family empowerment interventions.

We must be careful *to do no harm while we help the family increase its efficacy and caring* (Kerr & Bowen, 1988). Some of the attributes of families who have been engulfed in a series of difficult situations (Figure 3.4) are noted by Swick and Graves (1993, pp. 44-54):

Figure 3.4
Attributes of Families in High-Risk Situations

* A belief system that is predominantly fatalistic.

* A context that exudes a very low sense of control and suggests that the family is very dependent on extra-family happenings.

* People in the family seem to have low self-esteem.

* Family relationships are rigid with little role flexibility and family have little confidence in each other's role functioning.

* The family is mostly isolated from other school and community supports.

* The family either lacks a spiritual source of meaning or is overly rigid in its religious beliefs.

* Abusiveness and neglect seem prevalent in the family's recent history and in some cases in intergenerational stories.

A recursive, self-defeating style of life emerges when these behaviors and attitudes take hold of families. Indeed, the early childhood years offer the best opportunity to disrupt a cycle of fatalistic actions in families. Schools and communities acting in concert can create services and situations that prevent or limit the various risks that impact parents, children, and families. Several ideas are briefly noted as very influential in preventing or resolving many risk situations.

* Provide all expectant mothers and children with quality prenatal, maternal, and child health care (Brazelton & Greenspan, 2000).

* Assure that all families have their basic needs (food, clothing, housing, heat and other needs) met (Edin & Lein, 1997; Annie E. Casey 2008 Kids Count Data Book).

* Involve parents and family in meaningful adult education, family literacy, and parent education experiences (Swick, 1997, 2004).

* Provide and encourage parent use of job training and placement services, and provide needed supports such as transportation and child care (Edin & Lein, 1997).

* Offer quality child care to all families so that every family member feels secure while at work or play during the day (Brazelton & Greenspan, 2000).

* Provide a quality early childhood education program to help children and families have successful school and education experiences (Comer, 2001).

CASE APPLICATION: Identify and share strategies you believe will help families respond effectively in high-risk situations. Why do you see these as very helpful strategies? How would you use these strategies with families in very difficult situations?

DYSFUNCTIONAL: It is now agreed that even healthy families have some attributes of dysfunction; they are simply absorbed into the overall healthy pattern of stress responses and other problem-solving skills of family (Carter & McGoldrick, 1999). What happens in families that adopt dysfunctional responses is that certain perceptual and behavior patterns *appear to protect the family from change* (Boss, 1988) Change is inevitable in families and indeed is essential to our developmental growth. What initially appears to solve a family risk factor can quickly become THE FAMILY RESPONSE to that stressor even though that response is actually creating a dysfunctional pattern of living (Kagan & Schlosberg, 1989).

What happens in unhealthy family contexts is that problem-solving is usually replaced with more emotive-reactive thinking and thus family relations and responses are rigid, recursive, and often self-destructive. Swick (1991) explains some of the dynamics of this ineffectual learning system:

> *Unhealthy family relationship patterns* (which often lead to dysfunctionality) are characterized by their rigidity, insensitivity, and role distortion. Abnormal levels of emotionality along with excessive concentrations of power in one or two family members creates a volatile system, one in which the change process is resisted and often denied. In contrast to the *balance of power* found in functional families, an extreme imbalance of power is often present in the dysfunctional system. Too much is expected of one or two persons and usually these expectations are are based on inappropriate role assignments. In effect, dysfunctional families create excessive stress within their system of relationships by the way they rigidify roles and distort the balance of power. The system is out of balance before external change is ever engaged. (p. 101)

Three key stressors are linked to potential dysfunction (Figure 3.5) in families:

Figure 3.5
Key Stressors Linked to Family Dysfunction

---

1) Extreme and pervasive misconceptions about how children, adults, and families develop and function.

2) Highly distorted ideas about the roles different family members should perform.

3) A pervasive and chronic sense of fatalism that seems to embrace family living (Minuchin, 1984).

Misconceptions about development and family functioning: There is a strong connection between dysfunctional people and their growing up in a dysfunctional family context (Magid & McKelvey, 1987). Ineffective parenting seems to foster chaos and inappropriate developmental expectations for all involved. The use of abusive and harmful practices creates a sense of despair in many family members. Swick (1991) talks about how the dysfunctional syndrome works:

Dysfunctional syndromes are usually characterized by shame, guilt, denial of feelings, and punitive responses. In such a context the self is easily disabled, thus blocking the process of differentiation that is integral in healthy development. Healthy relationship patterns (inclusive of love, affection, guidance, and positive role modeling) are critical to the family's development of integrity over the life-span. This requires a family value system that promotes mutuality, trust, exploration, sharing, individuality, and teaming. Lacking in the needed resources to function in healthy ways, families at risk tend to rely on rigidly defined roles. Instead of a "we" environment emerging through positive and helpful relationships, an artificial and very insecure "I-focused" context takes shape. This self centered and narrowly defined system impedes the development of family bonding. (p. 111)

Distorted ideas about child and family roles: Dysfunctional families have distorted notions about what are appropriate roles for its members. For example, in many families where child abuse is prevalent it has been noted that role assignments are distorted. In a sense, the developmental pendulum is shattered and totally unacceptable and inappropriate roles are assigned to young children. A child may be assigned adult sexual or alcoholic role directions that attenuate the adult's distorted lifestyle and create a context for child pathologies. These debilitating and abusive role assignments preclude the growth process (particularly the process of self-differentiation) that must occur if secure and loving relationships are to flourish (Magid & McKelvey, 1987; Walsh, 1998).

Dysfunctional families have often experienced so many crises and negative stressors that they develop an ideology of pessimism and negativism. Failure to really resolve the alcoholic family dynamics or to even address them in any meaningful way is just one example of how this sense of defeatism develops. Despair, distrust, and a sense of powerlessness are predominant in most dysfunctional family contexts. What often happens is that the "dysfunction" absorbs so much family energy that the positive strengths of family members are missed. A sense of non-support, isolation, and low self-esteem begin to erode one's overall functioning.

Purposes and Uses of the Framework

Unfortunately, too often professionals use frameworks such as the one presented here to "judge" parents and families as opposed to better understanding them. It is important to the effective use of this framework to see it as a *tool for observing, engaging, and supporting parents, children, and families.*

Framework as observation tool: Using the three major elements of family functioning (structure, roles, and relationships) combined with the category-descriptors used in the framework (health, special needs, at-risk, and dysfunctional), early childhood educators can develop observational strategies that aim to gather data on family dynamics to then be used in helpful ways with parents and families (Dunst, Trivette, & Deal, 1988; Garbarino, 1992; Bronfenbrenner, 2005). The case of Mary Rand, as told by Swick and Graves (1993), highlights the need for an empowerment-based observation and intervention use of this framework. As Mary Rand tells the home visitor about her situations and perspective, we pick up with the story:

> Mary Rand explained that they were a poor but happy family, especially since the father left. She knew that "social services" was watching them, she said. The home visitor explained that she was there to help and not to interfere with the family's wishes in any way. She also explained that Mary could get involved in several ways, but could schedule things according to her family's needs. They developed a good relationship and over the first few months of the program developed a very supportive partnership. The home visitor helped the family take care of some very basic needs. She:
>
> * had the heat turned on with funds from a community group,
> * acquired some good used clothes for Mary and the children through a program at the church,
> * acquired a used car for Mary through help from a local church group,
> * acquired books and magazines for the home through the country's literacy program, and
> * nurtured Mary to get involved in the school's partnership program through monthly home visits, in-school activities, home-learning activities, and conferences with the children's teachers. (p. 136)

Framework as tool for engagement: The framework can also be used to help families engage in difficult changes that are essential to their long-term well-being. For example, a preschool program for homeless children and families the author works with use the framework to help parents see key need areas for engagement and for ways to then map out needed changes. One mother tells how this process enabled her to plan and act in new ways to help her family. "I found that by returning to school to complete high school I helped everyone in our family. Now I have a better job and am going at night to continue my education in computer training.

I am *engaged* (author's emphasis) in really seeing more positive things about my future and my children's. The Children's Garden (a preschool program for homeless children and parents) made the difference; they showed me how to start dealing with some of the constant problems we faced. Now I am seeing things differently and acting too!"

Framework as support tool: When we spot dysfunction do we attribute it to the victims or do we see a situation that can be changed? This is a critical question helping professionals have to ask and answer every time they relate to families with chronic and severe problems. For example, do we see homelessness as the "problem" of the family that is homeless or do we see it within a larger community ecology. Swick (1997, 2004) notes that in most cases of severe family homelessness high-support resources combined with strong educational and economic supports can indeed help families resolve these stressors. Supports such as adult education, child care, transportation, job training, counseling, life-skills education, needed housing, medical and health services, and other resources are powerful difference makers in the early childhood years (Swick, 1997).

One of the important perspectives for early childhood educators to adopt in using this framework is *that the framework must be seen as a dynamic continuum* (Swick, 1993). Three elements of this process offer help in our developing sensitive relationships with families. One, all families experience some aspects of each of the four category areas in the framework; that is, every family has special needs and faces some types of risk too! Second, the relationship process as it occurs in families holds the real promise for helping families develop strong and healthy family patterns. Third, the healthiest of families can have dysfunctional periods in their life-cycle.

Very important to our discussion, *the framework is most effective when used as a means for feedback and family strengthening* (Garbarino, 1992).

For example, if early childhood educators develop a trusting relationship with families, they can approach sensitive areas of family functioning, particularly when they are doing so in supportive and respectful ways. Swick and Graves (1993) describe a case study of a family where divorce had really negatively impacted everyone, especially the child. However, the teachers at the university child care center and allied helpers in the psychology department used their observations to help the father and the step-mother develop a positive plan for trying to resolve many serious family stressors. The important element in the case study is that it shows how helping professionals can use the framework to help families position themselves to solve their problems or at least to begin the process.

Also, the framework offers many opportunities for *strengthening the family* in ways that they gain in confidence and skills in being helpful to each other. Here are a few observations on possible opportunities for families in using this framework:

91

* Identifying the stressors in ways that the family avoids a blame and shame type of approach.

* Realizing that they have support people in the early childhood teachers and caregivers who help their children.

* Recognizing that by taking note of particular stressors and planning needed changes, they become more powerful in dealing with other family issues.

* Using the feedback to take note of each other's strengths and how to use them in enhancing the family.

* Extracting from this situation(s) possible helpful strategies that can be used in strengthening the family.

The Role of Culture in Influencing Family Dynamics

Every family is influenced in some fashion by the cultural dimensions of their past and present. The degree to which such influence embraces parents and children has much to do with several other factors such as the developmental stage of the family, how long the family has lived in a community, the intergenerational history of the family (is the family newly settled in the United States, for example), and the age of the parents and children in the family (Garbarino, 1992; Gonzalez-Mena, 1997). In relation to enhancing our ability to understand and support families, three dimensions of cultural influences are explored: 1) the role of beliefs and values in family decision making, 2) the early childhood professionals' understanding of how families respond to the cultural change process, and 3) the use of our knowledge of cultural differences to enhance families.

Cultural beliefs and values in families: Parental and family belief systems influence every facet of family functioning. For example, beliefs related to gender assignments within the parent dyad and the larger family ecology dictate the who, what, when, and where of many child rearing decisions. We develop our cultural beliefs through our interactions and learning in our family of origins, changing them only as we gain new insights and information. Rosier (2000) highlights this point in her discussion of mother's beliefs about parental involvement:

> As I emphasize throughout the book, mothers' practices were strongly influenced by their own experiences as children in family, community, and school settings. Amy recalled her own mother's strict parenting style with much admiration, and she clearly tried to reproduce tactics she viewed as highly effective and successful. (p. 20)

Thus, while one parent who has many positive and validating experiences with early childhood teachers may regularly conference with teachers, another parent may feel very insecure because her beliefs have been that teachers are indeed the source of knowledge and not to be questioned (Powell, 1989; Chavkin, 1993; Lawrence-Lightfoot, 2003). Interestingly, the author had a student who found that some parents she felt "did not care" about their children's education were very caring and concerned, but fearful they would seem unappreciative by speaking up at parent meetings. Chavkin (1993) makes this same point when she cautions teachers to gain insight into the dynamics of family culture and social beliefs before passing such judgments. Further, as Delpit (1995) notes, "we all carry worlds in our heads, and those worlds are decidedly different." (p. xiv) We need to have insights into these different worlds of the parents and families we relate to and then act on this information in sensitive and responsive ways (Kissman, 1999).

How families respond to cultural change: The process of "cultural change" involves many different elements: family culture, the predominant culture in the community, societal influences, supports and attitudes toward families who are different, and enabling supports or lack thereof in the community (Lynch & Hanson, 1998; Hanson & Lynch, 2004). Any change is disruptive of our pattern of living even if this change is positive and supportive of our well-being. As Garbarino (1992) suggests, the acculturation process is most effective in places where families are supported and positively valued. Even in such positive situations, most families learn to live bi-culturally or multi-culturally so that they are effective in the community and yet maintain and nurture their own cultural values. It appears that being bi-cultural has many advantages for strengthening parent and family life skills. Garbarino (1992) notes:

> The ability to live successfully in two cultures simultane-
> ously includes such factors as (1) the two cultures sharing
> norms, values, and beliefs; (2) having cultural translators,
> mediators, and models; (3) providing feedback by each cul-
> ture about one's behavior; (4) similarities in both cultures
> in conceptual and problem- solving style; (5) having lan-
> guage facility in both cultures; and (6) similarity in physi-
> cal appearance to mainstream culture. As we have seen,
> when the value systems of both cultures are similar, the
> child finds opportunities to grow and develop. (p. 194)

Most families find the unique balance between their particular cultural orientation and that of the larger community, usually using some of the values and life patterns from each setting to promote their growth in finding value in their cultural heritage.

Early childhood educators use cultural knowledge to support families: Early childhood professionals are sometimes perceived as a barrier by parents, children, and family. Gargiulo (1985) and Delpit (1995) both cite the lack of cultural understanding and possible corresponding insensitivities to families of different backgrounds as a barrier. Areas of stress and tension may range from simple ways of interacting and relating to each other, to more complicated differences due to language and educational variance. While we are not expected to know everything about cultural differences, it is important to show concern, be a learner (that is, acquire insights into the cultures of local and regional areas), seek the input of the parents and families, work with all available resources (bilingual translators or local cultural mediators), and respond respectfully and positively to family concerns and requests (Lynch & Hanson, 1998; Hanson & Lynch, 2004). Our goal should be to reach a level of cross-cultural competence that we are secure and growing in our relations with culturally different parents and families. Lynch and Hanson (1998, pp. 492-499) offer insights we can use as culturally growing early childhood educators:

* First, come to know your own personal and cultural identity.

* Second, learn about important values and beliefs of the parents, children, and families.

* Third, participate in activities in the school and community that can enhance your cultural insights about families.

* Fourth, avoid stigmatizing people as members of a culture; remember that within cultures there are many variations depending on situations, gender, social and economic circumstance, length of time in the community, education, and other factors.

* Fifth, look for the strengths of families from different cultural situations and emphasize these in your developing trusting relations with them.

Applying the Framework in our Understanding and Relating to the Situations and Strengths of Families

The framework of family types presented in this chapter (healthy, special needs, at risk, and dysfunctional) is intended to enhance our ability to understand and relate to the various situations in which families function.

Inherent in family responses to various situations is the presence of stress. *Stressors are integral to life and play a key role in our growth but can also impede our growth.* The nature of various stressors, the perceptions of the individuals involved, the dynamic patterns of stress reaction within families, and other factors impact how stress is played out in families (Seligman & Darling, 1989; Swick & Williams, 2008). For example, finding quality child care was not a stressor in families in the past for various reasons but mainly because mothers cared for the child in the home (Garbarino, 1992). In today's society finding child care is a major stress factor as well as the cost, the quality, and other variables that relate to the balancing act of family-work-community (Elkind, 1994). In a similar way what is stressful at one point in the family's life cycle is not stressful at another point. We find this contextual influence with culture also; what is stress inducing in one culture may actually be a positive influence in the family in another culture (Dent, 2000; Bronfenbrenner, 2005).

An important lesson for early childhood educators is to be sensitive to the various factors that impact family stress and family stress responses (Garbarino, 1992). It is also important that we realize that each person is unique. While each of us is influenced by our cultural and other social events, we are individuals and respond in our own unique way. We must avoid stereotyping and use the framework as a tool among other resources to strengthen our understanding and ability to relate effectively to parents, children, and families (Gonzalez-Mena, 1997).

Thus, the following indicators of how families respond to different situations are examples only, they do not represent static pictures of what is happening within any given family. Further, this opportunity is used to highlight many positive ways in which we can view and support families.

Healthy families as key to strong parent/family/community: The prevailing theme in the family literature is that parents, children, and families who respond in "healthy" ways to the various dynamics of life strengthen themselves and the entire community (Pipher, 1996). It is clear that families that use nurturing strategies to empower each other are valued people in the community. They are just as likely to experience stress and are certain to have real challenges in their journey. Yet it is in their approach to these issues that we find valuable attributes to nurture in our work with families.

Our main application of what we know about healthy families is to support their learning orientation, help them in gaining needed resources, and encourage their growth through flexibility approach (Bauer & Shea, 2003; Bronfenbrenner, 2005).

Special needs families seek care and understanding: The strength of many families *is in their ability to use special needs situations as points of growth* (Pipher, 1996). For example, the stress of a long term parent illness can erode everyone's usual functioning. A child is likely to behave more erratically and parents themselves report having less energy and motivation for their usual routines. Most families re-group and with support and understanding they actually may show real proactive growth (Garbarino, 1992). Swick (1993) tells how one mother began to turn things around through supportive help from a teacher.

> The turning point for me was a phone call from my daughter's teacher. She asked if Sue could go with some other students to an art show. I told her I doubted Sue would want to go. She said I think she will go if you encourage her and maybe you should come too. She went on: you know Ann, you and Sue will have to become a part of things again someday. Yes, I said, I know we have been in this house too much. Let me talk with Sue and I'll call you back. (p. 71)

Families in special needs situations respond more proactively when they have supportive early childhood educators helping them (Ahsan, 2004). Five areas of the situations of special needs families need our attention.

First, the *key elements of the situation* must be known. What has happened to the family that has disrupted their otherwise usual healthy functioning? Is it illness, a death in the family, economic dislocation, or other stressors? As we learn about the family situation we must be respectful and hold in confidence the information that is very sensitive to them. Know and respect the cultural beliefs of families that may impact their behaviors.

Second, *we need to know how the family has been particularly impacted* (Dunst, Trivette, & Deal, 1988). Each family reacts to stress uniquely and they process different forms of stress in different ways. For example, the emergence of stressors like divorce have already been in process; that is, the family has already developed some perceptions and behaviors on the dynamics of the divorce stress. The family has already experienced difficulties and challenges that led to the divorce decision. Yet there are some characteristics of the divorce situation that we can be cognizant of in our work with families (Wallerstein, Lewis, & Blakeslee, 2000):

> In every domain of the child's life, parents are less available and less organized, provide fewer dinners together or even clean clothing, and do not always carry out regular household routines or help with home work or offer soothing bedtime rituals. (p. 10)

Knowing how families in the divorce situation may react can be good information to use in then developing educational and support programs.

A third factor is to seek out *what can be done to help the family* resolve the situation or at least negotiate strategies that enable them to

96

cope with the key issues effectively (Seligman & Darling, 1989). Swick and Graves (1993) provide case examples of where early childhood home visitors were able to assist parents in getting needed surgery, obtaining funds to have the heat turned back on, providing literacy resources for their children, and other needed resource tasks. In some cases, families mainly want the support of caregivers and teachers.

A fourth element is *helping families access and use available and needed community resources* (Powell, 1998). Usually families with special needs can address the problems and challenges effectively with early support and help. Young families who experience homelessness provide an example of how multi-dimensional family supports can indeed help families to be more effective. Support services alone are not effective nor are professionally imposed "services" that may indeed alienate the family. As Nunez and Collignon (2000) point out, supports and related educational services need to be focused on strengthening the family. They use a "communities of learning" construct to pursue this need area:

> Communities of learning link education for parents and support services for the whole family into education programs for children. This coordination facilitates the ultimate goal of communities of learning: to immerse families in an educational environment with the support they need to make education a whole-family activity. Communities of learning provide an environment packed with supportive educators and peers who are working their way through the same challenges that homeless participants face. Here children can pursue their education while witnessing their parents embracing learning as well and families can focus on the future together. (pp. 119-120)

A fifth and very critical element deals with *supporting children in their coping with the special needs situation* within the classroom and school environment (Eddowes & Butcher, 2000). Three areas of emphasis should be considered: 1) helping the child recognize the nature of the need (at a level appropriate to his or her stage of development), 2) engaging the child in being proactive in addressing this special need, and 3) supporting the child during this time of stress with hopeful and caring interactions. For example, in cases where families have been displaced by unemployment or other economic crises, it is important for children to realize that this situation is solvable. Children need our support to see the positive features of their parents and family in such stressful contexts. An empowerment focused set of strategies is most effective:

* Provide a caring curriculum (Bronfenbrenner, 1979; 2005) where adult-child relations are nurturing and mutually supportive.

* Involve children in roles and activities where they help each

other with authentic needs so that they can become empathetic and competent.

* Engage children in appropriate counseling and play-therapy that sensitively responds to their special needs.

* Communicate often with parents and family about the child's functioning in the classroom and at home.

At-risk family situations call for early intervention and care: In at-risk family situations multiple risk factors that are chronic and intense combine to place the entire family system "at-risk" for eventual dysfunction. The key risk areas in families during the early childhood years are: poverty, ineffective parenting, inadequate home-learning environments, illiteracy, poor health care, malnutrition, lack of job skills, abusive situations, and chemical addictions (Swick and Graves, 1993). Typically, these risk areas develop in relation to each other and without intervention can become real obstacles to family growth. For example, poverty is often interrelated with illiteracy, chemical dependency, and lack of job skills. Further, these risk factors are more damaging when they become persistent and very intense in the context of the family's functioning (Sachs, 2005). In subtle yet often devastating ways, the stress of multiple risk factors like poverty and illiteracy can destroy the basic social learning system of people within the young family. Swick (1993) notes:

> Another significant but often overlooked process that occurs in young families under heavy stress is the short-circuiting or destruction of their social learning system. When young families are constantly responding to chronic stress they have little energy or faith for creating a proactive and nurturing ecology. In such contexts, families who are at risk develop behavior patterns that may be destructive of their integrity and are often dysfunctional (if not antisocial) within the larger environments of school, work, and neighborhood. (p. 103)

Thus, care and early intervention are two dimensions of the early childhood educator's response that can be powerful supports in helping families.

Care is the key to establishing trust with families in at-risk situations (Gonzalez-Mena, 1994). Most families under heavy stress need faith in the helpers who interact with them daily. Caring relations where specific supports are used to strengthen the family, assist them incoping with the risk situations. This process is more effective when the parent/family-professional relationship is one of trust and mutuality (Swick, 2006).

Intervention with parents and families in ways that support the family in resolving stressors is essential to truly strengthening families (Crouter

& Booth, 2004). Helping families achieve literacy, gain new job skills, return to school, obtain needed housing, access health and medical care, and achieve objectives they establish for themselves and their children are powerful interventions that impact the family in pervasive and sustaining ways. For example, comprehensive, multi-dimensional family support learning centers have positively influenced homeless families involvement in becoming educated, attaining housing, and furthering their empowerment in many other ways (Stronge & Reed-Victor, 2000).

Dysfunctional does not mean death: Re-energizing families through intensive interventions. Two patterns of thought seem to be associated with dysfunctional parenting and family life: chaotic, impulsive patterns, and rigid thought and behavior patterns (Kerr & Bowen, 1988). Both types of patterns seem to instigate individual and social behaviors that are destructive and anti-social. Healthy family relations are replaced with aggressive and often violent ways of living. Developmental benchmarks for child, parent, and family functioning are lost in a haze of distorted roles and relationships (Magid & McKelvey, 1987). McGoldrick, Broken Nose, and Potenza, 1999) discuss the dynamics of violence in relation to how it plays out in dysfunctionality:

> Violence in the family is not just aggression. It is abuse of power. The statistics show clearly that within families, it operates on the basis of the strongest victimizing the weakest. Thus, the greatest volume of abuse is directed against the weakest children, children under six. (p. 471)

We can see in this point on violence an attribute that permeates dysfunctional family living: power and role distortion creates a pattern of self-destruction for the adults and the children (Minuchin, 1984; Swick, 2008).

Yet, with intensive intervention that is directed toward educational and social supports, family dysfunctionality can be positively impacted. Three things must be recognized and then used as a basis for meaningful early childhood education action: 1) parents and families are the owners of their social and emotional relations; 2) any effective interventions must have the buy-in of the family as a total learning system; and 3) trained and nurturing counseling and psycho-therapeutic helpers are needed to guide the healing and restoration process (Pipher, 1996; Kerr & Bowen, 1988). With these elements serving as a framework, early childhood educators can then carry out various supportive and helping actions. First, we explore the three elements noted above. Then key support and helping roles are noted for the early childhood professional's consideration.

Parent and family ownership: Parents and families have developed counter-productive perceptions and behaviors because of their individual and combined experiences with particular stressors. Thus, they need to take on ownership of the transformation and healing processes. As Kerr and Bowen (1988) indicate, parent and child insights into the erratic, chaotic, and/or rigid repetitive refrains of their behavior and relationships are best altered when they are about the process of planning and probing their way into new venues. It may be one family member who steps forward to instigate the process. Or, it may be a combination of family members who gain perspective that "things can and need to be different," thus prompting the family membership to engage in therapeutic and behavior coping strategies (Minuchin, Colapinto, & Minuchin, 1998; Swick & Williams, 2008). Swick & Graves (1993) describe how a step-mother launched the new family into a change process for the better:

> Two days later, she [the step-mother] called and said they had agreed that Lisa should be in the play-therapy class and that they would meet with the psychologists to at least discuss the possibility of family therapy. This was the breakthrough that made the difference for everyone in the family. While the biological mother never did participate in the process, she finally agreed to change her way of functioning when Lisa was with her on weekends. Lisa progressed with amazing healing. The play therapy allowed her to act out many of her conflicts in a non-threatening environment. Within weeks the masturbation disappeared and the tantrums were subsiding. (p. 146)

Positive nurturing therapeutic settings were able to further support family change because of the "ownership" taken on by family.

Family-system buy-in to the intervention: Early childhood parent educators know very well the need for total family buy-in in the intervention strategies and activities. Far too often programs that seemed effective have been short-circuited because family members were not included or cultural beliefs were ignored (Minuchin, Colapinto, & Minuchin, 1998; Nunez & Collignon, 2000). We must be sensitive to both the participation of families and the means by which we involve them in the intervention process. As Lynch and Hanson (1998) note, in many culturally different families active participation is more about respect and validation as a person and family than it is about particular involvement strategies.

It is important that we use a shared-learning process to gain the input and "buy-in" of families in the interventions.

Several suggestions are noted for gaining and nurturing the buy-in of families:

* Use situations where you and the family are listening to each other and learning from each other.

*   Make available and co-participate in parent and family education sessions that provide enjoyable ways for parents and children and other family to strengthen the positive aspects of their lives.

*   Wherever decisions impact the family, engage them in the process and ask for their ideas regarding how strategies can be most helpful.

*   Encourage the family in question to set aside times for planned, meaningful and enjoyable family interactions.

*   Have families self-assess their growth through the intervention process. For example, how are family members using the materials of the home visitation process? What do they find most useful? Where do they think changes are needed and how would they facilitate that?

Trained nurturing counselors and helpers: Knowing our limits as family helpers is as important as the other strategies we use. A maxim in our profession is or should be: DO NO HARM! Thus, a key healing element in the lives of dysfunctional families is to be engaged with trained and nurturing counselors and helpers (Nunez & Collignon, 2000). Case studies presented by Swick and Graves (1993) in which families functioning in dysfunctional ways begin to show change and growth highlight five important points relative to the role of counseling and other therapeutic activities:

1) Counseling situations often provide the needed "mirror" for families to see the dysfunction(s) holding them back from change. While each case is unique, a parent can gain special insight via the family therapy system and then change ways of relating to other family.

2) Activities like play therapy often engage children in needed catharsis and reconstruction of roles that otherwise may seem too threatening to undertake. Children and adults need secure and caring situations within which they can then act out new possibilities in their lives.

3) All family members benefit from counseling settings where each is able to re-validate themselves and others in the family.

4) Early childhood educators need to connect with the counseling and therapeutic activities of families and "support and enrich" the process.

5) Families need to be the ultimate therapists in the sense of continuously involving themselves in activities that strengthen each other.

Interrelated with the above elements on helping families in dysfunctional situations are key support and helping roles such as the following (Seligman & Darling, 1989):

* Be consistently warm and supportive in your interactions with the family.

* Be positive and encouraging in your relationships with them.

* Suggest activities and resources they see as valuable in helping them further enhance their family. Specific and family-initiated ideas are best.

* Communicate often and in ways that both support and remind families to indeed continue with their growth and renewal efforts.

* Relate to the total family as a learning and growing system. Avoid putting family members in conflict situations with other family; show respect and validation for their need to be a part of their family.

* Be sensitive to the cultural identity of the family. What are cultural and language factors that you need to aware of and how can you be most effective in this regard?

* Always choose to see the best parts of the family and help the family see their strengths. This approach is very supportive of them at this time of stress and difficulty.

* Respond to the family in ways that promotes mutuality and where they can then help you out and others in the program. In many cases the best antidote to dysfunction is seeing one's self as a valid helper of others.

Strategies that Strengthen Families

Families are about constant change and hopefully positive and meaningful growth. We know, however, that as presented in this chapter, many families struggle with contextual, societal, and related stressors and often face risks and special needs that take them beyond their limits. Family empowerment is and must be our goal as early childhood professionals and as caring citizens too! In an issues statement on families and young children Swick (1997) notes the following as key elements of a foundation for family support strategies:

1) *Early childhood educators and families need to be intimately involved (as partners) in the planning and nurturing of healthy environments.* Understanding is best achieved when people are working with each other on a common goal or theme. Beginning early, parents and educators should be interacting,

supporting, planning, assessing, and collaborating with each other to create healthy places and systems.

2) *Through the creation of dynamic school-family partnerships, a family-centered "curriculum for caring" must emerge and support our understanding of the families we serve.* Such a curriculum needs to address issues inherent in the process of family development as well as related issues that link families and children to needed resources. Within this construct, we need to assure that the following elements are fostered: a) all family members need self-esteem nurturing, b) promotion of prosocial caring in all families, c) the nurturing of caring and culturally sensitive people, and d) the need for more community caring for families.

3) *The work of families is too critical to be left in the family domain.* Communities must be more engaged in helping families. We need a human team of nurturers who care for children and their parents. We are all linked in a human chain of growth and renewal and thus we are all responsible to assure the strength of this chain.

To truly strengthen families strategies like the following must be integrated into every dimension of family and community life (Children's Defense Fund, 2000):

1) <u>Health and wellness</u>: Provide for parents and children:

   a) prenatal care for all women.

   b) community awareness on the importance of prenatal care and family health.

   c) nutrition and health services.

2) <u>Parenting and family education and support, and needed child and family services</u>: Provide the following as essential family support services:

   a) Parent education that emphasizes the social and emotional needs of young families.

   b) Parent training and support for families with special needs in the areas of literacy, network building, health, child care, and related need areas.

   c) Family preservation strategies that identify and intervene at the earliest point possible in the family's development.

   d) Parent/family mental health centers that promote positive life styles.

   e) Family support services that enable parents and children to become involved in various school and community activities.

f) Provisions for quality child care and early education re-sources and services.

g) Literacy, job training, and related adult education (and enabling resources so that parents can use these resources).

h) Assure that all families have needed basic services: food, heat, health care, and other supports.

The perspectives and behaviors of early childhood professionals with parents are important for empowering families, particularly those in difficult situations. Several *professional perspectives related to empowering families* are noted (Dimidjian, 1989; Dunst, Trivette, & Deal, 1988):

* Maintain an active sense of empathy with the child and family.

* Be open and responsive to the real problems children and families face; involve them in articulating needs and possible strategies for resolving them.

* Work toward achieving synchrony with the family's need to connect their stressors to workable solutions.

* Be a caring early childhood educator who is supportive in words and action. Benard (1992) advocates that our caring can best be achieved through two such roles: 1) "teacher as positive model" and 2) "teacher as confidante."

* Have high expectations for the children and families you work with in relation to their skills and their potential to be growing and developing persons. Hilliard (2002) says that our verbal and nonverbal responses to diverse language and socio-cultural styles of living send powerful signals that we may NOT expect much of the child or the parent. If we see their language as deficient or their cultural perspectives as inhibiting the child and them, our low and negative views can further erode their power to grow and learn. Thus, we must be vigilant in our development of high, positive expectations for the parents and their children.

* Be family-centered in your thinking and overall functioning. The child is living in an ecological setting called the family where all of his important values and beliefs are evolving.

Of course, there are many *strategies teachers can use* to bring this caring and empowering philosophy alive in their work with children and families. LeTendre (1990) and Swick, Da Ros, & Kovach (2001) offer some examples of strategies that have proven effective in strengthening children and families.

* Provide children and adults with mentors who support, validate, and enrich their lives. Mentors often prove to be key people in our finding new and creative ways to resolve otherwise highly negative stressors.

* Connect parents and families to needed counseling and therapeutic resources. As Bronfenbrenner (1979) has so wisely noted, all of us need counseling and therapy throughout our lives in the sense of learning how to grow and meet life's many issues and stressors.

* Make sure children, parents, and families receive needed health, medical, speech, and related services that help them grow and learn.

* Engage parents and children in needed educational enrichment and support activities. Preventive or remedial tutoring can make the difference in a young child getting the needed foundation for life long learning. In this same perspective, adult education may help the parent achieve new economic goals that then increase the family's total functioning.

* Use parent education groups and personal visit situations to foster in parents a sense of caring inquiry that becomes their way of learning and problem-solving. As Rohner (1986) found, caring parents have close, warm, and nurturing relations with children. They are more responsive to children's needs and protect and support them in positive ways.

* Educate and validate parents' use of informal, social learning opportunities. We learn real life skills and perspectives from each other that often serve to enhance our self-esteem and our ideas about our importance to others.

* Encourage and foster in parents a sense of their educational responsibility and power with their children. Activities such as storytelling, reading with the child, shared social outings, and other experiences that strengthen the parent-child bonds are vital to the total family system.

SUMMATIVE DISCUSSION OF APPLICATION POINTS

Within the paradigm of ecological systems interactions, Bronfenbrenner (1979, 2005) articulated the concept that parents and families were typically victims and/or co-participants of being in high-risk situations such as the risks produced by chronic poverty. Thus, a key foundation point in this chapter is that families are at-risk because of a combination of personal and environmental factors. The "framework" presented in this regard is that parents and families function within a continuum construct: healthy, special needs, at risk, and dysfunctional.

The major concept of this framework is that our functioning is the result of situational factors as well as our skill in responding to the various stressors. In this sense, the following four application points are noted for your analyses:

1) Understanding that family functioning is grounded within a contextual framework that impacts how families learn and grow helps us realize more clearly how we can assist families. For example, seeing how a comprehensive homeless family program can empower parents and children to gain not only housing but all of the needed interacting elements such as education, food, counseling, and other resources is enlightening of our potential to be effective early childhood helpers.

2) Understanding the dynamics of how particular stressors like poverty impact families further strengthens our role as helpers so that we can be a positive influence. For example, this understanding might lead to our engagement in linking families with needed educational, economic, job training, and other supports that they can use to empower themselves.

3) Realizing how the family functioning framework can be used to help families is another important application point. The framework, for example, could be used to identify parent, child, and family needs and thus engage the helping professional in supporting them to achieve some skills and perspectives for dealing with their situation effectively.

4) Seeing the framework as helpful in developing strategies that enable families to resolve and/or prevent particular risk factors from eroding their power or debilitating them is also empowering. For example, the major goal of most early childhood parent and family strengthening programs is to disrupt the cycle of failure that may be impacting parents and children through early interventions such as parent education, family supports, and early childhood education.

Helpful Web Sites

African American Resources: <www.rain/org/-kmw/aa.html>

Chicano/Latino Net: <www.latino.sscnet.ucla.edu>

Resources for Native American Families: <www.familyvillage.wisc. edu/frc_natv.htm>

The Council for Exceptional Childrenn:

Kids Count Report on Children and Violence: <www.cait.cpmc.columbia. edu/dept/nccp>

Safety Net – Domestic Violence Resources: <www.cybergrrl.com/dv.hyml>

Institute for Children and Poverty: <www.opendoor.com/hfh/icp.html>

References

Ahsan, N. (2004). Domestic violence and family support programs: Creating opportunities to help young children and their families. In S. Schecter (Ed.), <u>Early childhood, domestic violence, and poverty: Helping young children and their families</u> (pp. 59-86). Iowa City, IA: School of Social Work, University of Iowa.

<u>Annie E. Casey Kids Count Data Book 2008</u>. Baltimore, MD: The Annie E. Casey Foundation.

Bauer, A., & Shea, T. (2003). <u>Parents and schools: Creating a successful partnership for students with special needs</u>. Columbus, OH: Merrill Prentice Hall.

Benard, B. (1992). Fostering resiliency in kids: Protective factors in the family, school, and community. <u>Illinois Prevention Forum</u>, 12 (3), 1-16.

Bond, J., Thompson, C., Galinsky, E., & Prottas, D. (2003). <u>Highlights of the National Study of the Changing Workforce</u>. New York: Family and Work Institute.

Boss, P. (1988). <u>Family stress management</u>. Newbury Park, CA: Sage.

Brazelton, T., & Greenspan, S. (2000). <u>The irreducible needs of children</u>. Cambridge, MA: Perseus Publishing.

Bronfenbrenner, U. (1979). <u>The ecology of human development and learning</u>. Cambridge, MA: Harvard University Press.

Bronfenbrenner, U. (2005). <u>Making human beings human: Bioecological perspectives on human development</u>. Thousand Oaks, CA: Sage.

Burland, J. (1984). Dysfunctional parenthood in a deprived population. In R. Cohen, B. Cohler, & S. Weissman. (Eds.). <u>Parenthood: A psychodynamic perspective</u>. New York: Guilford.

Caldwell, B. (1989). A faltering trust. In D. Blazer. (Ed.). <u>Faith development in early childhood</u>. Kansas City, MO: Sheed and Ward.

Carlsson-Paige, N. (2008). <u>Taking back childhood: Helping your kids thrive in a fast-paced, media-saturated, violence-filled world</u>. New York, NY: Hudson Street Press.

Carter, B., & McGoldrick, M. (Eds.) (1999). <u>The expanded family life cycle: Individual, family, and social perspectives (Third Edition)</u>. Boston: Allyn and Bacon.

Chavkin, N. (1993). <u>Families and schools in a pluarlistic society</u>. New York: State University of New York Press.

Children's Defense Fund. (2000). <u>A status report on children – 2000</u>. Washington, DC: Children's Defense Fund.

Coloroso, B. (2000). <u>Parenting through crisis: Helping kids in times of loss, grief, and change</u>. New York: Harper Collins.

Comer, J. (2001). Schools that develop children. <u>The American Prospect</u>, 12 (7), 3-12.

Comer, J., & Haynes, N. (1991). Parent involvement in schools: An ecological approach. <u>Elementary School Journal</u>, 91 (3), 271-278.

Crouter, A., & Booth, A. (2004). <u>Work-family challenges for low-income parents and their children</u>. Mahwah, NJ: Lawrence Erlbaum Associates.

DeJong, L., & McKinney, L. (2002). What a school district learned from parents about family learning activities. <u>Dimensions of Early Childhood</u>, 30 (2), 19-26.

Delpit, L. (1995). <u>Other people's children: Cultural conflict in the classroom</u>. New York: The New Press.

Dent, D. (2000). <u>In search of Black America: Discovering the African-American Dream</u>. New York: Touchstone.

Dimidjian, V. (1989). <u>Early childhood at risk</u>. Washington, DC: National Education Association.

Diss, R., & Buckley, P. (2005). <u>Developing family and community involvement skills through case studies and field experiences</u>. Columbus, OH: Pearson.

Dunst, C., Trivette, C., & Deal, A. (1988). <u>Enabling and empowering families: Principles and practices</u>. Lexington, MA: Lexington Books.

Eddowes, E., & Butcher, T. (2000). Meeting the developmental and educational needs of homeless infants and young children. In J. Stronge & E. Reed-Victor. (Eds.). <u>Educating homeless students: Promising practices</u>. Larchmont, NY: Eye on Education.

Edin, K., & Lein, L. (1997). <u>Making ends meet: How single mothers survive welfare and low-wage work</u>. New York: Russell Sage Foundation.

Elkind, D. (1994). <u>Ties that stress: The new family imbalance</u>. Cambridge, MA: Harvard University Press.

Erickson, M., & Kurz-Reimer, K. (1999). <u>Infants, toddlers, and families: A framework for support and intervention</u>. New York: The Guilford Press.

Erikson, E. (1959). <u>Identity and the life cycle</u>. New York: W.W. Norton.

File, N. (2001). Family-professional partnerships: Practice that matches philosophy. <u>Young Children</u>, 56 (4), 70-74.

Galinsky, E. (1990). Why are some teacher-parent relationships clouded with difficulties? <u>Young Children</u>, 45 (5), 2-3 + 38-39.

Garbarino, J (1982). <u>Children and families in the social environment</u>. New York: Aldine de Gruyter.

Garbarino, J. (1992). <u>Children and families in the social environment (Second Edition)</u>. New York: Aldine de Gruyter.

Gargiulo, R. (1985). <u>Working with parents of exceptional children: A guide for professionals</u>. Boston, MA: Houghton Mifflin.

Gonzalez-Mena, J. (1994). <u>From a parent's perspective</u>. Salem, WI: Sheffield.

Gonzalez-Mena, J (1997). <u>Multicultural issues in child care. (Second Edition)</u>. Mountain View: CA: Mayfield.

Hanft, B., Rush, D., & Shelden, M. (2004). <u>Coaching families and colleagues in early childhood</u>. Baltimore, MD: Paul H. Brookes.

Hanson, M., & Lynch, E. (2004). <u>Understanding families: Approaches to diversity, disability, and risk</u>. Baltimore, MD: Paul H. Brookes.

Hilliard, A. (2002). Language, culture, and the assessment of African American Children. In L. Delpit & J Dowdy. (Eds.). <u>The skin that we speak: Thoughts on language and culture in the classroom</u>. New York: The New Press.

Huston, A. (1991). <u>Children in poverty</u>. New York: Cambridge University Press.

Kagan, R., & Schlosberg, S. (1989). <u>Families in perpetual crisis</u>. New York: W.W. Norton.

Kelly, J. (2006). Supporting children's development by strengthening families who are homeless. <u>CHDD Outlook, 17 (2)</u>, 2-4.

Kerr, M., & Bowen, M. (1988). <u>Family evaluation</u>. New York: W.W. Norton.

Keyser, J. (2006). <u>From parents to partners: Building a family-centered early childhood program.</u> Washington, DC: National Association for the Education of Young Children.

Kissman, K. (1999). Respite from stress and other service needs of homeless families. <u>Community Mental Health Journal</u>, *35 (3)*, 241-249.

Klein, B. (1985). Families and handicapped children: A personal account. In K. Powers. (Ed.). <u>Lives of families</u>. Atlanta, GA: Humanics Limited.

Lawrence-Lightfoot, S. (1999). <u>Respect: An exploration</u>. Reading, MA: Perseus Books.

Lawrence-Lightfoot, S. (2003). The essential conversation: What parents and teachers can learn from each other. New York: Random House.

Le Tendre, B. (1990). Implementing accelerated schools: Issues at the state level. Presentation made at the American Educational Research Association Conference, Boston. (ERIC Document, ED 321 366).

Lynch, E., & Hanson, M. (1998). Developing cross-cultural competence: A guide for working with children and families. Baltimore, MD: Brookes.

Magid, K., & McKelvey, C. (1987). High risk: Children without a conscience. New York: Bantam Books.

Maslow, A. (1968). Toward a psychology of being. New York: D. Van Nostrand.

McGoldrick, M., Broken Nose, M., & Potenza, M. (1999). Violence and the family life cycle. In B. Carter & M. McGoldrick. (Eds.). The expanded family life cycle: Individual, family, and social perspectives (Third Edition). Boston, MA: Allyn and Bacon.

Minuchin, S. (1984). Family kaleidoscope. Cambridge, MA: Harvard University Press.

Minuchin, P., Colapinto, J., & Minuchin, S. (1998). Working with families of the poor. New York: The Guilford Press.

Nunez, R., & Collignon, K. (2000). Supporting family learning: Building a community of learners. In J. Stronge & E. Reed-Victor. (Eds.). Educating homeless students: Promising practices. Larchmont, NY: Eye on Education.

Pipher, M. (1996). The shelter of each other: Rebuilding our families. New York: G.P. Putnam.

Powell, D. (1989). Families and early childhood programs. Washington, DC: National Association for the Education of Young Children.

Powell, D. (1998). Reweaving parents into the fabric of early childhood programs. Young Children, 53 (5), 60-67.

Rohner, R. (1986). The warmth dimension: Foundations of parental acceptance-rejection theory. Newbury Park, CA: Sage.

Rosier, K. (2000). Mothering inner-city children: The early school years. New Brunswick, NJ: Rutgers University Press.

Sachs, J. (2005). The end of poverty. New York, NY: The Penguin Press.

Scarf, M. (1995). Intimate worlds: Life inside the family. New York: Random House.

Schwartzman, J. (1985). Families and other systems. New York: Guilford.

Seligman, M., & Darling, R. (1989). <u>Ordinary families, special children: A systems approach to childhood disability</u>. New York: Guilford.

Small, M. (2001). <u>Kids: How biology and culture shape the way we raised our children</u>. New York: Doubleday.

Spacapan, S., & Oskamp, S. (1992). <u>Helping and being helped: Naturalistic studies</u>. Newbury Park, CA: Sage.

Stinnett, N. (1979). <u>Building family strengths: Blueprints for action</u>. Lincoln, NB: University of Nebraska Press.

Stronge, J., & Reed-Victor, E. (Eds.). (2000) <u>Educating homeless students: Promising practices</u>. Larchmont, NY: Eye on Education.

Swick, K. (1991). <u>Teacher-parent partnerships to enhance school success in early childhood education</u>. Washington, DC: National Education Association.

Swick, K. (1993). <u>Strengthening parents and families during the early childhood years</u>. Champaign, IL: Stipes.

Swick, K. (1997). Strengthening homeless families and their young children. <u>Dimensions of Early Childhood</u>, 25, 29-34.

Swick, K. (2004). <u>Empowering parents, families, schools and communities during the early childhood years</u>. Champaign, IL: Stipes.

Swick, K. (2006). Families and educators together: Raising caring and peaceable children. <u>Early Childhood Education Journal</u>, <i>33 (4)</i>, 279 – 287.

Swick, K. (2008). The dynamics of violence and homelessness among young families. <u>Early Childhood Education Journal</u>, <i>36 (1)</i>, 81-86.

Swick, K., & Graves, S. (1993). <u>Empowering at-risk families during the early childhood years</u>. Washington, DC: National Education Association.

Swick, K., Grafwallner, R., Cockey, M., & Barton, P. (1998). Parents as leaders in nurturing family-school involvement. <u>Contemporary Education</u>, 70 (1), 47-50.

Swick, K., Da Ros, D., & Kovach, B. (2001). Empowering parents and families through a caring inquiry approach. <u>Early Childhood Education Journal</u>, 29 (1), 65-71.

Swick, K., & Williams, R. (2008). How attention to family stress dynamics can prevent homelessness among very young families. In M Jalongo. (Ed), <u>Enduring bonds: The significance of interpersonal relationships in young children's lives</u>. (pp. 91-106) New York: Springer.

Wallerstein, J., Lewis, J., & Blakeslee, S. (2000). <u>The unexpected legacy of divorce: A 25 year landmark study</u>. New York: Hyperion.

Walsh, F. (1998). <u>Strengthening family resilience</u>. New York: Guilford.

Parenting And Parent Education: Nurturing Meaningful Parent, Family, And Community Partnerships

---

CAPSULE: Parenting is about the process of constant change and renewal. The parenting journey requires us to be ongoing learners. Parent education and family literacy strategies can be positioned to support and enhance parents and families in their growth process. The emphasis in this chapter is on explicating how parents and other caring adults can foster healthy and meaningful family life. It is also about showing how parents develop their partnership behaviors through this early process of parent education and support. Finally, the challenges to this process are reviewed and suggestions offered to advance the educational and support strategies we use with parents and families that strengthen them to be effective family and community leaders.

Chapter Four Objectives:

1) To strengthen your understanding of the developmental and dynamic nature of parenting, inclusive of the many roles parents carry out to nurture healthy functioning in the family.

2) To enhance your perspective about the functioning of parents to include the essential "integrity" elements such as parental self-image, locus of control, social support, and the developmental status of parents.

3) To enhance your knowledge of the important roles that parents perform, the development of these roles in relation to family life, and our job as early childhood educators in nurturing these roles in parents.

4) To further strengthen your understanding of how culture and education influence parenting, especially in relation to how parents impact the family's total learning system.

5) To increase your knowledge and skills of using parent education and family literacy strategies as early intervention efforts to further empower parents and family.

6) To enhance your understanding of the potential of various parent education strategies in increasing parent and family literacy skills.

7) To strengthen your knowledge and skills of using parent education as a venue to create strong parent-teacher and family-school relations.

8) To empower you as an early childhood professional in understanding and applying the major concepts and strategies of parent education and family literacy in your work with parents and family.

My first experience as a father was very humbling. I had a great deal of cognitive knowledge about early childhood, parenting, marriage and family life. Yet as parents will validate, the actual experience of parenting is a holistic process where emotions and affect play key roles in our growth and functioning. We find ourselves as Galinsky (1987) shows in a continuous growth process, learning every minute of our parenting lives.

The intent of this chapter is to engage the reader in a dialogue about parenting and parent education in ways that will stimulate them to reflect and assess their status as early childhood educators who might nurture and enrich parents. We begin by exploring the process of parenting as developmental and dynamic; and then extend this inquiry to a construct called parental integrity. In this discussion we quickly see that parental functioning is interrelated with the total growth of parents (LaRossa, 1986; Swick, 2001).

The chapter also examines key parental roles and how parents negotiate and respond to these roles within a very complex society. Cultural and educational factors are also important to our discussion of parenting; thus we review key findings on the impact of culture and education on the parenting process. The final sections of this chapter are devoted to a critical analysis of parent education and family literacy as well as related parent and family empowerment strategies. We pay special attention to the role parent education and family literacy can play in the lives of families dealing with very difficult risk factors.

114

Parenting as Developmental and Dynamic

Parenting is dynamic in that it encompasses many roles, responsibilities, and complexities. Parenting is about our continued growth as adults and our relationships with our children. As Gonzalez-Mena (1994) notes:

> Parenting is a balancing act between getting totally wrapped up in the life of another person and standing apart – remaining a separate individual. To be a parent you have to be able to do both. You have to be involved and sensitive, yet not lose yourself in your children. (p. 13)

Swick (1993) takes note of two processes that strongly influence how we parent and how we grow as parents: 1) the developmental dynamics of parenting, and 2) the cultural facet of parenting.

Developmental dynamics: The developmental dynamics of parenting such as young parents negotiating their career-family balancing act clearly influence parenting in various ways. For example, parents struggling to meet job demands and/or returning to school may reduce their time for parenting (Rosier, 2000). Parents who report the stress of jobs and careers often experience barriers to carrying out roles they would like to be performing (Galinsky, 1999).

An important part of these parenting dynamics is the presence or lack of social support (Gonzalez-Mena, 2006). How we respond to the developmental challenges of parenting are influenced by available supports and our skills in relating to and nurturing these supports.

Cultural facet of parenting: Parenting is carried out within one's ever developing cultural framework. Culture is really the combination of beliefs, values, and actions that comprise our often taken-for-granted ways of living (Gonzalez-Mena, 1997). It is the mosaic of socio-cultural habits and rituals that comprise our perceptions and actions in parenting and family living (Rogoff, 2003).

Many parent educators have learned that the cultural beliefs and values of families are very powerful in shaping child care rituals such as feeding, toilet training, sleep patterns, bathing, and many other activities. Further, many of these behavior patterns are deeply rooted in accepted social and cultural practices that are highly valued and expected in one's community. While they may appear at odds with our understanding of quality care-giving, they may be very effective within a given culture.

Likewise, culture plays a role in how parents perceive and then act in relation to other social systems like school, church, and formal social support agencies (Garbarino, 1992; Gonzalez-Mena, 1997). The author recalls a recent discussion with a group of teachers who shared that they initially thought poor parent attendance at conferences and group meet-

115

ings showed that the parents were not very caring. Upon closer insight they found that practically all of the parents cared but many were reacting to their cultural, social or economic situations. For example, one group of parents worked the night shift at a local factory and could not attend such meetings. Another group worked in service industry jobs and had long travel days and were late getting home. A few parents thought they would be showing disrespect by coming; it might appear that they were challenging the teachers and their cultural values dictated high respect of teachers.

Another insight is that even within any particular culture there are differences in how parents and families believe and function (Lynch & Hanson, 1998). Just as we all have a culture, each of us is unique in our personal and social behavior. We are very distinctive in how we parent and do other social and cultural roles. Rogoff (2003) explains that individual reflection on cultural practices is one way we change and improve our cultural habits.

Parenting is also a developmental process where several factors are integrated into one's style and system for carrying out various parenting roles (LaRossa, 1986). Beyond the romantic mythology of first-time parenthood is the reality of new roles, new schedules, and more complex challenges.

Given supportive contexts and relationships, parents begin their parental roles during the nine months prior to the arrival of the first child. This period is identified as the _image-making stage_ in Galinsky's (1987) "stages of parenthood" scheme. During this aspect of parental development the major emphasis is on creating a vision of the kind of parent we want to become. It includes our childhood memories of being parented.

Given a positive approach to one's image-making as a parent, the next stage of development is a relatively seamless connection of love and affection for and with the baby. Galinsky (1987) terms this stage _nurturing_ because parents invest heavily in attaching themselves to the baby. One of the image-making processes is the beginning of "seeing one's self" as a loving and caring parent. This is no easy task as parents must transform their marital and/or friendship relations to make room for attachment to the child (Fishel, 1991; Honig, 2002).

This "nurturance" stage of development is foundational to all of the dynamics needed in healthy families. Swick (1993) captures the power of this developmental facet of parenthood:

> The nurturing stage is where parents make their unconditional commitment to the child, a unifying and energizing attachment; it is this "bonding" that makes healthy family life possible. This is not a static or mechanical process but rather a spiritual process where parents struggle to

define their selves in relationship to the infant, seeing in themselves the nurturer as lover and guide for the child and for themselves as they pursue this challenging and rewarding journey of parenting. (p. 226)

As the child develops and shows the signs of becoming an individual person, parents recognize and engage in the third stage of parenthood: authority (Galinsky, 1987). This is not about being punitive or rigid in our development of adult-child boundaries within the family, but is about becoming adult in the understanding, responsive, and guidance sense (Swick, 1987; 2004).

One of the big tasks children face is processing all of their experiences —that is, making sense of the world. This becomes more complex as they attend preschool programs and then eventually enter the formal school years. Here parents enter the *interpretive stage* of parenting. They become their children's helpers in learning how to make sense of different experiences. For example, children often have more questions than one can imagine any person having. Yet this is the "stuff" of parent-child relationships. It is the really powerful learning laboratory of young children. As parents often share with each other, the key is to interpret the experience in a way that the child is constructing their understanding and thus eventually the parent moves on to other interpretive roles and activities.

Later in the evolving role of parents, the *interdependent* and the *departure* stages are experienced. They are not reviewed here as our focus is on the family in the early childhood years. Consult Galinsky (1987) for an elaborate and rich description of these two stages of parenthood.

APPLICATION POINT: Given the dynamic and challenging nature of parenting, early childhood educators can create three support resources to assist parents in dealing with these challenges: 1) places and activities where parents can network and share with each other, 2) information centers that make available parenting and family materials on issues and topics of concern, and 3) easy access to services and support for dealing with daily and emergency situations. What support strategies can you develop for helping parents respond to the changes in their parenting lives in ways that further enrich and strengthen them?

Parental Integrity: Meaning and Applications

Parental beliefs provide the foundation for action in family dynamics. Each person's ability (and their perception of that ability) to live in what

117

they define as a quality manner is reflective of their *parental integrity* (Dunst, Trivette, & Deal, 1988).

Four factors interact to influence how parents develop their parental integrity:

Figure 4.1
Factors that Influence Parental Integrity

Locus of control
Personal self-image
Developmental status
Interpersonal supports

Locus of control: The degree to which parents perceive that they control their behavior and the environment in which they live is termed *parental locus of control*. Two constructs are important to this paradigm, perception and control. Perception refers to how parents see themselves functioning; do they believe in their ability to influence their own lives and that of their family in positive ways? Parental locus of control is interrelated with several internal and external forces (Galinsky, 1999).

Personal self-image: Our image of our selves is a composite that we construct from many life experiences (Hallowell, 2002). Parental self-image is linked to how parents perceive and act in several different personal, parental, marital, and family situations (LaRossa, 1986). Integral to self image are several perceptual patterns: views of self and others, personal happiness, future views of local and global events, one's sense of efficacy, martial and friendship harmony, and work place satisfaction (Hamner & Turner, 2001). Low self-image detracts from a parent's ability to be in caring and nurturing relations with their children. Positive self-image energizes parents to further grow and learn in their parenting journey. In practically every dimension of parenting and family life, parent self-image emerges as key to healthy growth and learning (Hanson & Lynch, 2004).

Developmental status of parents: Family development is often sequenced in patterns such as: initial stage, formative stage, style organization stage, maintenance/refinement stage, and consolidation stage (McHenry & Price, 1994). It is important to remember that parents' maturation and development occur within dynamic systems and the process is ever evolving. Although many factors impact the developmental status of parents, it is clear that partner relations (marital dyad or adult friendship dyad) and parent-child relations function to support or inhibit the growth of parents (Powell, 1998).

Interpersonal supports: Perhaps the key to nurturing and sustaining parental integrity is the availability of and parent skill in developing and using interpersonal support resources (Bronfenbrenner, 1979, 2005). For example, even prior to the birth of the baby parental use of prenatal care, participation in parenting education classes, and overall involvement in preparing one's self and the family for the arrival of the baby are healthy signs of parenting (Powell, 1989). Access to quality child care, support from a caring work environment, help from nurturing and supportive relatives and friends, and access to needed basic life resources provide parents with a powerful system for launching and then sustaining the family (Galinsky, 1999).

Key Parenting Roles: Their Development and Importance

It has been said that the "average" parent performs over 150 different roles during any given day. Clearly, parents epitomize the best aspects of multi-tasking as they carry out very critical roles. Initially, some of the important roles parents do are reviewed: personal development, community participant, family leader, role model, and nest builder. Then we look very closely at the "Parent as Teacher" role.

One of the interesting findings of Galinsky's (1999) research with children (an in-depth interview study) was that *children were very proud of their parents' personal and work achievements*. That is, children want parents who have personal interests and are doing positive and interesting things (Cowan and Cowan, 1992; Swick, 2005).

Interrelated with parents' personal growth is their *involvement as community participants*. We can only "grow" personally when we have social opportunities to contribute and support others in the community.

An essential role for all parents is that of *being a family leader*. Consider the many relationship patterns (marital, parent-child, child-peer, family-school, as examples) that must be negotiated. Research is very clear that parents (or other competent adult surrogates) must be the orchestrator and guide in assuring that these relationships enhance and not impede the family's well being (Fishel, 1991; Swick, 2004).

The *parent as role model* impacts us throughout our lives. Bronfenbrenner (1979, 2005) has noted that children are more influenced by what parents do to and with each other than by what parents do with them as children. Siegel (2000), in her work with families in case-therapy over several years, found that the marital relationships of parents is a significant influence in children's social and emotional learning.

Parents as nest builders is where parents work at developing an environment where children observe, feel, and participate in caring and nurturing relationships (Garbarino, 1992). While this "nest" is initially viewed mostly as the physical and social supports that comprise "family", it is also the life long emotional and spiritual home of the parents and the child (Chavkin, 1993).

119

Siegel (2000) reports that building relationships (marital and family) that are mutually respectful and nurturing is important to the development of loving and secure family environments. Children observe and then process the caring behaviors they see in their parents' interactions (Bronfenbrenner, 1979).

Parent As Teacher: The integration of all of the dimensions of parenting occurs within the role of "Parent as Teacher." As Galinsky (1999) found in interviews with children, what children valued most in their relations with their parents was the continuing learning they gained through the many activities their parents were able to share with them. Teaching and learning are integral features of what healthy parents do throughout their lives.

Burton White (1988) found that the most prevalent attribute of healthy and strong families was the teaching and guidance accomplished by the parents. White (1988, pp. 167-169) identifies the following as the key elements parents should seek to achieve during the early years:

* Help children feel loved and cared for in every aspect of their lives.

* Help children acquire a sense of competence in their daily relationships.

* Help children gain an interest in exploring the environment.

* Help children become delightful, caring, and competent.

* Help children maintain a balanced interest in themselves and their environment.

* Help children achieve the optimal learning foundations in language, social skills, and intellectual development.

Parenting as a Learning Process: Cultural and Educational Influences

Becoming a parent is a process of continuous learning and inquiry; it is all about gaining insights and understanding about how we grow and learn (Gonzalez-Mena, 1994; LaRossa, 1986). Swick, Da Ros, and Kovach (2001) note four means that parents use to pursue their growth and integrity: 1) the continuing search for and refinement of one's knowledge, skills, and attitudes that enable them to protect, nurture, and educate the child; 2) an intentional and sensitive focus on responding to the demands inherent in the child's growth and that occur in their own growth as parents; 3) the search for and sustaining of supports that strengthen parents to be capable nurturers of their children; and 4) the recognition and responsiveness to the need for continually refining their identity in relation to the complex processes of parenting and family dynamics.

120

Two ways parents continue their learning about dealing with child, family, and parenting issues are through self and child experiences and in interactions with others who have significance to the parent. The real-life content of parenting is in the dynamics of the parenting process itself; hopefully, to be enriched through parent education and family literacy.

As Fraiberg (1977) so aptly suggested, it is through reflective and affirming approaches to living that parents continually renew their conception of growth and learning. Our relationship with important adults is also a source of renewal and growth. Parents need mutually enriching relations with other adults and professional helpers. They need to gain immediate help and important knowledge, skills, and attitudes that engender in them the attributes of caring and nurturing (Emde, 2001).

Responding sensitively and intentionally to the changing growth of their children and themselves is essential to parents' nurturance of everyone's well being in the family (Gonzalez-Mena, 1994). In our rather individualistic society, this is a major adjustment for many parents. To be really responsive to our own personal growth needs and those of our children requires that we envision this process in a more ecological framework. This is so because sometimes (often in a rapidly changing world like ours) the critical needs are dramatic and can impact each of us in critical ways. Thus, we need very strong and nurturing attachments (Garbarino & Bedard, 2001).

Pipher (1996) uses the Sioux word *tiospaye* to represent the web of multiple attachments where people find the safety and nurturance to deal with the inevitable developmental, social, and ecological challenges and changes that arise in all parenting and family contexts. Pipher notes:

> What tiospaye offers and what biological family offers is a place that all members can belong to regardless of merit. Everyone is included regardless of health, likeability, or prestige. What's most valuable about such institutions is that people are in by virtue of being born into the group. (p. 23)

Seeking and then using supports that specifically strengthen one as a parent is integral to helping parents be capable nurturers of their children (Hamner & Turner, 2001). With the challenges of finding a balance between work and family, attaining quality child care, and developing a sustaining and enhancing set of relationships that nurture and support them as parents, we can clearly see the need for strong parent supports. Swick, Da Ros and Kovach (2001) point to three ideas as essential in this regard: 1) the parents as sharing and helping each other, 2) parent as mentor and mentorees, and 3) intergenerational family relations.

In practically every culture, some form of social support (such as networking) is a part of parenting (Lynch & Hanson, 1998; Hanson &

Lynch, 2004). Beyond the obvious benefits of *networking* such as gaining knowledge and resources from other adults is the very key value of being validated as a parent. Gonzalez-Mena (1994) suggests that parents need at least one and hopefully two or three caring and capable adult intimates they can depend on for processing all of the stressors of parenthood. As Powell (1989) found in his "kitchen talk" observations, sometimes the best parent education occurs in the kitchen at break time where parents themselves help each other with some very stressful and important problems.

The particular challenges of first-time parenting or of parenting a special needs child show very clearly the value of *a mentoring approach* (Galinsky, 1987; Kotre, 1999). The mutuality and enhancement aspects of parent mentoring are noted by Swick, Da Ros, & Kovach (2001):

> Even very secure parents recognize the need for having access to a "significant other adult" who has experienced parenting issues and grown in the process. All parents face new challenges that are more manageable when they can interact with a more experienced parent. Mentoring is a multidirectional process where mentors learn too! (p. 70)

Intergenerational family relationships offer a rich context for social, cultural, educational, and related supports for parents as they negotiate the various challenges of the family journey (Swick, 1987, 2004). In particular, the cultural knowledge that is transferred to a new parenting generation can become an empowering and sustaining source of energy if appropriately handled. For example, Hamner and Turner (2001) note that many African American families point to "grandparents" as the most supportive people in their lives.

Perhaps the most challenging task many parents face *is responding to the need for continued growth and renewal in themselves* (Galinsky, 1987, 1999). Parental involvement in growth and renewal efforts that sustain and enrich their personal lives is integral to their being positive and effective parents (Cowan & Cowan, 1992). For example, parents must negotiate their understanding of how their personal identity can be transformed in healthy ways while expanding their web of social and spiritual involvement through the family-community context. This is a process where parents literally experience a revolution in how they see the world, their children and family, and themselves. At the core of this process are the growth and renewal strategies parents use to help them successfully handle this part of their lives.

Parental self-perceptions set the stage for this renewal and growth process. How do I see myself as a person? What are my most effective ways of learning and growing? Who are my really supportive and positive helpers? These and other questions can be used as one strategy of helping parents examine their "self" as a growing person. As Swick (1991) notes:

> For parents to be able to carry out the teaching and modeling roles, they must have the foundation of faith in themselves that evolves from their growth as nurturing persons. (p. 53)

Parent Education as Early Intervention and Prevention

The goal of early childhood parent education / family literacy is to create a family-school-community system that promotes school and life success in the lives of children, their parents and families (Brown & Swick, 2002; Marshak, 1997; Powell, 1989; Swick, 1996; Weiss, 1988). This goal is reflective of the emerging recognition that human development and learning occur within a systems structure and that systematic and nurturing early intervention can indeed prevent many risk factors (Brazelton & Greenspan, 2000).

Thus, a more encompassing construct of parent education / family literacy has emerged and includes four key components (Swick, 1996, 2004):

Figure 4.2
Key Components of Parent Education / Family Literacy

Parent Education

Adult/Family Literacy

Child Development Services

Family Support Services

The Parent Education component is oriented toward helping parents realize their nurturing skills in supporting and enhancing their development, their children's optimal growth, and the healthy functioning of the family (Hamner & Turner, 2001; Ruddick, 1995). This is a collaborative process between parents and their helpers that aims to increase parent confidence and skills in being effective family leaders. The content of parent education attempts to address two broad areas of concern: parents' personal and parental competence, and parental understanding of child and family development (Swick, 2004).

A major feature of most programs is an empowerment emphasis where parents engage in all of the dimensions of the program planning and development process; it becomes "their" program structure with the help of professionals in early childhood education as a support strategy. The focus on early intervention in parent education programs (Figure 4.3) has multiple goals (Powell, 1998; Bronfenbrenner, 2005).

Figure 4.3
Focus on Early Intervention in Parent Education

* Support parents in increasing their personal efficacy so as to further increase their strength and skill in parenting.

* Enhance parents' parenting education attitudes, knowledge, and skills.

* Increase parental confidence and competence in family life skills and management.

* Increase parents' knowledge of appropriate child and family development as well as parental insights into their own growth and change.

* Strengthen parents' educational involvement with their children.

* Enhance parents' ability to locate and use needed community resources to further enhance their development as well as their children's.

The Adult / Family Literacy component aims to encourage and support parents in enhancing their personal educational competence through adult education, job training, and through personal literacy experiences (Swick, 2004). Family literacy activities are designed to engage parents, children and other family in meaningful and enjoyable literacy (Brizius & Foster, 1993).

Parental involvement in increasing parents' educational skills is interrelated with their increased participation in their children's early education (Greenspan & Benderly, 1997; Weiss & Jacobs, 1988). As parents shared with Swick (1993), when we (the parents speaking) are taking classes ourselves we are good examples for our children and they notice it and tell us how proud they are that we are in school too!

Child Services are far reaching and include a major emphasis on the prevention of risk factors that might negatively impact their school readiness and success (Brazelton & Greenspan, 2000). For example, key risk areas such as poor health, developmental delays, and lack of enriching early learning experiences are often targeted in quality programs. The quality of day care, providing improved early learning experiences, and assuring children the needed services for appropriate and successful development are important elements in all early childhood programs.

Parent-Family Services provide the web of care and nurturance that aim to strengthen the total family system (Pipher, 1996). Children and parents who lack food, heat, clothing, housing, and other essential services are unlikely to reach optimal development and learning modes (Swick & Graves, 1993). Regardless, it is also important that family system interventions capitalize on the strengths and skills of families (Dunst, Trivette, & Deal, 1988).

124

SAMPLE OF QUALITY EARLY CHILDHOOD PARENT EDUCATION / FAMILY LITERACY PROGRAM – PROJECT ENHANCE

In a growing but moderate sized coastal city, the school district has established a comprehensive early intervention focused parent education / family literacy program. Each elementary school has an early childhood family center that includes: parenting classes and seminars, an early childhood program (with programs for children birth-school entry), on-site adult education classes, a strong parent-child element in the early childhood programs, family support services (with an effective referral system), and a well trained and educated staff. Continuing education, community involvement, local advisory committees, parent training, health services (some of the centers have on-site health and medical services), family-friendly transitions into the K-12 programs, positive parent-teacher relations, and supportive programs that help each center evaluate and strengthen their programs.

Parent Education and Family Literacy Programs / Practices

The growth of parenting education and family literacy activities is amazing and now reaches beyond any individual's projections. Literally thousands of programs and strategies exist globally (Swick, 2004).

Within an empowerment paradigm, parent education acquires a broader and more encompassing meaning. It is now seen as a resource and support effort that engages the parents in various venues that help them to strengthen themselves and their children. The diversity of programs, resources, activities, and venues through which parenting education and family literacy are delivered is evidence of this highly complex process. As Powell (1989) notes:

> The image of parent education as an expert telling a group of mothers about the ages and stages of child development is neither complete nor accurate as a portrayal of many of today's programs. Consider the following contrasts: Some programs focus on family- community relations while others teach parents how to stimulate a child's cognitive development. Some programs prescribe specific skills and styles in relating to young children while other programs encourage parents to become informed decision makers in the use of child development information. (p. 89)

Since Powell's statement, the diversification of parent education and now family literacy have continued with amazing changes. For example, more recently a resurgence of fathering-related programs and a new emphasis on teen parenting as well as foster-parenting has emerged. Recognition of the special needs situations that many parents face has also impacted a major increase in that form of parenting education. In a similar way, prevention programs aim to disrupt many of the risks that tend to create life long problems for parents and children (Swick, Da Ros, & Kovach, 2001).

Seven distinguishing features of emerging parent education and family literacy programs and practices are important to our understanding of how these efforts can be of high quality and yet realistically linked to the empowerment of parents and families (Powell, 1998; Hamner & Turner, 2001):

1) They are reflective of and interrelated with the parent and family culture.

2) They use an ecological approach to promoting the development and learning of parents, children, and family. All aspects of the human development system (family, community, society) are considered and integrated into the educational and support process.

3) Program activities are community-based and sensitive to local needs and resources.

4) These programs define education broadly and thus provide services in each of the domains typically included within the concept of social support, needed validation and feedback to continue their growth process.

5) An emphasis is on using multiple strategies to intervene and disrupt any behavioral or contextual syndromes that may cause long term damage to the parent, child, and family.

6) These programs use innovative parent-directed and multilateral strategies to empower parents and families.

7) They foster a strong interdependence between family and community through using all possible community resources.

Parent education / family literacy is a strategy that hopes to promote parent and family empowerment and thus foster children's school readiness and success. To achieve this ambitious mission, parent education / family literacy use all possible resources to create the most family strengthening system possible (Amatea, 2009).

SAMPLE EARLY CHILDHOOD PARENTING PROGRAM THAT USES MULTIPLE STRATEGIES

Elwood School, a small rural school in a Midwestern U.S. community, takes great pride in offering multiple early childhood family strengthening services within a flexible and very nurturing culture. For example, adult education (especially English as a Second Language [ESL] services) is offered at the school during the day, in the evening, and in other very accessible locales such as a local factory and at the technical college site. The school provides on-site child care, various parenting programs, job training resources (including transportation to a nearby training program), and many other family literacy resources. Ms. Lattel, the principal, notes: "our success in reaching and involving parents is in our attitudes, our services, our family-friendly approach, and our love of our parents and children and all who are a part of their lives."

While there are many ways to organize a review of parent education and family literacy programs and practices, *a developmental and family-specific approach is used to highlight the critical role that education and support can play in the lives of parents, children, and families.*

The Developing Parent As Focus

Parent education is realizing the need to support the "developing parent" in becoming effective in all of their roles. The classic work of Ira Gordon (1975) noted the significance of the parents' personal development in relation to their overall functioning as parents. He (Gordon) found that improved parental self-image positively influenced all aspects of the parent-child relationship. In addition, Powell (1989), Galinsky (1987), and Swick (1991) suggest that the personal, developmental needs of parents are vital to empowering parents in the more direct parenting roles.

In particular, the parent as nurturer role is receiving attention in many parent and family programs. Parent-Child Centers, Healthy Start, and a variety of other program structures emphasize the strengthening of parental self-image as a means of fostering strong parent leadership (Powell, 1998; Swick, 2006).

Programs like The Western Carolina Center's Family, Infant, and Preschool Program emphasize the role of the helping professional in assisting parents in strengthening their personal development. Dunst, Trivette, and Deal (1988) focus on increasing parent control skills, strengthening parental confidence in their roles with children and others in the family, and on helping parents become the key leaders in their personal growth.

The importance of helping new parents deal with risk factors in their development is seen when intergenerational dysfunction occurs because risk behaviors were never identified and addressed (Karr-Morse & Wiley, 1997). For example, Hetherington and Kelly (2002) found that children of divorced parents tended to repeat this same pattern of marital conflict unless there was some intervention that enabled them to negotiate resolutions to the risk factors in their lives. A similar intergenerational story is seen in the lives of adults who were abused as children. Child abuse patterns tend to destroy our sense of security and also distort our "map" of how to relate to our selves and to others (Swick, 2005). But effective and meaningful parent education can help people reconstruct their ideas about how to live productively and in caring, nurturing ways (Hamner & Turner, 2001).

Thus, parent education and family support have a very important mission in relating to the needs of parents and children in at risk situations. The focus should be on *three elements* (Swick, 1993):

Figure 4.4
Important Elements for Supporting Parents

---

1) Helping parents and families gain control over the forces that are eroding their power.

2) Engaging parents in experiences where they can gain a sense of self-worth and self-direction.

3) Nurturing in parents the proactive beliefs essential to their being effective family leaders.

These elements have been successfully carried out in various ways. Home visit programs (utilizing trained professionals and paraprofessionals) have used family supports, counseling, and educational activities to position parents to gain the needed skills and perspectives to address some key risk areas. Other strategies include: parent networking, group meetings and activities, therapy, family strengthening resources, and specific supports such as literacy activities, adult education, and job training (Swick, 2004).

CASE APPLICATION: The "developing parent" needs an experiential form of parent education and support. In what ways can you as an early childhood professional support parents by developing activities that both engage them and help them become learners? For example, how might you use conferences as a time to engage parents in furthering their own knowledge of children and themselves? Give some examples you plan to use with parents in this regard and explain one of them in detail.

The Marital / Friendship Relation As Focus

The marital relationship has a very powerful impact on children and on family dynamics. Cowan and Cowan (1992) found in the research from their "Becoming a Family Project" that:

> The more unhappy mothers and fathers feel about their marriage, the more anger and competitiveness and the less warmth and responsiveness we observe in the family

during the preschool period – between the parents as a couple and between each parent and the child. (p. xi)

The "map" of anxious and high-stress relationships seems to then increase and further complicate marital and family relations in kindergarten and beyond.

Parents need to be cognizant of the role their marital or friendship partnership plays in the entire family (Siegel, 2000). Regardless of the formal marital status, parents need strong and nurturing adult relationships to provide an emotional and spiritual foundation to the family's growth and functioning (Bronfenbrenner, 2005).

As Siegel (2000) notes the marital relationship is perhaps the most impacting factor in the children's development of a schema of how to handle emotional and social relationships:

> The marital relationship observed by the child acts like a blueprint upon which all future intimate relationships will be built. For this reason, it is important for parents to step back and examine the lesson plan they have created for their own children. Parents should ask themselves what their children might be noticing and question whether they are helping them create the best possible future. (p. xvi)

Parent educators and other early childhood helpers need to integrate this area of family life into the parent education program. For example, Cowan and Cowan (1992, p. 5) points to five dimensions of marital partnership (Figure 4.5) that have a dramatic influence on the family. These five points can be interrelated with various parent education and family literacy activities.

Figure 4.5
Five Dimensions of Marital Partnerships That
Influence Family

---

1) The inner life of both parents and the first child, with special emphasis on each one's sense of self, view of the world, and emotional well being or distress.

2) The quality of the relationship between the husband and wife, with special emphasis on their family roles and patterns of communication.

3) The quality of the relationships among the grandparents, parents, and grandchildren. The family is a total system and many parent educators have noted how often they do focus on helping parents realize the need for including other family in positive and nurturing interactions with their children.

4) The relationship between the family and helpers from outside the family need attention. Work, church, friends, child care, and other community helpers should be the focus of home visit lessons and / or group meetings.

5) The quality of relationships between each parent and their first child.

Further, *four elements of the marital / adult friendship system have been shown to be very influential in families:* 1) relationships, 2) the marital dyad, 3) intra-family system patterns, and 4) family-environment interface. These and other marital dynamics can be addressed through parent education. Cowan and Cowan (1992) present the "couples groups" strategy as one parent education approach:

> The couples groups provided an experience that we (the authors) wish we could have had as we became parents fifteen years earlier. In the last few months of pregnancy, the group leaders helped couples take a look at their current lives, anticipate what their lives would be like once the baby arrived, and make explicit some of their unexplored pictures of life as a family. (p. 9)

Several things happen in these groups but the most influential experiences revolve around couples' communicating more with each other and gaining insight into their marital strengths and needs. Cowan and Cowan (1992) point to four observations in this regard:

1) The manner in which married couples handled parenting in the early months of the baby's life seemed to set the stage for later functioning too!

2) Parents who said they had some continuing conflicts with their parents also had similar issues with their children.

3) Parents who fought with each other a great deal also reported having conflicting relations with their children.

4) *The really big news* is that parents' marital relations seem to act as a crucible in which their relationships with their children take shape.

Based on their extensive work with couples they point to the following as risk indicators in a marriage that very likely will negatively impact the total family system:

* Major distress before the baby is born in any of the arenas of family life.

* Serious ambivalence in one or both spouses regarding the pregnancy.

* Low self-image and major depression or disappointment in one or both of the parents.
* Negative views of each other as spouses.
* Chronic "strain and stress" within the marriage.
* Consistent poor communication within the marital or family relationship.

In terms of guidelines and "best practice" for developing parent education that strengthen parents' marital (or friendship) system (Figure 4.6), they (Cowan & Cowan, 1992) note the following.

Figure 4.6
Best Parent Education Practices to Strengthen
Marital Relations System

---

* Share and develop expectations about parenting and family life as a couple.
* Carry out regular feedback or "checkups" as a couple in relation to how you feel about your parenting – individually and as partners.
* Set aside "talk-time" with each other as a couple at least once a week.
* Develop a "parenting/family" agenda together so that problems and concerns are discussed openly and addressed as a team.
* Develop a flexible, experimental approach to parenting – develop a style that is nurturing of the changes that come so quickly during infancy and toddlerhood.
* Nurture the marriage relationship and avoid the "loss of intimacy" syndrome that erodes the very foundation for having healthy family life.
* Line up and use support people you as a couple feel can help your family grow in positive ways.
* Locate or develop a small but supportive network with friends who can discuss the issues of early parenting with you.
* Seek a balance among the many dimensions of being a person, spouse, parent, and contributor to the community.

Fishel (1991), Galinsky (1987), and Feeney, et al. (2001) emphasize educational and social support interventions early in the parent relationship system in order that harmony, proactive problem solving, and marital effectiveness are nurtured. Fishel (1991) uses a questionnaire where parents examine their ideas and perceptions of parenting, marriage, and family relations. Galinsky uses biographical questions to engage each parent in thinking through where they are at in the developmental stages of becoming a parent. This enables the partners to have a basis for then sharing their perceptions and questions with each other. Feeney et al. involve parents in looking at their attachment, nurturance of each other, and their support systems – hoping to stimulate the parents to strengthen these aspects of their lives.

CASE APPLICATION: Identify some of the common stressors that parents face in working toward having healthy marriages. What support resources and parent education strategies can be used to help parents in their efforts to respond effectively to these stressors? Share an example of how support resources might make a difference in marital relations that ultimately also positively impacts everyone in the family.

Focus On Meaningful Relationships With Children:

Parenting education programs that focus on helping parents establish and nurture meaningful relationships with their children emphasize several points (Swick, 1993; Swick, Da Ros, & Kovach, 2001):

* Involve the parents in all aspects of planning the parent education programs.

* Organize programs that address the holistic nature of parenting.

* Emphasize a caring approach where parents are supported and validated in using their personal and cultural knowledge in combination with other learning modes to enhance and strengthen their parenting.

* Use a family-centered approach to parent education and involve all family in the process.

* Create and sustain the needed enabling activities (child care, meals, needed transportation, and essential materials/resources) to advance parents' growth and strong participation.

* Engage the parents in reviewing and refining the program in ways that they see as making it more relevant to their needs.

An innovative approach to empowering parents in their parent-child relations is the strategy and content used in the *Family Literacy Program*. As noted by Darling (1989), the family literacy approach seeks to disrupt whatever literacy barriers or other social and educational impediments that may be creating dysfunction in the family. Programs that reach parents during pregnancy or early in the newborn's life offer powerful opportunities to develop warm and responsive relations with children (Zigler et al, 2002).

While the *Family Literacy Program* is designed to focus mainly on parents and families in high-risk situations, the concepts and practices are applicable to all programs that aim to empower parents and children. This program provides early intervention to break the cycle of illiteracy through combining quality early childhood education, adult education, parent-child time, parent education, and family support resources (Brizius & Foster, 1993). In addition to providing parents with child development knowledge, skills, and experiences, the program is responsive to parent-determined needs. In particular, the parenting aspect of the program engages parents in gaining knowledge of child learning, observing models (the child's teachers) of how to interact with the child, and using their information and skills during PACT (Parent and Child Time). These experiences are then supported during parent discussion time where parents have opportunities to share, ask questions, and gain new ideas about how they might use these skills at home (Swick, 1991, 2004).

Sample Early Childhood Family Literacy Program
Lawsonville's Community Power Strengthens
Families

Lawsonville is a small to mid-sized community of about 150,000 people. A small industry community, it is seeking to strengthen the literacy of the people to enhance its' opportunities for attracting more sophisticated and better paying industries. With help from a small state education department grant, Lawsonville Schools have opened two early childhood family literacy centers. The aim of these centers is to strengthen the total family's literacy and overall readiness for school. The centers serve children from 0-5 and their parents/families. Three attributes make these centers very special places of learning and support: comprehensiveness, family-sensitive scheduling, and family empowerment.

The centers offer all of the elements of a high-quality family literacy program plus many needed family services via a strong family counseling and referral program. Very importantly, these two centers schedule their program efforts in relation to the needs of the participating families. For example, each center has an evening cycle where all of the elements (adult education, early childhood, parenting sessions, parent-child time, and related job skills activities) are offered and in ways that parents can attend.

The family-friendly philosophy of the centers is seen in their scheduling of activities, provisions for family meals once each week, inclusion of transportation, and supportive counseling.

One of the most significant features is that each center involves parents in the operations of the program. For example, a "leader-ship" program engages parents in helping manage the evening meals, organizing some of the learning environment for the children, and functioning as trusted advisors to staff. Each family crafts their own goals and strategies for achieving these plans. Families are guided to use the entire family as a learning team, thus empowering each other to be effective learners.

Another widely used early childhood parent program that emphasizes strengthening parent-child relations is *Parents as Teachers*. This program's curriculum is often referenced as "Born to Learn" and the up-dated materials integrate recent research on brain development that clearly impacts the parent and family role in children's growth and learning (Eliot, 1999). The foundation of this program is based in the research of Burton L. White, which focused on the critical areas of children's early learning and development and the role of family in this growth process (White, 1988). The PAT program is now a nationally recognized parent education strategy. This program aims to help parents support their children's healthy growth and thus prepare them for a successful school experience. The core strategies that have served this program's work over many years include: providing parents with information on appropriate child development and care (this includes information on prenatal care), home visits to families as needed and to support their social, cognitive, and language interactions with their child, health and developmental assessments (and needed referrals) for the children, vision and hearing checks for all children, provisions for a parent and family resource center (including library resources), and the delivery of monthly group meetings (Olsen & Fuller, 2003).

Branon City Parents as Teachers Project

A small city, Branon City Schools pride themselves in having a state validated and nationally recognized Parents as Teachers program. Unique in that the program goes beyond the typical home visits, group meetings, assessments, and related support activities, this project features three very successful strategies: father involvement, a special program for teens, and a highly effective bilingual, multicultural facet to the project.

Father involvement: In Branon every new father gets a certificate that reads "A Very Important Father Helps His Child Learn." Fathers are heavily recruited to be a part of the group programs on child development and learning and to show leadership in advocating for quality early learning for all children in the community. Over half of Branon City's new fathers have been enrolled in the PAT program and several have distinguished themselves in making improvements in family child support resources in the community.

PAT for Teens: Parents as Teachers child development and parenting emphasis has been adapted for involving all teens in the community. Programs are offered in schools, at churches, and in neighborhood groups. Thus far over 60 percent of the teens have participated. Some are teen parents but most are teens who will one day be parents.

Bilingual, Multicultural: Branon's population is now 15 percent Hispanic.

Many are young parents with very young children. Branon PAT has translated all program materials into Spanish, hired and trained several Hispanic parent educators, and is recruiting strongly to gain more Hispanic involvement. Culturally enriching activities like international family nights are regular features at the meetings.

While all parents face special needs situations, teen parents need additional support to solidify their early relationships with their children. In this regard, the emotional stress of parenthood is a critical need area for support for teen parents.

Resource Mothers is a program concept that aims to reach teen mothers during pregnancy and equip them with needed cognitive, social, and emotional skills for effective parenting (Schorr, 1997). As Swick (1991) comments:

> With a focus on gaining the trust and involvement of these very young soon-to-be mothers, Resource Mothers provides needed information on prenatal care, parenting, and support resources, and, just as important, offers continuity of help so that risk factors being confronted can be dealt with effectively. (p. 61)

Focus On The Preschool Years

The preschool years are now widely accepted as the critical period for children's growth and learning (Brazelton & Greenspan, 2000). Research on the early growth of the brain suggests that serious deprivation or abuse can cause permanent damage to the child's learning system. Serious neglect, experiential deprivation, malnutrition, abuse, or other chronic negative impacts do indeed bring about serious degradation of children's functioning (Small, 2001; Restak, 2003).

Perhaps the most obvious need for parents is gaining a solid base in understanding their child's development. As noted previously, the *Parents as Teachers* program includes content on children's growth. Another program that includes such content is the *Minnesota Early Learning and Development (MELD)* program. A very adaptive and parent-responsive program, MELD includes a variety of materials, activities, and resources on child development.

This program is especially responsive to cultural and ethnic differences among families and several of its programs are in Hispanic and Hmong languages (Swick, 2004). The program recommends using a variety of delivery strategies including group meetings, home visits, community meetings, technology, and individual counseling.

Children's behavior and social relations is another parent-expressed need for parent education during the preschool years. Cataldo (1987) indicates the following as areas of most importance during the preschool years (Figure 4.7):

Figure 4.7
Important Parent Education Topics
for the Preschool Years

---

* Communication behaviors of children that are appropriate for their development and how these behaviors are best nurtured by parents and caregivers.

* Parent-child communication that fosters warm, positive, and harmonious family relations.

* Child social skills and behaviors appropriate to their development and how parents can facilitate these behaviors in their children.

* Social skill areas such as peer relations, empathy, play, child care, school adjustment, development of self confidence, and self-care skills are all important to healthy child growth. Supporting parents in helping their children achieve these needed skills is a role for parenting education programs.

* Distress and related conflict-resolution skills and strategies are also important to the entire family's coping and social functioning.

* Related cognitive and language skills also support parents in their work with young children.

Discipline is the most requested parent education program in the preschool and early school years. Unfortunately, many parents (and teachers) still incorrectly see discipline as punishment. The work of Cataldo (1987) and Brazelton and Greenspan (2000) clearly point to the need for an empathic and caring understanding of the discipline construct. Cataldo reminds us *that discipline is purposeful, aiming to help us become self-managers.* In the same regard, Brazelton and Greenspan indicate, "All learning, even of limits and structure, begins with nurturing care, from which children learn trust, warmth, intimacy, empathy, and attachment to those around them" (p. 145).

One program that includes a strong focus on discipline and self-management throughout is the *Systematic Training for Effective Parenting (STEP)* program. This program was developed by Don Dinkmeyer and Gary McKay and is based on the work of Alfred Adler. The program uses a variety of positive parent skills and parent-child communication strategies to promote socially responsible behaviors in children. As indicated by Hamner and Turner (2001, p. 137), the STEP program calls for the following to nurture in children socially responsible behaviors (Figure 4.8):

Figure 4.8
STEP Strategies for Effective Parenting

* Democratic relationships based on mutual respect; a feeling that the child deserves to be treated with both firmness and kindness.

* Encouragement that communicates respect, love, support, and valuing the child as a person.

* The use of natural and logical consequences to replace reward and punishment, which enables the child to develop responsibility, self discipline, and judgment.

* A basic understanding of human behavior that helps parents to maintain a consistent approach to human relationships.

Within these broad guidelines for positive discipline *early childhood educators need to play close attention to guidance and behavior guidelines that are developmentally and culturally appropriate.* Gonzalez-Mena (1997) notes that while our culture is very focused on a self-directed concept of discipline, other cultures (including many Hispanic cultures) emphasize a common values approach and are more didactic in their means of teaching children. We need parental input on parent education programs that focus on discipline.

Of concern to the entire community and an essential parent education topic in the preschool years is that of *Health Education and Development* (Greenspan & Benderly, 1997). The content of this emphasis area should include information and resources on the following: the protection and safety of the child, needed childhood immunizations, basic health and well-care strategies, nutrition and emotional health, safety-proofing the home, regular child health check-ups, and other related health and medical issues significant to the entire family (Brazelton & Greenspan, 2000). Attention to the mother's prenatal care during pregnancy offers an opportunity to begin this important educational process. Through a combination of home visits, group meetings, parent networking, print materials, and the use of well designed videos, parent education content in this area can alert parents (and simply remind them) of the following key points (Brazelton & Greenspan, 2000, Chapter 2):

* Take care of your self during pregnancy by not smoking, avoiding alcohol or drugs, eating nutritious food, developing a good sense of self, and beginning your journey of parenthood in a positive way.

* Establish a really nurturing and helpful support team.

* Before bringing the baby home check your house and surrounding area for any toxic substances (for example: lead) that might cause harm to the child.

* Place all poisons or other household cleaning items in a safe place.

* Establish the pattern of doing regular medical check-ups by visiting the pediatrician often during your pregnancy.

* Be sure to provide yourself and your child with nutritious and enjoyable food.

* Maintain a calm and yet stimulating environment for you and your family.

* Love and nurture your child and form strong bonds with the child.

* Be sure any item (poisons, guns, or other items) that can cause harm to the child or other family is removed from the environment.

* Observe your child and yourself regularly for any signs of ill health (mental or physical) and attend to these quickly.

Early childhood educators can reach beyond the educational interventions noted above and advocate for and help to establish community-centered health and medical services for all children and families. Services like community-wide immunization days, well-care for children, reminders through newspaper and television specials, and home safety specials are valuable reminders to young families about the important role that health and safety play in the developing child's life (Eliot, 1999).

With the recent research on brain development receiving global attention, all parents are interested in *promoting children's early learning and development* (Brazelton & Greenspan, 2000). Clearly, children's early learning is linked to their safe, nurturing, healthy, and responsive involvement in family (Eliot, 1999). Given that children and parents have attended to the key health, safety, nutrition, and related features of a productive family setting, Hamner and Turner (2001, chapters 1, 2) offer the following parent education framework for promoting children's learning:

Stage of Development Theme

Infancy Attachment, Trust-building, Provide Safety/ Provide natural stimulation through play

Toddlerhood Child-proof safety, Promoting autonomy, self-help, Social and intellectual learning, Language stimulation, Encourage curiosity.

Preschoolers Nurturing the "Growing Child" and Using appropriate play materials and activities. Parental involvement in children's learning, Family-center and Family-school involvement.

In addition, early childhood parent educators emphasize helping parents become especially engaged in roles such as the following to enhance and support their children's early learning (Gonzalez-Mena, 1994; Swick, Da Ros, & Kovach, 2001):

* Emotional and social responsiveness
* Proactive and caring involvement in the family
* Nurture your child's interests
* Play with your child
* Provide a stimulating and yet secure home learning environment
* Model the social, cognitive, and language you want your child to develop
* Be a keen observer of your child's development and
* Promote in your child and in yourself a positive self-image.

During the early years, over seventy percent of parents will need to select an out-of-home care center or place for their child. Parents are very interested in receiving guidance and support in making good choices related to the early care and education of their children. The challenges parents face in this regard include at least three issues (Hamner & Turner, 2001):

Figure 4.9
Three Important Issues in Selecting Out-of-Home
Child Care

---

1) Choosing care that is high-quality and that they feel secure and happy with in relation to their child's well-being.

2) Finding care that is accessible (close to work or home) and affordable for the family budget.

3) Developing and sustaining strong involvement in the center or school in which the child is placed.

The National Association for the Education of Young Children (1509 16th St., NW, Washington DC 20036) offers many resource pamphlets and books as well as other resources for early childhood professionals and parents to use in parenting workshops. Swick (1993) cites the excellent "What to look for" list on parent guidelines for selecting quality child care by Magid and McKelvey (1987, pp. 286-290) and recommends its use in parenting education efforts:

Quality Child Care: What to Look For

Caregiver

* There should be no more than 1 – 3 infants or very small children per adult caregiver.

* One caregiver has the responsibility for your infant in particular.

* At least one person should be a fully certified early childhood professional and ALL staff should have at least some substantive formal child development training and be enrolled in continuing early childhood education.

* The staff should work well together and there should be continuity of staff from year to year.

* All staff should voluntarily submit a state law enforcement check on their background so that parents and others are assured of their good character.

* Staff should be nurturing , loving and warmly interact with children.

* Staff should praise, encourage and support children as they develop self-help skills.

* Staff should talk and interact in positive ways with the children and parents regularly.

* Staff should invite and seek out continuing parental involvement in all aspects of the program.

Facilities:
* The surroundings should be safe and clean with plenty of room for the infants, toddlers, and preschoolers.

* Specific appropriate areas are set aside for nap and quiet times and specific places exist where each child can place their special items and materials.

* A fenced yard with plenty of space for play, running, jumping, and other physical activities exists. Staff supervise and interact with the children's play.

* The overall environment is safe, well maintained, clean and neat (but messy in a child's way of play), and nurturing.

* Nutritious food is served in a family style manner, and healthy habits of sanitation and cleanliness are followed regularly.

  Safe action toys are plentiful as are more manipulative indoor/outdoor materials like blocks and water play resources.

* The facility is licensed, approved by local health and fire departments, and meets all other regulatory requirements.

Program:
* Active, creative, and child-appropriate learning activities are prevalent in the daily program.

* The program is flexible within a well organized daily plan that emphasizes the individual needs of each child and family.

* Children experience a balance of indoor and outdoor play that capitalizes on their imagination and creativity.

* Parents are regularly involved in the program.

Focusing On The Changing Needs Of Parents

Three "sets of parent needs" emerge during the preschool years that early childhood parent education programs should address: 1) the emerging parent identity needs, 2) creating a viable family system, and 3) developing an effective work-family balance (Galinsky, 1999; Powell, 1998).

Establishing a parenting identity is very challenging within the social and economic situations most parents experience (Garbarino, 1992). Parent educators have found that "themes" that comprise the actual work of parents provide the substance for parenting education programs and supports: provide security and physical care for the child, nurture and love the child, meet the basic physical and health needs, attend to the child's social and emotional needs, engage the child in stimulating learning activities, guide the child's behavioral development, model healthy and nurturing life style, recognize and nurture this emerging "parent self", and foster healthy and nurturing family communication (Cataldo, 1987; Gonzalez-Mena, 1994; Bronfenbrenner, 2005).

Creating a viable family system is the structural challenge that today's parents point to as the most difficult and yet needed element for being effective (Galinsky, 1999). The birth of the first child introduces dramatic changes in scheduling, use of time, personal activities, and relational activities. For example, as people become parents they note that they need support, ideas, role models, resources, and opportunities to meet other parents who have been successful (Cowan & Cowan, 1992; Heretick, 2003).

Developing an effective work-family balance is an issue that parents and families deal with over the life span. Children report that they worry most about how hard their parents work and the stress their parents experience in trying to be a parent and a worker (Galinsky, 1999). Parent education programs usually address this need in home visits and in group meetings where parents can share and discuss strategies with other parents (Powell, 1998). When the "balance" issue is placed within the larger set of challenges in terms of managing the family-environment stress that all families experience, *The Family Matters Program* and other programs like it offer many good ideas (Cochran, 1988). This program works to help parents achieve attitudes and skills for relating family needs to potential resource groups and agencies in the community. It also engages parents in actually using specific family needs to plan goals and strategies for addressing some of the needs of the family. Some of the major issues parents and families consistently note are (Heymann, 2000; Elkind, 1994; Thornton, 2001): networking effectively with parents and other helpers, finding opportunities to use one's skills in the workplace, managing the needs of children, finding and affording child care, relating effectively to the many people who can be of help to the family, and finding resources to maintain their personal growth. In relation to these needs, Powell (1998) suggests that early childhood professionals:

1) Develop family resource centers where parents and family can find help in strengthening their skills for managing family stress.

2) Provide regular outlets where parents can network and share with other parents and helpers.

3) Encourage and support other community and school groups to offer family support programs that aim to specifically equip parents with life skills.

4) Integrate needed parent and family management skills into parent education programs like Equip for the Future does.

5) Offer programs on family-work stress management, finding quality child care, and using community resources effectively – in ways that many parents can attend.

Early childhood parent educators use various delivery strategies to reach as many parents and families as possible. Some of these strategies are highlighted as follows.

Home Visiting. Home visiting (also known as personal visiting by many early childhood educators) is a delivery strategy that offers optimal conditions for support, education, and parent and family directed activities (Olsen & Fuller, 2009). The visits typically occur within the family's setting, offer opportunities for one-to-one interactions with a caring professional or para-professional, engage parents and children [and other family] in hands-on learning, and create an atmosphere for communication (Hamner & Turner, 2001). In home visits the goal is to educate, support, and enable the parents and other adult family to become the leaders and instigators of home learning. It is a collaborative strategy where professionals and parents create a positive cooperative learning environment (Powell, 1998).

Group Meetings. Group meetings offer a guided social and educational setting where parents and professionals can learn about and support each other in their common goal of child, parent, family, and community empowerment (Couchenour & Chrisman, 2000). While the most popular use of group meetings has been to provide parents with information on a variety of topics, *more contemporary uses* include: parent sharing, networking, and joint problem-solving (Barbour, Barbour, & Scully, 2008). The keys to successful group meetings are: gain needed parent input, advanced planning (to clarify goals and activities), share work load where everyone contributes to the program, organize time and place that is convenient for families, have a relevant and motivating program, include parents and children as presenters in the program, advertise thoroughly, remind parents with notes or phone calls, and make the total environment family-friendly (Swick, 1993; 2004).

Parent Discussion Groups. Emerging from the group meeting concept is the use of *parent discussion groups* (Powell, 1998). These are nurturing and highly supportive meetings that are co-structured and co-facilitated by parents and professionals. Usually the topics emerge from parent perceived needs and/or other family-school issues that a significant group of parents and professionals desire information and opportunities for discussion. Three elements of successful discussion groups are: parent empowerment, constructive problem-solving, and parent-professional networking (Powell, 1998).

Conferences. Parent-teacher, parent-child-teacher, and/or family-early childhood conferences typically have one of the following goals in mind: to share information, to up-date each other on some aspect of family or school life, or to problem-solve a situation (Barbour & Barbour, 2001). The main guideline for establishing effective conferences is in the *collaboration* of professional and parent/family (Lawler, 1991; Swick, 2004). Parents and family should be joint planners with the professionals in developing and implementing conferences. *Group conferences* have become more prevalent as some families have common concerns or interests. As Lawler (1991) has suggested, responsiveness, planning, parent participation, family-friendly practices, and an overall school culture that values parents, are critical to successful conferencing.

Parent Participation In The Classroom. A major goal in early childhood family programs is to create and foster strong parental involvement in the child's learning, development, and education. Most early childhood programs create many opportunities for parents to become a part of the classroom learning activities. One program that has achieved this strategy is the Family Literacy component – Parent and Child Time Together (PACT). The PACT engages parents in a joint learning activity with their child on a regular basis (in some cases three or more mornings a week). In other approaches, parents contribute through reading to the children over their lunch time, help through after-school enrichment work, share their special talents in the classroom, or do other such activities. As Cataldo (1987) and Couchenour and Chrisman (2000) indicate, parental involvement in the classroom sends a strong positive message to the child: we (parents and teacher) are both your teachers and we care that you have the best learning experiences. In addition, parents gain support from teachers for their contribution and teachers feel validated by the additional work of the parents and other family.

Additional delivery strategies are noted in other parent involvement sections in this book.

Comprehensive Family Support / Strengthening Programs and Practices

While individual parent education / family strengthening programs certainly have many positive attributes and contribute important supports to parents and families, *the need and emerging practice is to create comprehensive family strengthening systems* (Schorr, 1997; Bronfenbrenner, 2005). This is particularly so with families who are in high-risk situations or have been negatively impacted by chronic stressors over long periods of time. However, the use of comprehensive, integrated services is good for all families, especially when combined with other social, educational, and economic services that support families and communities (Hanson & Lynch, 2004).

For example, Nunez and Collignon (2000) describe a family-centered program in New York City for homeless families. Conceptually and programmatically the efforts aim to support the entire family in becoming empowered to live and grow in healthier ways. As they note, parents and children who are in a shelter situation face very stressful lives and to simply meet the housing need without addressing the other needs is futile. Their effort has created "Communities of Learning" with three very important elements: 1) education for homeless children, 2) family support services, and 3) education for homeless parents.

In the Family Support component of these comprehensive family centers, *three major services are emphasized:* 1) providing for basic needs (food, shelter, clothing), 2) health care, and 3) meeting mental health needs. In the New York City model these "centers" are housed at homeless shelters (or nearby facilities) and called Family Inns. The goal in meeting essential family needs is to help the family meet emergency situations and then to position themselves to become more independent in self-care (Nunez, 1996).

The Parent Education component is inclusive of parenting, personal, and job / career educational goals and strategies. Thus, parents are enrolled in various literacy, adult education, job skills, and life skills training activities and courses.

The Early Childhood Education component is ideally offered in the same facility with the adult education and parenting / family services. The goal here is twofold: 1) to provide children with quality learning and development experiences, and 2) to empower the total family as a learning system, including the support this provides for parents to then seek work or continue working when they attain it (Nunez & Collignon, 2000).

144

After School and Summer Enrichment are also integrated into this program. Children in the preschool or in the formal school years enroll in various activities that relate to their specific interests and needs. In many cases these activities are linked with the school's efforts to assure a more "mainstream" environment for all of the children

Family Literacy: A major integration process in bringing together the different components of comprehensive family strengthening programs is *family literacy* (Brizius & Foster, 1993). The family literacy construct actually brings together the elements of adult literacy/training, parent education (including life skills training), parent-child time, and early childhood education.

Another program approach that seeks to provide comprehensive outreach services is **Healthy Families** (Schorr, 1997). *Healthy Families America* is a national early childhood family strengthening program that aims to intervene with young families to prevent abuse, neglect, and other dysfunctional behaviors from emerging. The program began in Hawaii and is now being implemented in several states. It may have different titles such as Healthy Start, Healthy Families, or other similar titles. The program begins at birth in the hospital with the home visitor using a stress index to help parents understand their stressors and to offer support in solving serious stressors. Home Visitors are key to the intervention process; they meet with the family and build a nurturing, trusting relationship that allows for strong parent/family collaboration in the intervention effort. Families are linked to needed services, provided regular support visits, and encouraged to continue their education and that of their children.

This model raises an important issue about comprehensive family strengthening efforts – the intensity and duration of such services (Forest, 2003). Programs must not only provide integrated and comprehensive services but provide them in the doses and longevity that truly empower families.

Further, effective comprehensive family strengthening efforts address critical issues that assure full participation of parents and families (Schorr, 1997). Consider the following issues and corresponding strategies (Forest, 2003):

*   Assure that staff are "family-friendly" and "parent responsive" so that parents and families feel wanted and valued.

*   Create "spaces" in the program environment that are especially suited and designated for parents.

*   Assure that transportation and scheduling of events are organized to support optimal parent and family participation.

*   Schedule activities in flexible ways that offer family alterna-

tives in terms of their matching family/work schedules to events in the program.

* Provide child care at all events and activities that dictate this service so that all parents who want to be a part of the activity are able to do so.

* Assure that all program activities are affordable or that scholarships, reduced fee schedules, or other financial support is used to support parent and family involvement.

* Link services to each other and with parent/family needs in mind so that quality services are provided in efficient and family-friendly ways.

Addressing the Needs of High-Risk Populations

Families experiencing chronic and/or intense stress resulting from various risk factors such as poverty, illiteracy, chemical addictions, economic problems, health stressors, mental health issues, homelessness, and other problems need positive and supportive attention from early childhood professionals. Swick and Graves (1993) present an empowerment approach for early childhood professionals to use in responding to the needs of high-risk families. These are families who typically have experienced severe stress and have seen their resources depleted or badly eroded. Further, the traditional stereotypes of families "at-risk" no longer are adequate to describing and understanding the multiple family situations that cause severe and damaging stress (Elkind, 1994; Heymann, 2000; Hanson & Lynch, 2004).

Swick and Graves (1993) identify five initial concerns for early childhood professionals working with parents and families in high-risk situations: 1) understanding context, 2) developing trust, 3) fostering mutuality, 4) developing a shared sense of purpose and action, and 5) nurturing open and honest communication.

Context is the setting in which parent/family and professionals interact and seek to become mutual helpers. Parents and families in trouble seek helpers who have similar goals and values, and who seem genuinely interested in their total family (Spacapan & Oskamp, 1992; Minuchin, Colapinto, & Minuchin, 1998; Swick, 2005).

Closely related to context is the *need for trust* within the helping relations of parents/families and professionals (Swick & Graves, 1993). Parents want someone who is consistent and reliable in their relations as well as caring. Swick and Graves (1993) delineate some of the questions parents noted when they were asked about the kind of person they seek in a helper.

1) Is this a caring person?

2) Is this person interested in our family beyond tomorrow?

3) Is this person really skilled in helping us with our concerns?

4) Does this person have integrity?

Mutuality is essential to any helping situation. Early childhood parent educators need to create learning environments that support parent-professional mutuality. This simply means that we engage parents in leadership, and work toward empowering them as important leaders in the parent education and family strengthening effort (Schorr, 1997).

Developing a shared sense of purpose and action is linked to our mutually respectful and beneficial interactions. As Powell (1998) suggests, parent educators are more effective when parents and families see the purpose and activities as reflective of their desires and needs. Swick and Graves (1993) also noted the value of including parents in all aspects of goal setting and implementation.

Open and honest communication provide the binding energy to the parent-teacher relationship (Swick, 1997). All aspects of the partnership and the emerging parent education activities benefit from open, honest communication. Parents point to the integrity and warmth of home visitors as very important to their being interested in program work (Schorr, 1997).

SUMMATIVE DISCUSSION OF APPLICATION POINTS

Meaningful parent education and family literacy experiences enhance every family member in their journey to grow and learn. Yet obstacles abound in the real contexts where early childhood professionals seek to establish trusting and nurturing programs and services: parental fear of authoritative systems like education, negative parent experiences with programs in the past, lack of communication and transportation, inadequate resources, poorly trained staff, poor scheduling of activities, lack of parent and family involvement, and a variety of other issues.

Fortunately, research and application work in the various quality parent and family programs offer us several application ideas:

1) Use multiple assessments to establish valid needs along with potential resources to use in addressing these needs.

2) Parent and family input is essential in every facet of the program or service development, implementation, and evaluation.

3) Acquire and use an understanding of local cultural, social, and educational needs and strengths in *selecting goals, strategies, and approaches to parent education*.

4) Build quality program elements into the mix such as: appropriate and relevant goals, high-quality staff, strong family involvement, several venues for families to access available

services, content and process that is connected to family needs at the local level, and many leadership development activities for parents and staff.

5) Use evaluation and assessment to empower the program: study strengths and needs, locate gaps that need attention, seek parent and community input, form review teams for feedback, – and then design refinements that use this information.

Suggested Websites

Home Instruction Program for Preschool Youngsters (HIPPY): <www.c3pg.com/hippy.htm>

I Am Your Child:

National Parent Information Network:

Parents As Teachers (PAT) National Center: <www.patnc.org>

Zero To Three:

Parent Center: <www.parentcenter.com/general/34754.html/>

Child Welfare Leage of America (CWLA): <www.cwla.org>

National Network for Family Resiliency: <www.nnfr.org>

Mother-Child Home Program: <www.motherchildhome.org>

References

Amatea, E. (2009). Building culturally responsive family-school relationships. Columbus, OH: Pearson.

Barbour, C., Barbour, N, & Scully, P. (2008). Families, schools, and communities: Buidling partnerships for educating children. Fourth Edition. Columbus, OH: Pearson.

Brazelton, T., & Greenspan, S. (2000). The irreducible needs of children. Cambridge, MA: Perseus Publishing.

Brizius, J., & Foster, S. (1993). Generation to generation: Realizing the promise of family literacy. Ypsilanti, MI: High Scope Press.

Bronfenbrenner, U. (1979). The ecology of human development. Cambridge, MA: Harvard University Press.

Bronfenbrenner, U. (2005). Making human beings human: Bioecological perspectives on human development. Thousand Oaks, CA: Sage

Brown, E., & Swick, K. (2002). Parent education/family literacy: First Steps effective practices report. Columbia, SC: University of South Carolina Institute for Families and Society.

Cataldo, C. (1987). Parent education for early childhood. New York: Teachers College Press.

Chavkin, N. (Ed.). (1993). <u>Families and schools in a pluralistic society</u>. Albany, NY: State University of New York Press.

Cochran, M. (1988). Parental empowerment in Family Matters: Lessons learned from a research program. In D. Powell (Ed.). <u>Parent education as early childhood intervention</u>. Norwood, NJ: Ablex.

Comer, J. (1997). <u>Waiting for a miracle: Why schools can't solve our problems – and how we can</u>. New York: Dutton.

Couchenour, D., & Chrisman, K. (2000). <u>Families, schools, and communities: Together for young children</u>. New York, NY: Delmar Thomson Learning.

Cowan, C., & Cowan, P. (1992). <u>When partners become parents: The big life change for couples</u>. New York: Basic Books.

Darling, S. (1989). <u>Family literacy project</u>. Louisville, KY: The Keenan Family Trust Literacy Project.

Delpit, L. (1995). <u>Other people's children: Cultural conflict in the classroom</u>. New York: The New Press.

Dunst, C., Trivette, C., & Deal, A. (1988). <u>Enabling and empowering families: Principles and guidelines for practice</u>. Lexington, MA: Lexington Books.

Eliot, L. (1999). <u>What's going on in there? How the brain and mind develop in the first five years of life</u>. New York: Bantam.

Elkind, D. (1994). <u>Ties that stress: The new family imbalance</u>. Cambridge, MA: Harvard University Press.

Emde, R. (2001). From neurons to neighborhoods: Implications for training. <u>Zero to Three</u>, 21 (5), 30-34.

Feeney, J., Hohaus, L., Noller, P., & Alexander, R. (2001). <u>Becoming parents: Exploring the bonds between mothers, fathers, and their infants</u>. New York: Cambridge University Press.

Fishel, E. (1991) <u>Family mirrors: What our children's lives reveal about ourselves</u>. Boston: Houghton Mifflin.

Forest, C. (2003). <u>Empowerment skills for family workers</u>. Ithaca, NY: Cornell Family Development Press.

Fraiberg, S. (1977). <u>Every child's birthright: In defense of mothering</u>. New York: Basic Books.

Galinsky, E. (1987). <u>The six stages of parenthood</u>. Reading, MA: Addison-Wesley.

Galinsky, E. (1999). <u>Ask the children: What America's children really think about working parents</u>. New York: William Morrow.

Garbarino, J. (1992). <u>Children and families in the social environment. Second Edition</u>. New York: Aldine de Gruyter.

Garbarino, J., & Bedard, C. (2001). <u>Parents under siege: Why you are the solution, not the problem, in your child's life</u>. New York: Free Press.

Gonzalez-Mena, J. (1994). <u>From a parent's perspective</u>. Salem, WI: Sheffield.

Gonzalez-Mena, J. (1997). <u>Multicultural issues in child care. Second Edition</u>. Mountain View, CA: Mayfield.

Gonzalez-Mena, J. (2006). <u>The young child in the family and the community.</u> Fourth Edition. Columbus, OH: Pearson.

Gordon, I. (1975). <u>Research report of parent oriented home-based early childhood education programs</u>. Gainesville, FL: Institute for Human Development, University of Florida.

Greenspan, S., & Benderly, B. (1997). <u>The growth of the mind and the endangered origins of intelligence</u>. Reading, MA: Addison-Wesley.

Hallowell, E. (2002). <u>The childhood roots of adult happiness</u>. New York: Ballantine Books.

Hamner, T., & Turner, P. (2001). <u>Parenting in comtemporary society. Fourth Edition</u>. Boston: Allyn and Bacon.

Hanson, M., & Lynch, E. (2004). <u>Understanding families: Approaches to diversity, disability, and risk</u>. Baltimore, MD: Paul H. Brookes.

Heretick, D. (2003) <u>The empowered family: Raising responsible and caring children in violent times</u>. Toledo, OH: Mercy Health Partners.

Hetherington, E., & Kelley, J. (2002). <u>For better or for worse: Divorce reconsidered</u>. New York: W.W. Norton.

Heymann, J. (2000). <u>The widening gap: Why America's working families are in jeopardy and what can be done about it</u>. New York: Basic Books.

Honig, A. (2002). <u>Secure relationships: Nurturing infant/toddler attachment in early care settings.</u> Washington, DC: National Association for the Education of Young Children.

Karr-Morse, R., & Wiley, M. (1997). <u>Ghosts from the nursery: Tracing the roots of violence</u>. New York: Atlantic Monthly Press.

Klass, C. (1996). <u>Home visiting: Promoting healthy parent and child development</u>. Baltimore: Paul H. Brookes Publishing.

Kohn, A. (1990). <u>The brighter side of human nature: Altruism and empathy in everyday life</u>. New York: Basic Books.

Kotre, J. (1999). <u>Make it count: How to generate a legacy that gives meaning to your life</u>. New York: The Free Press.

LaRossa, R. (1986). <u>Becoming a parent</u>. Newbury Park, CA: Sage.

Lawler, S. (1991). <u>Parent-teacher conferencing in early childhood education</u>. Washington, DC: National Education Association.

Lynch, E., & Hanson, M. (1998). <u>Developing cross-cultural competence: A guide for working with children and their families</u>. Baltimore, MD: Paul Brookes.

Magid, K., & McKelvey, C. (1987). <u>High risk: Children without a conscience</u>. New York: Bantam Books.

Marshak, D. (1997). <u>The common vision: Parenting and education for wholeness</u>. New York: Peter Lang.

McKenry, P., & Price, S. (1994). <u>Families and change: Coping with stressful events</u>. Thousand Oaks, CA: Sage.

Nunez, R. (1996). <u>The new American poverty: Homeless families in America</u>. New York: Insight Books, Plenum Publishers.

Nunez, R., & Collignon, K. (2000). Supporting family learning: Building a community of learners. In J. Stronge & E. Reed-Victor (Eds.) <u>Educating homeless students: Promising practices</u>. Larchmont, NY: Eye on Education.

Olsen, G., & Fuller, M. (2003). <u>Home-school relations: Working successfully with parents and families</u>. New York: Allyn & Bacon.

Olsen, G., & Fuller, M. (2009). <u>Home-school relations: Working successfully with parents and families</u>. Third Edition. New York: Allyn & Bacon.

Pipher, M. (1996). <u>The shelter of each other: Rebuilding our families</u>. New York: G.P. Putnam's Sons.

Powell, D. (1989). <u>Families and early childhood programs</u>. Washington, DC: National Association for the Education of Young Children.

Powell, D. (1998). Reweaving parents into the fabric of early childhood programs. <u>Young Children</u>, 53 (5), 60-67.

Restak, R. (2003). <u>The new brain</u>. New York, NY: Rodale Books.

Rogoff, B. (2003). <u>The cultural nature of human development</u>. New York: Oxford University Press.

Rosier, K. (2000). <u>Mothering inner-city children: The early school years</u>. New Brunswick, NJ: Rutgers University Press.

Ruddick, S. (1995). <u>Maternal thinking</u>. Boston, MA: Beacon Press.

Schorr, L. (1989). <u>Within our reach: Breaking the cycle of disadvantage</u>. New York: Anchor Books.

Schorr, L. (1997). <u>Common purpose: Strengthening families and neighborhoods to rebuild America</u>. New York: Anchor Books.

Siegel, J. (2000). <u>What children learn from their parents' marriage</u>. New York: HarperCollins.

Small, M. (2001). <u>Kids: How biology and culture shape the way we raise our children</u>. New York: Doubleday.

Swick, K. (1987). <u>Perspectives on understanding and working with families</u>. Champaign, IL: Stipes.

Swick, K. (1991). <u>Teacher-parent partnerships to enhance school success in early childhood education</u>. Washington, DC: National Education Association.

Swick, K. (1993). <u>Strengthening parents and families during the early childhood years</u>. Champaign, IL: Stipes.

Swick, K. (1996). Early childhood parent education / family literacy: A prevention of school failure strategy. <u>Occasional Papers</u>, 1 (2), 1-8.

Swick, K. (2001). Nurturing decency through caring and serving during the early childhood years. <u>Early Childhood Education Journal</u>, 29 (2), 131-138.

Swick, K. (2004<u>). Empowering parents, families, schools and communities during the early childhood years</u>. Champaign, IL: Stipes.

Swick, K. (2005). Helping homeless families overcome barriers to successful functioning. <u>Early Childhood Education Journal</u>, 33 (3), 195-200.

Swick, K. (2006). Families and educators together: Raising caring and peaceable children. <u>Early Childhood Education Journal</u>, 33 (4), 279-287.

Swick, K., & Graves, S. (1993). <u>Empowering at-risk families during the early childhood years</u>. Washington, DC: National Education Association.

Swick, K., Da Ros, D., & Kovach, B. (2001). Empowering parents and families through a caring inquiry approach. <u>Early Childhood Education Journal</u>, 29 (1), 65-71.

Thornton, A. (2001). <u>The well-being of children and families: Research and data needs</u>. Ann Arbor, MI: University of Michigan Press.

Weiss, H. (1988). Family support and education programs: Working through ecological theories of human development. In H. Weiss & F. Jacobs (Eds.). <u>Evaluating family programs</u>. New York: Aldine de Gruyter.

Weiss, H., & Jacobs, F. (Eds.). (1988). <u>Evaluating family programs</u>. New York: Aldine de Gruyter.

White, B. (1988). <u>Educating the infant and toddler</u>. Lexington, MA: DC Heath (Lexington Books).

Wuthnow, R. (1995<u>). Learning to care: Elementary kindness in an age of indifference.</u> New York: Oxford University Press.

Zigler, E., Finn-Stevenson, M., & Hall, N. (2002). <u>The first three years and beyond</u>. New Haven, CT: Yale University Press.

Chapter Five

Building Strong Partnerships between Families, Schools, and Communities

---

CAPSULE: The bases for having strong partnerships between families, schools, and communities during the early childhood years are examined. In particular, the nature of partnerships is discussed with special relevance for helping parents, families, schools, and communities craft such collaborative schemes. Further, the needed strategies for achieving partnerships are presented and evaluative activities are identified that hold promise for continual improvement in these vital partnership arrangements.

Chapter Five Objectives:

1) Gain insight and understanding of the important constructs within the partnership process.

2) Learn about and apply parent and teacher leadership development strategies that help to nurture strong family, school, and community partnerships.

3) Gain insight and skills for using strategies on developing and enhancing parent/family, school, and community partnerships during the early childhood years.

4) Enrich your understanding of the major attributes of a "family-community friendly" school.

5) Synthesize the material presented in the chapter into a workable framework for promoting strong parent-teacher and family-school-community partnerships.

6) Explain and apply some of the strategies and activities in the chapter that help to empower the partnership efforts.

7) Discuss and simulate examples of how evaluation can help to refine and strengthen the partnership process.

Because of its interdisciplinary nature and multi-faceted service structure, early childhood education thrives on effective partnerships. This chapter examines several topics relevant to the development of effective and growing partnerships among families, schools, and communities. Initially, the discussion focuses on important constructs that shape the partnership process and their implications for building strong relationships. Then, the critical elements of parents and teachers as the leadership team are reviewed. The value and practice of beginning partnerships during the early childhood years is also examined. The remaining sections of this chapter attempt to respond to four important questions: 1) What does a family-community friendly school look like? 2) What are the essential aspects of a framework for having a strong partnership? 3) What are some helpful strategies for strengthening the family-school-community partnership? 4) In what ways can programs evaluate and improve their partnerships?

Important Constructs within the Partnership Process

Any partnership that hopes to last and have a meaningful impact on the collaborating parties requires certain elements as shown in Figure 5.1.

Figure 5.1
Elements for Having Lasting Partnerships

---

*   A sense of common purpose
*   Trust in each other
*   Mutuality in all relationships
*   Specificity of roles
*   A structure for program actualization
*   Resources for functioning
*   Evaluation to refine and improve

The author experienced the importance of these elements in helping staff and parents in a *Head Start* program develop a family involvement effort. What I noticed was that as staff and parents realized they had a common mission, their sense of trust, purpose, and mutuality took on a sense of urgency. They felt connected in having some activities they felt would improve the lives of their children. Thus, as the following brief notes make clear, each element played an important role in having strong family involvement.

Common Purpose: Partnership efforts thrive on having a common purpose. For example, Comer (1997, 2000) points out that schools that have a strong parent-teacher-community advisory group tend to have a better understanding of what their partnership is trying to achieve. A clear implication for family-school-community partnership leaders is to gain input from parents, teachers, citizens, and others into the development of the partnership's mission (Epstein, 1991). Another implication is to publish and display this statement of purpose (Ferguson, 2008). Finally, early childhood leaders need to continuously review this purpose in light of the activities happening in the partnership (Bauer & Shea, 2003).

Trust in Each Other's Worth: Partnerships that thrive regardless of the stressors experienced have an underlying sense of trust in each other's value and worth (File, 2001). For example, an *Even Start* program the author assists through consulting work has strong partnerships with local social service and health agencies. When the program was in need of a major financial boost, these partners stepped forward and shared funding, training, and other resources.

Mutuality: Closely linked to trust is a sense of mutuality in all helping relationships (Swick, 2001, 2004). The growth and renewal of partnership efforts is dependent upon the sharing of tasks and activities in ways which empower the partners (Comer, 1997, 2000). Most early childhood education programs actively promote and value this "mutuality of helping relationships" with parents, families, and communities.

Specificity of Roles and Actions: Couchenour and Chrisman (2000) remind us that partnerships only come alive through relationships that result in activities meaningful to the partners. It is crucial for parents and teachers to identify and articulate specific roles and activities each is to perform. Likewise, community involvement efforts must also have clear roles and functions for their partners (Goldberg, 1997).

A Structure for Actualizing the Partnership: Some form of partnership board, council, or other group structure for planning, implementing, and refining the partner's work is essential in achieving the desired goals (Epstein, 1991; Bagin et al, 2008). The structure should be formed with input from all parties, have an appointed leader, articulate its procedures for operating, have scheduled meetings, and use all other needed means for communicating and actualizing its purpose.

CASE EXAMPLE: A community *"Healthy Start"* program that is partially funded by the state but mostly a project of local civic, church, and business leaders – achieves many improvements for children and families because it has a strong management team that articulates priorities, seeks people's input, and evaluates the program regularly. Without this structure many child and family advances would not exist. This team has included all elements in

the community and attempts to address issues that
indeed impact every group in the community.

Resources: Time, skilled people, materials, funding, transportation, space and facilities, and other "resources" are essential to actualize any partnership effort (Swick, 1991, 1993, 2004). One reason many partnerships are formed is to help each other have access to resources important to each party's functioning. In early childhood education, for example, programs like *Even Start* and *Head Start* could not exist without intensive resource sharing. This is also seen in many faith-based programs where churches use community resources to have a quality program for children and families (Couchenour & Chrisman, 2000).

Evaluation and Improvement: The focus of evaluation should be on the mechanism that empowers the partnership to achieve its purpose. Is the partnership creating a strong helping relationship process? Is the partnership achieving its goals to help others? What challenges are emerging that need attention? These and other questions can serve as guides to our review and improvement of various elements in the partnership (Powell, 1998; Barbour et al, 2008).

Parents and Teachers: A Leadership Team

Parents and teachers are society's leadership team in renewing the foundation for an enriched culture in each generation (Ryan et al, 1995). Parents and teachers play specific roles in carrying out their leadership functions. Important to our developing strong partnerships is our understanding of the attributes in parents and teachers (and the partnerships they form) and of how we can facilitate these processes. First, we look at the parental attributes that promote healthy partnerships as presented in Figure 5.2.

Figure 5.2
Parental Attributes that Promote
Healthy Partnerships

---

* Warmth

* Nurturance

* Active Listening

* Follow Through

* Problem-Solving

* Cultural Sensitivity

In addition, attributes such as a strong sense of efficacy, marital happiness, family harmony, and caring have been cited as highly desirable in parents as they engage in partnership activities (Swick et al, 1998). Parental integrity is linked to parents' involvement efforts and

Swick (1991, 2004) notes that integrity is comprised of four elements (See Figure 5.3): self-image, parent efficacy, parent development, and parent interpersonal skills. Each element is briefly reviewed.

Figure 5.3
Four Elements that Comprise Parental Integrity

---

* Parent self-image
* Parent efficacy
* Parent development
* Parent interpersonal skills

Parent Self-Image: Strong partners in any endeavor have a positive and resilient self-image. In particular, Swick (1991, p. 35) comments that "parents who have a positive self-image tend to see their children in a more meaningful sense, to spend more time with them in learning activities, and to have a more positive attitude toward teachers and the educational process."

Parent Efficacy: Having a sense of mastery over one's regular life routines (efficacy) is highly related to strong partnership skills. Schaefer (1982) and Goodnow & Collins (1990) found a strong correlation between parents' self efficacy early in the child's life and their later involvement in the child's kindergarten. Interestingly, parents gain a stronger sense of efficacy through positive involvement with the school; efficacy building experiences add to one's sense of harmony with the total life system (Comer, 1997, 2000).

Parent Development: Parents who are intentionally engaged in growth experiences and positively responding to their family and related life challenges are more effective in various partnership roles. Swick (1991) states the essence of this process:

> The developmental gains parents acquire through the maturation process, which is indeed an intentional endeavor, provide them with "perspective-taking" – a skill that is integral to working with others in productive ways.
>
> Negotiating the marital, friendship, and family challenges that arise in the early years of family development successfully adds a new dimension to parents' perspectives about their development, one that strengthens their attitudes and skills for relating to new challenges. (p. 36)

Parent Interpersonal Skills: Perhaps the binding force in partnership efforts is the interpersonal skill level of the partners. Parents need strong and reciprocal relationships that promote their caring and nurturing, because partnerships require this approach. Thus, a beginning point for parents is to have a strong social network of friends and helpers as people who validate them (Swick, 2006).

Four Application Strategies:

1) Help parents realize that self-care is the source of energy they need to care for children and others.

2) Educate parents about self-care strategies they can use to strengthen their self-image.

3) Engage parents in developing and nurturing strong interpersonal support systems that empower them and their children.

4) Support parents in understanding and relating to their developmental changes and challenges in effective ways.

Teachers also have particular attributes whicht are positively related to having meaningful and beneficial partnerships.

Swick et al (1998) note four teacher attributes essential to having trusting and enabling partnerships: sensitivity, flexibility, reliability, and accessibility.

Sensitivity: Teachers who respond warmly and with skill to unique and stressful parent/family needs are identified as strong partners by parents and family (Gonzalez-Mena & Eyer, 2001). Teachers with a sensitive perspective are responsive and more focused on the strengths of families They value cultural differences and make efforts to support these differences as enriching the school and the community (Delpit, 1995).

Accessibility: Both physical and social/psychological access to teachers is cited as a major support for ongoing healthy parent-teacher relations (Riley, 1994). Parents note teachers who listen to their ideas, take time to meet with them, are generally accessible, and have stronger and more lasting partnerships with them (Swick, 1997).

Flexibility: Adapting to parent schedules, gaining input from parents on needed changes, and adjusting to parent work schedules are some instances of teacher flexibility cited by parents as helping them become effective partners (Powell, 1998).

Reliability: This is the attribute that sustains partnerships. Consistency of action and follow-up work provide parents and teachers with a sense of continuity and value that enriches their partnership. For example, Fuentes, Cantu, and Stechuk (1996) found in Migrant Head-Start programs, teachers viewed as reliable and caring were noted by parents as very strong teachers and models for their children.

Swick and McKnight (1989) and Couchenour and Chrisman (2000) point to five additional teacher attributes for promoting strong partnerships with parents and families (See Figure 5.4):

Figure 5.4
Teacher Attributes that Promote Strong Partnerships

---

1) Positive teacher attitudes toward parents combined with a strong belief in extending school learning into the home.

2) High parent involvement teachers were described as caring, belonging to a professional association in early childhood, and as valuing parent and family input.

3) Teachers who have had teacher education about parent involvement or who are currently engaged in such education.

4) Teachers who have supportive administrators and see this support as positive.

5) Teachers with a family-friendly philosophy and a developmentally appropriate practices belief system.

A third aspect of the parent-teacher leadership effort is the *joint roles they carry out to establish and maintain their partnerships* (Epstein, 1991). Four teacher-parent partnership roles have been noted (Swick, 1991, 2004): collaboration, communication, planning, and evaluation.

Collaboration is the core of the teacher-parent partnership process (Comer, 1997). It involves parents and teachers in joint goal setting, mutual sharing of the workload, and continuous growth experiences to enrich their partnership efforts. As noted by Koch and McDonough (1999):

> Collaborative practices emphasize the importance of partners teaching each other about personal experiences, goals, and possible solutions. The aim is not to convince others of solutions and competence but to ask questions and understand experiences in ways that illuminate resources and spur people to action. (p. 11)

Communication is the means by which parents/family and teachers enrich and renew their partnership efforts (Kaufman, 2001). Teachers use various means to achieve this process: regular telephone contacts, daily notes, conferences, home visits, and the use of technology.

Planning is the process parents and teachers use to sharpen their vision of how to enhance and empower their children's lives and their own (Comer, 2000). This planning process must be continuous with a focus on using the talents of parents and teachers in ways that strengthen the total educational program (Henderson et al, 2007).

Evaluation provides the partners with a system that energizes the total partnership structure (Diehl, 2002). Early childhood professionals need to respect and seek out parent and family input on the relevance, utility, and effectiveness of programs serving them and their children.

CASE APPLICATION: Identify two issues that parents and teachers could work on together; explain how parents and teachers could use joint efforts to be effective in dealing with these issues. What challenges are they likely to face and how might they overcome these problems? What success stories can you share with them to empower their work? What kinds of training activities would you involve them in to enhance their skills in the partnership efforts?

Developing Partnerships During the Early Childhood Years

The early childhood years offer an opportune time for families to strengthen their bonds and become positioned to be productive people in society (Caldwell, 1989; Greenspan, 1999). It is during this period of family formation and early parental development that responsive attitudes and behavior patterns are most likely to emerge (Galinsky, 1987). Several beneficial outcomes have been noted (See Figure 5.5):

Figure 5.5
Benefits of Forming Early Parent/Family/Professional
Partnerships

---

* Parents gain support in their early development as parents.

* Parents gain new resources and knowledge when the partnership fosters a learning approach.

* Teachers and caregivers gain new perspectives and respect for parents, children and families.

* Families can identify and address key risk factors before they become chronic stressors.

* Families and schools/early childhood groups can learn to empower each other (Schorr, 1997).

What are some effective ways to initiate partnerships with parents and families during this formative period of their lives? The material shared in this part of the chapter present three examples of important themes and strategies to begin this partnership process effectively.

Initially, early childhood educators *should focus on supporting parents in developing their personal and parental efficacy and integrity* (Powell, 1998). As Swick, Da Ros, and Kovach (2001, p. 65) note: "The impact of parents' efficacy in using a caring inquiry approach is seen in the love and nurturance they share with their children." Powell (1989) and others (Gonzalez-Mena, 1994; Siegel, 2000; Brazelton & Greenspan, 2000) have noted the importance of engaging parents early in educational and support activities.

An encouraging pattern is emerging where schools and community groups are supporting parents in shaping their early identity as parents and family leaders. For example, *South Carolina's First Steps to School Readiness* program emphasizes community partnerships to enhance parents and families during the period from pregnancy to 7-years of age. It emphasizes engaging parents in needed health services, literacy, adult education, parent education, job training, counseling, and related support activities.

Another program that aims to support parents in this process is the *Family Resource Program* which uses a multi-faceted, comprehensive "center" where parents can access programs, resources, counseling, activities, and related social and health services to empower them and their families (Swick, 1991).

In effect, the initial focus of efforts to help promote strong parent-teacher partnerships must be on the early parenting behaviors – those behaviors and attributes so essential to the family's long term health and well-being (Brazelton & Greenspan, 2000).

A second partnership theme should be on *helping parents develop and enrich their relationships with their children* (Greenspan, 1999). Of utmost concern is the attachment relationship between parent and child. Feeney et al (2001) suggest that positive and nurturing attachment relationships between parent and child establish the security and warmth for long term loving and growing relationships.

It is this parent-child relationship building emphasis that is at the core of the Parents as Teachers (PAT) project. Based on the research work of Burton L. White (1988), this nationally validated program provides parents and family with key information and insights relative to child development, parent-child relations, and parenting/family life. The program includes home visits for parents who want this service and group meetings along with support resources as needed. The revised version of PAT (Born to Learn) uses recent brain development research to emphasize the role of parents in creating supportive and stimulating home learning environments (Eliot, 1999).

The third partnership theme emphasizes *the early partnership learning and experiences of parents as formative in their long term involvement with school and community* (Swick, DaRos, & Kovach, 2001). Two interacting and partnership experiences of parents happen in their marital (or intimate friendship) relations and in their formation of family relationships and links to family support systems. Siegel (2000) found that parents who successfully negotiated marital dynamics also had very successful relations with their children's teachers and were proactive in community relations too! Learning to develop and effectively use social support arrangements in family and community is also empowering of parents for other involvement situations such as in parent-teacher partnerships (Powell, 1998).

Swick (1991) notes two important partnership-building attributes that can be nurtured through early supportive involvement of parents, and that are crucial to their life long relationship skills.

> The challenges of early parenthood create a strong need in parents for validation of their competence or for their potential to become competent. This need is met through strong partnerships with close intimates or through relationships with helping professionals who have the ability to humanize their involvement with the parent. In effect, the parent is asking for a vote of confidence in his/her worth as a new and growing parent. Through many discussions, interactions, and nurturing experiences with significant others, parents may resolve this validation issue enough to support their continued growth. Later, parents will repeat this process as they interact with their children's caregivers and teachers, in effect asking for support for their identity and not just for their child's. Growing parents also want to contribute to their helpers and to the community. They seek, through their partnerships, a sense of mutuality that they too are helpers, not just receivers of help. (p. 64)

Ultimately, the goal of early parent involvement experiences is both educational (helping parents solidify their identity and empower themselves to be effective parents) and transformational (engaging parents in developing strong leadership/partnership skills (Comer, 2000). One program in Maryland that featured this leadership approach to empowering parents and teachers for partnership skills and perspectives was the *HOST (Helping One Student at a Time)* project. It engaged parents in mentoring, nurturing, and support roles with their preschool children and other children who could benefit from these services. But they also helped each other in their parenting challenges and thus opened each other up to new parent involvement possibilities. As noted by Swick et al (1998):

> Their modeling of positive interactions with teachers and their advocating of doing home learning activities were two elements that parents and teachers cited as especially important to increasing parent involvement in their children's education. The importance of parents

seeing and relating to other parents from the community who are actively engaged in their children's education is very influential in building a total commitment in parent and family involvement. (p. 49)

The major elements in the program that supported the development of parent leadership are continuous parent education, and the inviting philosophy of participating teachers. Further, the personalized attention children received certainly encouraged parents to be more responsive to their child's development and learning.

Key Application Points: School and comunnity groups should strive to develop parent / family early childhood experiences that:

* Strengthen parental, family, and child bonds.

* Empower parents to be growing and learning people in all aspects of their lives.

* Involve parents and family in shaping personal/educational goals that will strengthen their lives.

* Support parents and family in gaining insights that help them relate more effectively with their children and each other.

A Family/Community Friendly School

Partnerships happen in specific environments and are impacted by the "culture" that has been nurtured within such settings (Comer, 2000). Early childhood programs need to recognize and nurture an arrangement that is friendly and supportive of parents, family, and community. Eight attributes that comprise a family/community friendly center or school program are noted (See Figure 5.6) with some examples of how these attributes can be actualized (Henderson et al, 2007):

Figure 5.6
Eight Attributes of Family-Friendly Schools

---

* Trust and acceptance
* Craft a mutually enhancing culture
* Value cultural diversity
* Address special needs in empowering ways
* Value and use parent leadership
* Ongoing communication
* Celebration rituals
* Continuous improvement

Trust and Acceptance: Trust and acceptance supports all that happens in parent-teacher or family-school-community partnerships (Couchenour

& Chrisman, 2000). It is where parents and family feel important to the overall functioning of the program. One way to nurture this sense of trust and acceptance is to visit parents in their homes (as they permit and desire) and to ask for their ideas about what is needed in a partnership program (Hamner & Turner, 2001).

Crafting a Mutually Enhancing Culture: Parents and families want to feel and sense that they are an important part of the early childhood center or school program (File, 2001). They value having mutuality – a process where people contribute to and learn with each other (Swick, 1993). One way to establish this sense of mutuality is to invite parents to share their talents and skills in the early childhood program (Eldridge, 2001).

Valuing Cultural Diversity: An inviting early childhood center or school culture shows respect and active support for families of different cultures (Couchenour & Chrisman, 2000). Three questions program leaders can use to engage staff and parents in reviewing the school's cultural focus are (Swick, Boutte, & Van Scoy, 1995/96): 1) Are staff good role models of multicultural learning? 2) Do parents and staff plan and advocate for healthy and positive cultural activities? 3) Is the program active in using anti-bias curriculum criteria?

Special Needs are Addressed in an Empowering Way: Responding to stressful family situations, parent or family trauma, or children's special learning needs in empowering ways communicates to parents and family that we understand and value the roles and situations of all people (Kaplan, 1986). For example, is our early childhood staff skilled in understanding and responding to the special needs of children? Is our facility accessible to people with various physical challenges? Do we view learning differences as opportunities to challenge each other with new ways of teaching and learning? (Koralek, 2007).

Valuing and Using Parent/Family Leadership: Every early childhood center or school should ask: Is there education happening here that strengthens parents and family in further developing their leadership? (Comer, 2000). An "inviting" environment should be such that parents and family feel their investment of time, talents, and energy will reap increased knowledge and skills in their growth process. Consider the seven items noted by Swick et al. (1998) that spark parent involvement in leadership enhancing roles:

1) Assist other parents and families in becoming effective educators of their children.

2) Support increased parent and family involvement in school and classroom activities.

3) Encourage and facilitate parent involvement in parent education and networking activities.

4) Involve parents in classroom support roles such as tutoring, working with small groups of children, and other tasks.

5) Encourage and assist parents in carrying out home learning activities.

6) Support parents in connecting with their child's teachers.

7) Engage parents in advocacy activities that improve the lives of all children in the community.

Ongoing Communications: One of the six national standards of the National Parent-Teacher Association is that schools will hold regular two-way communication between family and school (National PTA, 1998). As Gelfer (1991) and Comer (2000) suggest, the communication process invites parents into continuous dialogue about their children's education, their learning and growth, and ways they can partner with school and community to strengthen this total educational process. For example, one school holds "town meetings" twice a year to engage parents and community in the decision making process. Through these meetings, the parents and citizens were able to successfully engage city council into re-instituting budget funds they had planned to cut from the school's budget (Swick et al, 1997).

Celebration Rituals: Validation is an integral part of our growth as individuals. Comer (1997) notes that his parents received plaudits from teachers and community leaders for the great job they did as parents. Likewise, inviting early childhood programs recognize and celebrate the involvement activities of parents. One way to do this is to have a "Wall of Parent/Family Fame" where pictures, news articles, and other features about things parents and families did in school and throughout the community are posted in an appealing way (Drake, 2000).

Continuous Improvement: Family-responsive programs happen because they are under continuous review and refinement (Powell, 1989). Important to this effort is "learning from families" the things that work, activities that are no longer in need, and ideas on ways to better involve and support families (Lopez, 2002; Caspe et al, 2006).

Three application strategies for building family-friendly early childhood programs.

1) Include all families in the development of "friendly and nurturing" activities such as special celebrations, sharing of cultural events and experiences, and in the work of the program.

2) Interrelate the program's work and activities with the work and lives of parents and other adult caregivers. By connecting the various parts of the lives of families, programs can indeed

schedule activities to support and respond to family-work needs and stressors.

3) Invite and involve parents and other family in various ways: sharing their talents, serving on advisory groups, decision making teams, school or center improvements, and in other supportive activities.

A Framework and Strategies for Strong Parent-Teacher and Family-School-Community Partnerships

A framework for helping parents and professionals develop strong and viable partnerships must have a solid *philosophical base*. Key principles of this philosophy are noted (Barbour & Barbour, 2001; Swick, 1994):

* Parents and teachers work toward common goals as developed by them in mutually supportive efforts.

* Teachers invite and involve parents and family in various program and curriculum decisions and improvement efforts.

* They (parents, teachers, and families) communicate regularly in ways that enhance and strengthen their partnership.

* They engage in helping roles that strengthen the school and the home learning environment.

A *dynamic framework* for organizing, supporting, and carrying out the involvement and partnership process is presented. Integral to actualizing the framework is the commitment of parents and teachers to "collaborating" in assuring that these elements are used effectively. Three categories provide the structure: 1) planning, 2) implementation, and 3) evaluation. The elements in each of these categories are briefly reviewed and applied to the development work needed.

Planning Process: Seven interacting elements comprise the partnership planning effort (See Figure 5.7):

Figure 5.7
Elements that Comprise the Planning Cycle

---

* Needs Assessment
* Goals/Objectives
* Setting Priorities
* Selecting Strategies
* Organizing Resources
* Continual Assessment

Needs assessment should be based in the research on effective practices in parent/family involvement. For example, Epstein (1995) found teachers who used surveys, questionnaires, and other tools to gain parent input on important partnership needs, reported strong and more effective parent participation. The critical part of this process is that parents and teachers have authentic dialogue about the needs, use a data based approach to gather important information on these needs, and are culturally sensitive to how different families in the community might see "needs" from varying perspectives (Sanders & Epstein, 1998). In all communities it is especially important to take the "cultural view" of various groups and families (Cooper, 2005).

Setting goals/objectives should emerge naturally from the needs-assessment process. As Epstein and Dauber (1991) point out, goals and objectives in successful family-school partnerships are constantly being adapted based on data from new needs assessments. The process is highly dynamic and early childhood professionals need to be open to continuing to return to the assessment process. Needs assessment data should be organized into thematic objectives that guide the overall thinking and planning of the partnership team. For example, in many early childhood parent education programs "parent networking" and "parent leadership training" have emerged as important goal areas (Powell, 1998). And, as Rich (1987) found in her work, parents' objectives often revolved around what teachers expected of their children, how they could help (e.g., homework), and in what capacity did teachers want parents to function.

A question all of us ask of others who request our help is: What is it that you really want? Thus, *setting priorities* among varying agendas is significant to the viability and harmony of parent-teacher and family-school-community partnerships (Swick, 1991*).*

Three facets of prioritizing are related to having successful efforts (See Figure 5.8):

Figure 5.8
Prioritizing Family Involvement Goals

---

1) Truly gaining some consensus on the most important goals for the project.

2) Identifying needed and available resources to help achieve the priorities.

3) Establishing a plan to achieve these goals (Epstein, 1995).

But setting priorities is more than a task of listing items. ***It involves very sensitive listening to the nonverbal and community indicators of risk*** that may be impeding if not destroying the fabric of families, schools, and communities. The prioritizing process should reflect a team effort (Koralek, 2007).

Participation in *selecting strategies* is also important to the success of the planning process. Finding some consonance between goals and strategies involves more than a simplistic matching process. Rather, early childhood professionals need to be sensitive to parent and family wishes on how they see particular strategies. The use of multiple strategies for partnership activities increases the potential for having more parents involved (Swick, 1993, 2004).

Resource organization offers parents and teachers opportunities to see how the program and activities might best be supported. For example, resources include use of parent and teacher talents, engaging community in support and leadership roles, identifying space and material needs, and organizing these resources into a manageable program effort (Berger, 2000).

Implementation design and provisions for *continual assessment* are two additional elements that call for shared planning. Questions such as the following should guide the planning work that parent-teacher partnership teams undertake (Swick, 2004):

* What activities are important to the success of the program?
* When, where, and how can these activities happen in ways that engage the partners in meaningful learning and growth?
* What resources are needed and how can these resources be deployed?
* Who will be needed to comprise the leadership team that guides the implementation work?

Implementation Process: Actualizing a parent-teacher or family-school-community partnership efforts involves several strategies. It is a team effort that requires strong professional-parent leadership (Epstein, 1995).

Parent-professional and *parent-parent dialogue* are essential to the success of all the involvement strategies used. It is through dialogue that inquiry and various helping activities acquire some direction and potential positive impact on children, parents, families, schools and communities (Ryan et al, 1995; Hoover-Dempsey et al, 2005)).

Three important questions that need to guide this dialogue are (See Figure 5.9):

Figure 5.9
Key Questions to Guide Parent-Teacher Dialogue

---

1) What strategies suit the achievement of our goals and best relate to the learning styles of our parents and families?

2) How can these strategies be deployed to optimize parent and family participation and to then sustain such involvement over the family's life span?

3) What supportive and challenging training and education efforts can nurture parents, family, and professionals to positively impact the learning and growth of children and of the adults involved?

Several partnership strategies are reviewed in relation to their value for strengthening parent-teacher and family-school-community relationships in Chapter Six (Communication Concepts and Strategies for Strengthening the Partnership). In addition, the following strategies are presented as means to highlight the different ways parents and teachers can partner to the advantage of children, families and the community.

PARENTS IN HELPING ROLES: Any partnership is strengthened when parents take on helping roles such as coordinating parent meetings, reading to small groups of children, mentoring children, carrying out clerical tasks to free teachers to teach, helping with after-school and summer enrichment, sharing their talents, assisting in areas where they have expertise, and in many other roles (Rich, 1987). These helping efforts need to be well organized so as to gain the real value of the sharing of parent skills and talents.

PARENTS AS FAMILY EDUCATORS: An essential area of children's learning that parents and family can provide real leadership in is that of *family learning beyond the school* (Epstein, 1991). Children whose parents and family extend and enrich their learning beyond the classroom do better in school and in life (Chavkin, 1993; Comer, 2000). Five areas in which parents can and have had a powerful influence on strengthening their partnerships with teachers and thus further empower their children for success are (Fuller & Olsen, 1998):

1) Model literacy and inquiry skills, perspectives, and attitudes. Let children see you reading, learning, questioning, and reflecting, often and in various ways.

2) Organize a highly literate environment that is appealing and filled with child-selected literacy materials.

3) Expose and involve your children in community learning activities such as libraries, museums, service learning, and various church, civic, and school related events and activities.

4) Monitor and support your child's homework and home learning efforts (but do not do the work for your child).

5) Communicate with your children's teachers and find out how their home learning is interrelating with their school learning.

PARENTS AND TEACHERS IN JOINT ACTIVITIES: Whenever parents and teachers (and, where appropriate, children too) learn, serve, and grow together through joint activities the family-school-community partnership is truly strengthened (Epstein, 1991). For example, recently the author joined a group of 4-year olds, their teachers, and their parents in sharing children's books with senior citizens at a community care center. It was truly amazing to hear the comments of parents as they joined teachers in planning and doing this outing with the children. One parent commented, "I had no idea my child could be so talkative with others." Another parent said, "My, Aliza is enthusiastic about reading – I think it is because she is sharing it with the older people at the center."

TECHNOLOGY AND HOME LEARNING: Several ideas have emerged that use technology to enhance the home learning environment (Chen, 2002). For example, some school districts use local television channels to plan and broadcast "homework hot lines" that review homework assignments and offer parents and children ideas on how to make the homework process a useful experience. In a unique approach to the homework help time, one school offers a video on particular topics and units that help parents see how home learning activities can be linked to particular content and topics. In addition, some innovative uses of technology for home learning include (Swick, 1991, 2004):

* Telephone calls to parents and children asking for their help in mentoring other children in need of assistance.

* Computer learning nights at school where parents, children, and teachers design special programs for sharing with others.

* Videotaping field trip experiences that have special significance for subjects under study in class.

* Developing web sites devoted to academic subjects of special challenge to children and parents.

LEADERSHIP AND ADVOCACY IN PARTNERSHIPS: As Comer (2000) suggests, the parent-teacher partnership offers the strongest advocacy system available to our society. Consider the following accomplishments of parent-teacher advocacy teams:

* One team in Baltimore, Maryland successfully engaged the county recreation department in cleaning up and enriching the parks in several neighborhoods. Previously parents felt these parks were unsafe and a real danger. Now they have become the pride of many people in the community (Swick et al, 1997).

* Another parent-teacher project that has real potential is where a team plans and conducts community wide educational programs on topics like drug prevention, immunizations, violence prevention, family reading nights, and other topics as identified by citizens (File, 2001).

* In South Carolina, several parent-teacher teams across the state noted the need for full-day kindergarten and developed a statewide citizen advocacy group to lobby the governor and legislator. They were successful and South Carolina now has not only full-day kindergarten but also many skilled parent advocates for children.

Leadership growth is linked to having long-term strong, caring parent-teacher partnerships (Schorr, 1997). Parent-teacher leadership involvement in training, school or community improvement, and curriculum development efforts are integral to building a talent pool of committed parents and teachers. Rioux and Berla (1993) describe three powerful leadership efforts:

1) Parent training in areas such as communication, positive discipline, family management, and advocacy – with the focus on engaging parents in applying these skills to their school and community work.

2) Parent service on school improvement groups, volunteer community efforts, and school-community planning teams can increase parent efficacy and serve to build a new leadership team for the future.

3) Parent assessment of school activities and involvement in shaping plans for improvements.

Evaluation and Refinement: Teacher-parent partnerships are in need of continual renewal and growth. The purpose of evaluation is to empower the partnership that aims to enhance and strengthen the child, parent, family, and teacher/school (Swick & Graves, 1993). This focus on empowerment includes five important elements related to the renewal and growth of the partnership process (Kellaghan, Sloane, Alvarez, & Bloom, 1993):

1) Articulation of the major goals of the partnership as developed by the parent-teacher and family-school team.

2) Identification of needs-assessment results related to needs, strengths, resources, resource-needs, and strategies the partners have established related to using the results.

3) Use of an inclusive set of evaluation instruments and processes that gain input from all the members, and that help shape a clear picture of the effectiveness of the partnership.

4) Targeting of evaluation to assess the most effective practices in the partnership growth process.

5) Organization and dissemination of evaluation results in ways that assure the use of these results to energize and guide the future work of the partnership.

The initial role in the empowerment evaluation of parent-teacher and family-school-community partnerships is to review why the partnership took place.

Parents and teachers need to ask questions such as the following as they review where the partnership is at (Rioux & Berla, 1993; Caspe et al, 2006):

* Are the original goals of the partnership still relevant to what is important to parents and teachers in the current partnership relationship?

* Is there consonance between the "claims" the partnership is trying to achieve and the actual substance of program activities?

* What are the strengths of the partnership efforts? Where are the gaps or needs for refinement?

* What indicators in child, parent, family, teacher, school, or community suggest that the partnership's claims are being achieved or at least that some progress is being made?

* What clear challenges for the partnership emerge from the evaluation results?

A second aspect of empowerment evaluation is to take stock of the kinds of relationships happening in the partnership (Powell, 1998). Progress toward long-term goals is only feasible when mutuality and nurturing relationships exist. For example, in one parent education program the author evaluated a focus group discussion with parents that suggested that decisions were made by one or two professional staff members. Parent surveys were distributed and completed but never really used in deciding on program activities. Once staff were alerted to this problem they followed through on gaining much more parent input. Another part of this

174

relationship assessment is to look closely at the quality of nurturance in the parent-professional relations. Helpful, supportive, and sincere parent educators can make a powerful difference in who participates in the program and how they contribute to its success.

Thus, *clarifying the claims (or outcomes) desired* is essential to then determining how the partnership is progressing. A program might have adult claims, child claims, and community claims – all of which are interrelated and dependent on specific teams carrying out particular tasks and roles. However, an evaluation effort might show that actual program activities are not addressing the claim areas noted. Thus, as Swick (1991, 2004) suggests, it is critical that the partnership team closely reviews claims and actual leadership efforts that are directed toward achieving these claims:

> Given the authenticity and utility of partnership claims, teachers and parents need to consider various indicators that will help them achieve these claims. What leadership resources do they have or need to become effective, not simply in attaining goals but rather in developing and growing through their collaborations? What kinds of activities do hey see as meaningful and doable? How do they hope to support each other and their children in pursuing their desired outcomes? How can they cooperatively shape and refine their partnerships as they explore working together?

A third element in empowerment evaluation of teacher-parent partnerships is to highlight the strengths and successes of the partnership process (Comer, 2000). Too often, program leaders and evaluators look for the deficits and thus miss the opportunity to target "effective practices" that are influencing program achievements. For example, Rioux and Berla (1993) report that one program evaluation used an "index formula" targeting criteria like high parent participation, father involvement, bilingual family involvement, teacher support, parent leadership, and community support as real strengths of the program.

Evaluation tools are varied and offer parent-teacher partnerships many ways to view their program work (Couchenour & Chrisman, 2000). Surveys and questionnaires tap the broad understanding of parents on various issues and needs. Focus and discussion groups offer more in-depth perspectives of small groups of participants on particular facets of the program. Interviews probe individual parent or teacher views on the partnership. Observational records, individual program activity assessments, check lists, and knowledge/attitude instruments can be used to evaluate particular outcomes. As various evaluation tools are considered, be sure to review how they serve your assessment functions. The goal is to enhance the partnership and thus selective data is more important than large quantities of data. We need to return to questions such as the following regardless of the tools and processes we used to answer them:

* What are our purposes?

* What resources and strategies are most effective in helping us make progress toward our objectives?

* Who is guiding the overall program system and how are they negotiating the challenges of the partnership?

* What are we learning about our partnership and our claims for enhancing the quality of life for families, schools, and communities?

* How can we use the evaluation process to truly enhance and strengthen our partnership efforts?

Strategies and Activities for Empowering the Partnership

The question is often asked: How can we keep our parent-teacher partnership growing and of high quality? The focus of this part of the chapter is to delineate some of the elements of an empowerment framework for nurturing strong partnerships, and ideas that should help program leaders achieve continuing growth.

Elements of the needed Framework: The basis of empowerment is in five processes noted throughout this book and highlighted here to show their core value to having healthy and enduring partnerships: 1) proactive assessment, 2) collaborative planning, 3) a prevention orientation, 4) comprehensive support, and 5) a systemic approach (Swick & Graves, 1993; Swick, 2004).

Proactive assessment is used continuously to help the parent-teacher partners come to an understanding of each other's needs, strengths, talents, goals, resources, and values, as well as their common goals and functions (Chen, 2002).

Collaborative planning is the process partnerships use to shape, implement, refine, and enrich their vision and agenda (Kirshbaum, 1998).

A *prevention orientation* focuses parent-teacher and family-school-community energies on empowering everyone (Schorr, 1997).

Comprehensive support for partnerships is like a foundation for a house. Support resources provide the energy that drives the partnership. For example, parent volunteers are the support for making many classroom activities high-powered (Kirshbaum, 1998).

School-family system approaches provide the structure for carrying out coherent and well-planned activities. Systemic approaches keep the partnerships within a visible and meaningful structure.

Elements and Ideas for Partnership Renewal and Growth (See Figure 5.10): Three particular ideas for empowering the partnership process are noted and explored:

Figure 5.10
Elements/Ideas for Partnership
Renewal and Growth

---

1) Supporting healthy family growth,

2) Alliances to strengthen families and schools, and

3) Shaping public policy for strong families and schools.

Supporting healthy family growth: Families are the key to partnerships and thus must have a healthy and nurturing system of relations (Swick, Da Ros, & Kovach, 2001). In effect, schools need to restructure and reframe the early childhood curriculum to be family-focused and not just child focused. The emphasis should now be on the preschool years, on family, and on ways early childhood professionals can support families.

Alliances to strengthen families and schools: Family-school and parent-teacher partnerships find their energy through their supportive alliances with various community groups and agencies (Schorr, 1997). In particular, communities need to be in unison with families and schools on having high-quality early childhood environments, responsive parent and family programs, and strong parent-teacher partnerships (Comer, 2000). Communities offer family-school partnerships three important resources: service, support, and collaborative learning (Hesselbein et al, 1998). For example, community services in the areas of health, recreation, mental health, social support, shelter, and related emergency services are vital to families. Likewise, support groups in the community can offer special services for helping families in distress or in responding to special child needs. And, very importantly, communities can promote collaborative learning arrangements through continuing education efforts (Meier, 2002).

Public policy for strong families and schools: Parent-teacher partnerships must be a part of shaping community policies that support their efforts for quality early childhood education for parents, children, and families. Brazelton and Greenspan (2000, chapters 6 and 7) advocate for policy development that achieves the following for all children and families:

* Safe, secure, and enjoyable neighborhoods

* Access to preventive health and medical care

* Availability of quality child care and early learning programs

* Access to enriching social and recreational activities
* Support services for families such as counseling, food, clothing, medicine, housing, and related essential services
* Opportunities for job training, job placement, and continuing education for new job skills
* Ongoing support for quality schools
* Available high quality after school and summer enrichment programs.

Evaluating and Refining the Partnership Process

While the topic of evaluation was reviewed in a previous section in this chapter, the process is connected to broader issues in partnerships in this part of the chapter. In particular, this section focuses on *program component evaluation tools and processes* (Swick, 1991). Three examples are noted to highlight the value of this assessment focus.

Assessing Parent Volunteer Programs: Three things stand out in the example of Lightwood Elementary School: 1) volunteer records of service, accomplishments, and impacts; 2) teacher comments on volunteer activities; and 3) recognition and validation using evaluation results. The records provided a strong base for seeing what activities were most needed, how they worked, who accomplished them, how much time was devoted to the activities, and other needed and valuable specifics. Teacher comments let parents know how much their efforts were appreciated and how teachers felt certain things might be even further strengthened. Recognition was based on the data kept in the service records and thus specific reinforcement was provided parents on actual work they achieved (Kirshbaum, 1998).

Assessing Parent-Teacher Conferences: A university early childhood center uses an all-purpose conference check-list for planning and evaluation functions. It includes several items worth noting (Swick, 1991, 2004):

* Purpose is clearly defined and communicated to all participants. (Communication is adapted to the language and needs of the parents and family.)
* The classroom environment is clean, appealing, and reflective of the work of the children and families. (The classroom reflects the many cultures of the center and of the world we live in.)
* Key conference topics are highlighted and sent to parents well in advance and their input invited through advance communication.
* Where needed a bi-lingual interpreter is available to help

parents whose language is other than English. Also, other English speaking families are engaged in the conference to create a family welcoming and supportive environment.

* Parent and family concerns are noted, used for further planning, and responded to in an effective and helpful manner.

* "Super Parent" badges (with parent and child names) are given to each parent. Refreshments and other supportive resources are provided too!

* Parents evaluate all conferences and make suggestions for improvement.

* Parents complete a written suggestion card to help the teacher better know their child and to know them as parents.

* Follow-up plans are noted and a schedule for future conferences set.

Assessing Family Lending Libraries: Busy parents enjoy having access to parent and child literacy resources at their child's early childhood program. Many programs find that through ongoing feedback forms from parents, record keeping on what is being used from the library, and an overall end-of-year assessment, they gain valuable insights on strengthening this part of the program. Here are three assessment suggestions noted by Kirshbaum (1998):

1) Keep good lending library records to see what items parents are reading and what the children like too!

2) Have a teacher-parent team review usage records, make suggestions for new acquisitions, and to offer other ideas for improvement.

3) Do a once-a-year overall focus group with the parents who are the real users of this service. What do they say about it? What requests do they have for next year?

Strong partnerships between families, schools, and communities require systemic planning and design. Intentionality, collaboration, and on-going renewal of the family-school-community system is vital to having safe, secure, and meaningful places for children and their families.

SUMMATIVE DISCUSSION OF APPLICATION POINTS

A review of the application points that stand out in the work of successful family-school-community partnerships include the following:

1) Programs need to craft a vision and sense of purpose that empowers them to act jointly on behalf of children and families. This work needs to be inclusive of all the varying needs and perspectives and organized in ways to achieve significant positive impacts on the participants.

2) Parents and teachers need to create a "culture" where they are leaders in the effort to enhance and strengthen the partnership so that children are empowered in their lives.

3) The partnership process should begin during parents' early development in parenting and thus help them to create patterns of functioning that are based in the partnership effort.

4) A partnership framework that includes the essential assessment, goal setting, prioritization of elements, strategy selection, resource organization, and implementation/evaluation activities – is more likely to achieve its mission.

5) Empowering the family-school-community partnership to grow and sustain itself is best realized through training of parents and teachers/staff, community education and support, obtaining needed resources, collaborative work strategies, articulation of key roles and activities, and ongoing assessment and refinement.

Suggested Websites

COMPASS Resources Parents and Teachers: <www.compassinc.com/resources.html>

Teacher/Parent/Trainer Site List: <www.edpro.com>

Center on Families, Communities, Schools and Children's Learning: <www.jhu.edu/news.info/educate/experts/epstein>

National Coalition for Parent Involvement in Education: <www.ncpie.org>

National/Network of Partnership Schools: <www.csos.jhu/edu/p200>

The Search Institute: <www.search-institute.org>

References

Bagin, D., Gallagher, D., & Moore, E. (2008). The school and community relations. Ninth Edition. Columbus, OH: Pearson.

Barbour, C., & Barbour, N. (2001). Families, schools, and communities: Building partnerships for educating children. Columbus, OH: Merrill Prentice Hall.

Barbour, C., & Barbour, N. (2008). Families, schools, and communities: Building partnerships for educating children. Fourth Edition. Columbus, OH: Merrill Prentice Hall.

Bauer, A., & Shea, T. (2003). Parents and schools: Creating a successful partnership for students with special needs. Columbus, OH: Merrill Prentice Hall.

Berger, E. (2000). Parents as partners in education. Columbus, OH: Merrill Prentice Hall

Brazelton, T., & Greenspan, S. (2000). The irreducible needs of children. Cambridge, MA: Perseus.

Caldwell, B. (1989). A faltering trust. In D. Blazer. (Ed.). Faith development in early childhood. Kansas City, MO: Sheed and Ward.

Caspe, M., & Lopez, E. (2006). Lessons from family-strengthening interventions: Learning from evidence-based practice. Cambridge, MA: Harvard Family Research Project.

Chavkin, N. (Ed.). (1993). Families and schools in a pluralistic society. Albany, NY: State University of New York Press.

Chen, M. (Ed.). (2002). Edutopia: Success stories for learning in the digital age. San Francisco, CA: Jossey-Bass.

Comer, J. (1997). Waiting for a miracle: Why schools can't solve our problems – and how we can. New York: Dutton.

Comer, J. (2000). Schools that develop children. The American Prospect, 12 (7), 3-12.

Cooper, C. (2005). Evaluating parent empowerment: A look at the potential of social justice evaluation in education. Teachers College Record, 107 (10), 2248-2274.

Couchenour, D., & Chrisman, K. (2000). Families, schools, and communities: Together for young children. New York: Delmar.

Delpit, L. (1995). Other people's children: Cultural conflict in the classroom. New York: The New Press.

Diehl, D. (2002). Family support America: Supporting "family supportive" evaluation. The Evaluation Exchange, 8 (1), 14-15.

Drake, D. (2000). Parents and families as partners in the educational process: Collaboration for the success of students in public schools. ERS Spectrum, 18, 34-39.

Eldridge, D. (2001). Parent involvement: It's worth the effort. Young Children, 56 (4), 65-69.

Eliot, L. (1999). What's going on in there? How the brain and mind develop in the first five years of life. New York: Bantam Books.

Epstein, J. (1991). Paths to partnership: What can we learn from federal, state, district, and school initiatives? Phi Delta Kappan, 67, 442-446.

Epstein, J. (1995). School/Family/Community Partnerships: Caring for the children we share. Phi Delta Kappan, May, 701-712.

Epstein, J., & Dauber, S. (1991). School programs and teacher practices of parent involvement in inner-city elementary and middle schools. The Elementary School Journal, 91, 289-305.

Feeney, J., Hohaus, L., Noller, P., & Alexander, R. (2001). Becoming parents:

Exploring the bonds between mothers, fathers, and their infants. New York: Cambridge University Press.

Ferguson, C. (2008). The school-family connection: Looking at the larger picture. Austin, TX: National Center for Family and Community Connections with Schools.

File, N. (2001). Family-professional partnerships: Practice that matches philosophy. Young Children, 56 (4), 70-74.

Fuentes, F., Cantu, V., & Stechuk, R. (1996). Migrant Head-Start: What does it mean to involve parents in program services? Children Today, 24 (1), 16-19.

Fuller, M., & Olsen, G. (1998). Home-school relations: Working successfully with parents and families. Boston: Allyn and Bacon.

Galinsky, E. (1987). The six stages of parenthood. Reading, MA: Addison-Wesley.

Gelfer, J. (1991). Teacher-parent partnerships: Enhancing communications. Childhood Education, Spring, 164-167.

Goldberg, S. (1997). Parent involvement begins at birth: Collaboration between parents and teachers of children in the early years. Boston: Allyn and Bacon.

Goodnow, J., & Collins, W. (1990). Development according to parents: The nature, sources, and consequences of parents' ideas. Hillsdale, NJ: Lawrence Erlbaum Associates.

Gonzalez-Mena, J. (1994). From a parent's perspective. Salem, WI: Sheffield.

Gonzalez-Mena, J., & Eyer, D. (2001). Infants, toddlers, and caregivers. Fifth Edition. Mountain View, CA: Mayfield.

Greenspan, S. (1999). Building healthy minds: The six experiences that create intelligence and emotional growth in babies and youjng children. Cambridge, MA: Perseus.

Hamner, T., & Turner, P. (2001). Parenting in contemporary society. Third Edition. Boston: Allyn and Bacon.

Henderson, A., & Raimondo, B. (2001). Unlocking parent potential. Principal Leadership, 2 (1), 9-17.

Henderson, A., Mapp, K., Johnson, V., & Davies, D. (2007). Beyond the bake sale: The essential guide to family-school partnerships. New York, NY: The New Press.

Hesselbein, F., Goldsmith, M., Beckhard, R., & Schubert, R. (Eds.). (1998). The community of the future. San Francisco, CA: Jossey-Bass.

Heymann, J. (2000). The widening gap: Why American's working families are in jeopardy and what can be done about it. New York: Basic Books.

Hoover-Dempsey, K., Walker, J., Sandler, H., Whetsel, D., Green, C., Wilkins, A., & Closson, K. (2005). Why do parents become involved? Research findings and implications. *The Elementary School Journal, 106 (2),* 105-130.

Kaplan, L. (1986). Working with multiproblem families. New York: Lexington Books.

Kaufman, H. (2001). Skills for working with all families. Young Children, 56 (4), 81-84.

Kellaghan, T., Sloane, K., Alvarez, B., & Bloom, B. (1993). The home environment and school learning: Promoting parental involvement in the education of children. San Francisco, CA: Jossey-Bass.

Kirshbaum, R. (1998). Parent power. New York: Hyperion.

Koch, P., & McDonough, M. (1999). Improving parent-teacher conferences through collaborative conversations. Young Children, March, 11-15.

Koralek, D. (2007). Young children and families. Washington, DC: National Association for the Education of Young Children.

Lopez, E. (2002). Learning from families. The Evaluation Exchange, 8 (1), 2-3.

Lynch, E. (1998). Developing cross-cultural competence. In E. Lynch & M. Hanson. (Eds.). Developing cross-cultural competence: A guide for working with children and their families. Baltimore: Paul H. Brookes.

Meier, D. (2002). In schools we trust. Boston: Beacon Press.

National Parent Teacher Association. (1998). National standards for parent/family involvement programs. Chicago, IL: National Parent Teacher Association.

Powell, D. (1989). Families and early childhood programs. Washington, DC: National Association for the Education of Young Children.

Powell, D. (1998). Reweaving parents into the fabric of early childhood programs. Washington, DC: National Association for the Education of Young Children.

Rich, D. (1987). Schools and families: Issues and actions. Washington, DC: National Education Association.

Riley, R. (1994). Strong families, strong schools: seven good practices for families to use their time. Vital Speeches, 60 (24), 745-749.

Rioux, W., & Berla, N. (1993). Innovations in parent and family involvement. Princeton Junction, NJ: Eye on Education.

Ryan, B., Adams, G., Gullotta, T., Weissberg, R., & Hampton, R. (1995). The family-school connection: Theory, research, and practice. Thousand Oaks, CA: Sage.

Sanders, M., & Epstein, J. (1998). The effects of school, family and community support on the academic achievement of African American adolescents. Urban Education, 33 (3), 385-409.

Schaefer, E. (1982). Parent-professional interaction: Research, parental, professional, and policy perspectives. In R. Haskins and D. Adams. (Eds.). Parent education and public policy. Norwood, NJ: Ablex.

Schorr, L. (1997). Common purpose: Strengthening families and neighborhoods to rebuild America. New York: Doubleday.

Seligman, M., & Darling, R. (1989). Ordinary families, Special children: A systems approach to childhood disability. New York: Guilford.

Siegel, J. (2000). What children learn from their parents' marriage. New York: HarperCollins.

Swick, K. (1984). Inviting parents into the young child's world. Champaign, IL: Stipes.

Swick, K. (1991). Teacher-parent partnerships to enhance school success in early childhood education. Washington, DC: National Education Association.

Swick, K. (1993). Strengthening parents and families during the early childhood years. Champaign, IL: Stipes.

Swick, K. (1994). Family involvement: An empowerment perspective. Dimensions of Early Childhood, 22, 10-14.

Swick, K. (1997). A family-school approach for nurturing caring in young children. Early Childhood Education Journal, 25 (2), 151-154.

Swick, K. (2001). Nurturing decency through caring and serving during the early childhood years. Early Childhood Education Journal, 29 (2), 131-137.

Swick, K. (2004). Empowering parents, families, schools and communities during the early childhood years. Champaign, IL: Stipes.

Swick, K. (2006). Families and educators together: Raising caring and peaceable children. Early Childhood Education Journal, 33 (4), 279-287.

Swick, K., & McKnight, S. (1989). Characteristics of kindergarten teachers who promote parent involvement. Early Childhood Research Quarterly, 4 (1), 19-30.

Swick, K., & Graves, S. (1993). Empowering at-risk families during the early childhood years. Washington, DC: National Education Association.

Swick, K., Boutte, G., & Van Scoy, I. (1995/96). Families and schools:

Building multicultural values together. Childhood Education, Winter, 75-79.

Swick, K., Grafwallner, R., Cockey, M., Roach, J., Davidson, S., Mayor, M., & Gardner, N. (1997). On board early: Building strong family-school relations. Early Childhood Education Journal, 24, 269-273.

Swick, K., Grafwallner, R., Cockey, M., & Barton, P. (1998). Parents as leaders in nurturing family-school involvement. Contemporary Education, 70 (1), 47-50.

Swick, K., Da Ros, D., & Pavia, L. (1999). Inquiry as key to early childhood teacher education. Childhood Education, 75, (2), 66-70.

Swick, K., Da Ros, D., & Kovach, B. (2001). Empowering parents and families through a caring inquiry approach. Early Childhood Education Journal, 29 (1), 65-71.

White, B. (1988). Educating the infant and toddler. Lexington, MA: D.C. Heath.

186

Chapter Six

Communication Concepts and Strategies for Strengthening the Partnership

---

CAPSULE: The power of any partnership effort is in the communicative relations that comprise the daily functioning of the members. This chapter focuses on ways to better understand and use the communication process to enrich and further empower parent-teacher and family-school- community partnerships. Of particular emphasis is the manner in which communication can be used to help the partners initiate and sustain efforts that help children and families achieve healthy family, school, and community life.

Chapter Six Objectives:

1) To further develop an understanding of how communication empowers early childhood family-school-community partnerships.

2) To refine and strengthen our understanding of how participant attitudes shape the communication framework.

3) To gain perspectives and skills for using communication as a process for shared-learning.

4) To articulate and apply important communication behaviors and processes to strengthen family-school-community partnership situations during the early childhood years.

5) To enrich and strengthen knowledge and skills in understanding and using various parent-teacher communication strategies and techniques.

6) To gain insight into various ways to use conflict as an opportunity for strengthening and enriching parent-teacher and family-school relations.

7) To strengthen skills in dealing with cultural differences in the communication process.

8) To sharpen skills in using nonverbal communication skills to empower parent-teacher and family-school relations.

9) To increase skills in responding effectively to the communication needs of multi-problem families.

Parents, children, and early childhood educators are involved in the communication process in every part of their daily relationships (Swick, 1997). In this chapter we explore several topics related to how families, schools, and communities can use communication to strengthen their partnerships. The empowerment nature of communication is presented along with an exploration of how attitudes shape a great deal of our communication. The shared-learning process that is an integral feature of communication is also presented. Essential communication behaviors, strategies, and problem-solving activities are then discussed in relation to developing and supporting strong partnerships. The role of culture in the communication process is examined with special attention to the way we can use cultural differences as a means to enrich our relationships and create positive environments for family-school-community communication.

Communication as the Key to Empowering Partnerships

Communication is indeed the major way that we empower each other. As Satir (1988) noted:

> Once a human being arrives on this earth, *communication is the largest single factor determining what kinds of relationships she or he makes with others and what happens to each in the world.* How we manage survival, how we develop intimacy, how productive we are, how we make sense, how we connect with our divinity – all depend on our communication skills. (p. 51)

In relation to parent-teacher and family-school-community partnerships, communication is the critical factor. Swick (1991) suggests the following principles as key to this process (Figure 6.1):

Figure 6.1
Keys to Communication as Empowerment

* Each person recognizes the need for involving others in arriving at decisions that affect them and their children.

* The development of "high regard" for each other's integrity and roles as advocates and models for children is also recognized.

* Each person works toward having empathetic and supportive attitudes toward the other.

* As a team, parent and teacher seek the most productive system

for arriving at roles and means by which to achieve a true partner-ship.

* Each person is sensitive to the cultural, personal, and individual values of the other and shows respect and validation for these at-tributes.

Gelfer (1991) and Swick (1997) caution early childhood educators to avoid communication behaviors that degrade partnerships. Swick (1993) (citing Satir, 1988) notes that communication styles like blamer (this is the fault-finder) or placater (this is the person who always wants to please the other person or group) really function to degrade everyone involved. Building trust is essential to having authentic, meaningful, and growth-promoting communication. Four communication behaviors that enrich partnerships are noted (Swick, 1993, pp. 311-314):

Figure 6.2

Four Communication Behaviors that Enrich Partnerships

---

1) The approachable person is an individual with whom people feel comfortable and secure.

2) Sensitivity is at the heart of all communication. The sensitive person communicates a desire to understand the other person in positive and supportive ways.

3) Flexibility provides the needed "space" and security for effective communication. Early childhood educators who provide parents and families with flexible conference times, are responsive to their complex schedules, and relate to their needs effectively, are seen by parents as very helpful and caring teachers.

4) *Dependability* is the bridge between parents and teachers as they develop trusting and growing relationships. This is the attribute where parents and teachers learn to depend on each other in providing continuity and security in the child's life. This is also the attribute that helps parents and teachers cre-ate long-term partnerships. They come to realize that their relationship is not perfect but one that is continually grow-ing.Meaningful parent-teacher and family-school-community relationships are best realized through the use of communica-tion processes that serve to continually renew and enrich the partners. Eight such processes are noted:

Meaningful parent-teacher and family-school-community relation-ships are best realized through the use of communication processes that serve to continually renew and enrich the partners. Eight such processes are noted:

1) *Trust* is the foundation of all significant relationship building

(Erikson, 1982). Our initial task in this world is to develop trust in our parents and significant caregivers. In "trust" we find the energy to be caring and decent people (Swick, 2004).

2) *Role Flexibility* is essential to the viability of relationships. We must be able to nurture as well as be nurtured. We must also be able to leave room for others to grow and take risks. We must be role-exchangers and flexible in how we respond to the stressful situations of others so we can be empowering of each other (Swick, Da Ros, & Kovach, 2001).

3) *Help-exchange* is central to all healthy relationships. Communication can only occur where there is an attitude and reality of help exchange. For example, where partners team up to achieve their goals, the outcomes tend to enhance them and their children (Swick, 1997, 2003).

4) *Responsive Listening* is the needed feedback process that adds substance and growth to the communicative relationship (Pipher, 1996). Responsive listening is more than just reacting to what someone says, it is about our total interaction with them (verbal and nonverbal). It is also about our intent, our perspective, and our respect for their growth (McKay, Davis, & Fanning, 1995; Sturm, 1997).

5) *Individuation* is our way of developing our identities through communication (Kotre & Hall, 1990). It is how we grow and develop our personalities. Without a strong individual the communication process would flounder. Satir (1988) says it very well:

Good human relations and appropriate and loving behavior stem from persons who have strong feelings of self-worth. Simply stated, persons who love and value themselves are able to love and value others and treat reality appropriately. (p. 33)

6) *Group functioning skills* is also an essential ingredient in communicative relationships (Swick, 2003, 2003a). It is through the "give and take" of dialogue and working together on common goals that our group functioning skills are sharpened and strengthened.

7) *Nurturance and 8) problem solving* are two additional communication processes that are important partnership efforts (Swick, 1993, 2004). Nurturance is the core of the renewal process in relationship building. It is about treating each other with warmth, mutuality, and a sense of uniqueness. Parents

often refer to teachers and caregivers who communicate effectively with them as warm and responsive (Galinsky, 1988).

Problem solving, Swick (1993, p. 308) notes, "might be called the action arm of the communication process." It is the perspectives, dialogue, and energy we bring to finding solutions and new possibilities to the complexities and challenges in our partnerships. Satir (1988) suggests that an open environment is most suitable to fostering and sustaining healthy and meaningful communication.

CASE APPLICATION: Select or hypothesize a communication situation where empowerment approaches can help and explain how you might achieve this process. Explain how you would use at least two communication strategies noted above to help parents and teachers work more effectively together. For example, parents often point to teacher attitudes toward them as a barrier to the communication process.

Participant Attitudes Shape the Communication Framework

The underlying attitudes that parents/families and their helpers have about themselves and each other play the major role in shaping the framework within which communication occur. For example, when caregivers use derogatory language to describe certain parents or families, they have already established a degrading perspective, and thus have little potential for having positive relations with the parents and families (Garbarino, 1992; Gonzalez-Mena, 2009).

A triad of beliefs, perceptions, and actions combine to reveal our attitudinal set. Swick (1993, p. 321) notes, "<u>Beliefs</u> about the communication process and about each other's role in that process shape the foundation upon which parents and teachers establish their relationships." Teachers and parents/family need to examine their beliefs in three areas: self, self-other, and the communication process itself (Swick & Souto-Manning, 2006). As Gargiulo and Graves (1991) indicate, teachers' lack of faith in their own self-worth is often a major obstacle in having positive relationships with parents and families. Teachers and caregivers who take care of themselves usually are caring and responsive to parent and family needs (Marshak, 1997).

Beliefs about others are the cumulative result of our experiences with "self" and "self-others" in various contexts (Satir, 1988). For example, caregivers who themselves are degraded by their supervisors without supportive continuing education opportunities are likely to "pass on" the negativity they experienced to parents and families (Swick & Graves, 1993; Swick, 2003a). In contrast, early childhood educators who have nurtured positive and rewarding parent/family involvement experiences are more prone to be highly positive with parents (Powell, 1998).

Our beliefs (parents and early childhood professionals) about the communication process itself is a powerful influence on how we interact with each other (Swick, Da Ros, & Kovach, 2001). *An empowerment communication philosophy* values dialogue that is rich with multiple voices and that is woven together through nurturing, trusting interactions (Noddings, 1995).

Perceptions are a composite of our beliefs as they relate to our views of others and the nature of events in our ecology (Bronfenbrenner, 1979). In relation to strengthening our partnerships, parent and teacher perceptions set the stage for our ongoing dialogue and actions. Swick, Da Ros, and Kovach (2001) recommend the following as perceptions that can enhance and strengthen parent-professional relationships (Figure 6.3):

Figure 6.3
Perceptions That Enhance Parent-Professional Relations

---

* Each person is unique, having special strengths, needs, challenges, and resources that are integral to their life journey.

* The source of power in each person's life is caring.

* The caring process is energized and humanized through inquiry that is responsive to the goodness and the fragility that is a part of our human journey.

* A caring form of communication is based on mutuality, trust, respect, and a strong sense of parent/family-teacher involvement.

Action is the venue we use to convey our caring and support for each other. Strong family-school-community partnerships are built on parent-teacher efforts that actualize the caring process. Gelfer (1991) and Swick (2004) articulate particular aims that our communicative relations with parents and families should seek to achieve:

* Promote a bond between family and the early childhood center or school experience.

* Help parents gain knowledge and perspectives about child development that enhances their relationship with their children.

* Engage parents in active roles to advance and strengthen their children's growth and development.

* Nurture parents to enrich their parent as teacher role.

* Support parents in meeting their family needs.

* Build a strong working partnership between parents and the professional early childhood staff.

Swick, Da Ros, and Kovach (2001, pp. 70-71) discuss ways we can use our communicative relations with parents and families to further empower them and our selves.

* Conduct a meaningful and enjoyable program on "family communication" and its importance to how children learn and how family-school partnerships are thus enriched..

* Develop and continually update a file of "counseling and family support resources" for families to use in various ways to renew and or further enrich their lives.

* Model good communication skills with children and parents; hold regular times for interaction and be receptive to parent and child inquiries and ideas.

* Invite counselors to do preventive mental health work with parents, families, and professionals in early childhood programs.

Communication: A Process for Shared Learning

Communication is about families and schools-communities building cultural rituals that help all who are involved (Marshak, 1997). *Four elements comprise this shared learning process:*

Figure 6.4
Communication Elements That Promote Shared Learning

---

1) Valuing parent and family input

2) Strategies for achieving partnerships

3) Feedback for parents and families

4) Engagement of each other in collaborative learning

Parent and family input need to be priorities in the communication activities of early childhood educators (Gonzalez-Mena, 1994). For example, a significant part of conference time should be guided by parent input and the nonverbal communication of children and parents should be "content" for our planning and work (Koch & McDonough, 1999).

Partnership building strategies should be integrated into our communication with parents and families (Comer, 1997). For example, some teachers find it invaluable to survey parents and families about their interests, concerns, and issues related to all facets of the center or school effort *prior to and during the year* (Katz, 1995). Additionally, parents and teachers find strategies that focus on sharing, working together in joint efforts, and in ways that enhance their common goal of advancing children's learning and development (Clark, 1999; Swick, 2004).

Feedback is the content of parent-teacher communication that helps to enhance and strengthen our lives. In particular, parents and families point to the feedback they receive from teachers and caregivers as essential to their goals and life enhancement (Gonzalez-Mena, 1994). An important part of shared learning is gaining insights from others about child development, parenting, and family life that help us as parents and early childhood professionals strengthen our skills and perspectives in helping children and each other grow and learn. Three examples of this process at work are noted by Swick, Da Ros, & Kovach, 2001):

1) One example is where parents use feedback to improve their literacy interactions with their children.

2) Another example is where parents use feedback to adjust their work-family schedules so that their time is increased with their children.

3) Finally, one parent shares that as caregivers impressed on her the need for her to assure her child that she loved her and was always interested in what she was doing at school she did these things more often.

Feedback also enhances teachers too! As Mr. Shelton told one group of parents, your insights reveal to me a world of your child that otherwise I would not likely know.

Collaborative parent-teacher activities enrich the entire early childhood learning environment (Swick, 1997, 2004). For example, parents and teachers might model service-learning work in the community and engage children in this effort too! Children thus see and participate with adults in prosocial activities and the family-school relationship takes on new and authentic meaning (Swick, 2001).

Important Communication Behaviors and Processes

While we reviewed some of the key communication attitudes and strategies in a previous section of this chapter, it is important to recognize the behaviors and processes that facilitate healthy parent-teacher and family-school partnerships. Four behaviors/processes that are recognized as highly enabling of parent-teacher communication are noted (Figure 6.5):

Figure 6.5
Four Important Communication Behaviors

---

* Nurturance

* Support

* Partnering

* Providing Feedback

Nurturance of each other creates an inviting and effective communicative relationship (Noddings, 1995; Swick, 2006). For example, teachers and parents point to the powerful influence of their nurturing relationship on the children. One teacher said that the children even did drawings of her and the child's parent in a loving embrace, suggesting the child valued this relationship and was eager to let them know.

Support for each other's goals and efforts appear to empower everyone involved including the children (Comer, 1997). Verbal and nonverbal support such as parents praising the work of the teacher and then actively engaging in helping out in the classroom, really sends the message that they value what the teacher does with the child. The same process is at work as teachers support parents and let the children know just how important their parents are to them and to everyone in the community (Edwards, 2000).

Partnering with each other is the most visible and often the most powerful means of strengthening communication (Swick, et al. 1997). Joint planning, shared learning, and regular conferencing are means to empower the total parent-teacher, family-school learning system.

Providing feedback in relation to the parent-teacher partnership is essential to ongoing communication (Swick, 1993). Feedback offers parents and teachers three important processes: 1) information for enhancing their efforts, 2) validation of each other's mission and involvement, and 3) challenges to further grow and learn in their respective roles (Gelfer, 1991; Swick, 2006).

Couchenour and Chrisman (2000, pp. 189-192) review two additional communication behaviors/processes important to successful partnerships: active listening and reflecting. They note that *active listening* is a process where the listener conveys their value and appreciation of the other person's message. This process of active listening is about being open to what the person is saying, avoiding being judgmental, and conveying sincere validation of the person's ideas (See Figure 6.6). Elements of this process are noted as:

Figure 6.6
Elements of Active Listening

---

* Attentive body position
* Appropriate eye contact
* Authentic facial expression
* Appropriate body positions
* Appropriate touch
* Meaningful verbal responses

Reflecting is also noted as very important to parent-teacher and family-school-community empowerment. This process involves early childhood educators in repeating back to the speaker what they said with supportive contextual tones used to show sincerity (McKay, Davis, & Fanning, 1995). It is also about our understanding of the message and how we interpret this message in relation to our concerns. It is an active reflection effort that usually engages the parent and teacher in mutual dialogue.

Parent-Teacher Communication: Strategies and Techniques

Early childhood educators should use a diversity of communication strategies and techniques to develop and nurture their partnerships with parents, families, and communities. The cultural, social, work, demographic, educational, and personal needs of parents and families require that we use communication efforts that are best suited to having successful and positive relationships with parents/families (Amatea, 2009). At this point we review several useful strategies/techniques that have proven effective in helping parents and teachers have nurturing and effective partnerships.

Conferences: Conferences provide the "context" for interactive communication among all parties involved. Conferences take various forms: formal, informal, individualized, group, telephone, interactive email, and other types (Couchenour & Chrisman, 2000, Swick, 2006). As Swick (1993) notes:

> Regardless of the type of conference, however, the emphasis is on sharing information, getting feedback from each other, being supportive of each other, planning school and home learning activities, and carrying out many other partnership actions. (p. 324)

Successful conferences are the result of teacher and parent planning and total school support for the effort to have meaningful partnerships. Conferences often focus on an individualized plan for enhancing child and family development and learning. Five questions that guide our communication during conferences (Figure 6.7) are noted by Swick (1993):

Figure 6.7
Questions to Guide Conferences

---

1) Have I left time for parents to express their ideas and concerns? It is best to allow parents time throughout the conference for having optimal input.

2) Have I expressed my major points clearly and in a non-threatening manner? Clarity helps parents understand and a non-threatening approach shows parents we are caring people.

3) Have I established a supportive environment where parents feel

comfortable in asking questions and sharing important information?

4) Have I reviewed my communication effectiveness and up-dated and improved how I communicate with parents regularly?

5) Have I been sensitive to the cultural and language diversity of parents and families in our school and community?

Planning the communication effort is very important. Be clear on purpose, date/time of conference, topics to be covered, parents' role (and your role), substance of materials to be used, and available supports such as child care, food, transportation, or other items. Swick (1993, p. 325) suggests: "Encourage parents to bring materials from home or to write down their observations to share with you. Make every attempt to use materials that are clear and understandable to parents." And it is important to re-emphasize the importance of having interactive relations with families.

For example, the following is a sample checklist for parents to use in preparing for the conference. You might use this list as a way of educating parents about their important role in the parent-teacher conference.

Sample Checklist for Parents in Preparing for Conferences

* What are some concerns that you want to ask the teacher?

* What are some interesting and important observations that you can share with the teacher about your child?

* What are some home learning strategies you have been using that you would like to share with the teacher?

* What ideas do you have about your child's learning at school that you can share?

* What topics or issues would you like future parenting programs to focus on?

Three communication reminders from Satir (1988) are important to making conferences and other strategies effective (Figure 6.8):

Figure 6.8
Satir's Reminders on Communication

1) Always begin and end the conference on a positive note, parents need to see the good things their children are about and how they can continue to nurture this process.

2) Never criticize, condemn, or complain unless it can be done constructively and is immediately linked to a productive strategy you and the parents can use to help the child.

3) Always show sincere appreciation, make the parent feel wanted and important, listen carefully, and be supportive of the parent.

Use the conference time to provide specific activities and supports that you and the parents can use in partnership to enhance the child and your family-school relationship. Swick (1993, 2004) suggests the ISP approach: Involve, Support, and Praise parents and family in the positive things they have accomplished and use this foundation to then make suggestions for further strengthening the parent-teacher relationship.

Post-conference efforts should include the finalization of an individualized educational plan for the child, a parent-teacher written statement on their support plans, and a positive follow-up note to parents thanking them and asking for their ongoing support and involvement. Regular follow-up contact strengthens the parental view of the importance of the communication effort. A sample parent-teacher conference follow-up plan is noted:

Sample Parent-Teacher Conference Follow-Up Plan

1) Need noted for teacher and parent to keep in touch with each other: ____
   _____
   _____

2) Specific activities parent, teacher and child will work on between this conference and the designated follow-up contact date: _____
   _____
   _____

3) Plan for parent, child, and teacher to conference jointly on progress toward meeting specific need(s) noted: _____
   _____
   _____

CASE APPLICATION: John's parents feel that he is being bullied during outdoor play time. Design a conference to use in responding to their concerns. What would you prepare for the conference? What advance materials would you send to the parents? What other issues might you cover in such a conference? Explain what your overall approach would be in trying to help the parents understand the total context of the situation.

Three additional conference types are noted because they are often used in early childhood education: group conferences, telephone conferences, and problem-solving conferences. The following points are drawn from Lawler (1991), Couchenour and Chrisman (2000), and Swick (1993).

Group conferences offer the opportunity for a group of parents and early childhood professionals who have a "common concern or issue" to meet and gain information, share perspectives, lay out strategies, and up-date each other on progress toward specific goals. For example, many teachers use the opening of the school period to have small group meetings that help parents gain proactive ways to make the school year successful.

Telephone conferences have become a useful way for busy parents and teachers to keep in touch. Short conferences often help to prevent problems or to lay the foundation for needed interventions. Parent or teacher initiated, these contacts offer quick, easy access, and a continuing way for handling daily tasks.

Problem solving conferences are directed toward a specific problem(s) identified by the parent/family and the professional as needing special attention. This type of meeting is geared toward finding positive and workable solutions, building trust, developing confidence in each other's skills and perspectives, and developing a foundation that solves the problem or at least offers hope for leading to a resolution. Lawler (1991) and Koch and McDonough (1999) offer excellent ideas for having effective problem solving sessions with parents and families:

* Remember, you are working with parents and not against them; focus on the positive and use a consensus building approach.

* Reassure and support parents as child problems may negatively impact their confidence – they need your support and continuing partnership in seeing the difficulty through to a successful situation.

* Use an exploratory, sensitive, and responsive approach to seeing the problem or issue from the parental perspective. Keep in mind that each parent will have his own idea regarding development and learning and related issues. Respect their views and use these opportunities to educate each other about various views on child development and learning (Gonzalez-Mena, 1997).

* You and the parent do not always have to have an answer to the problem that particular day or week. It is okay to have confusion and stress if we use them to build strength and trust in our partnership. If we do approach things positively, we will eventually solve most any issue (Galinsky, 1990).

* Above all else nurture in yourself and in the parents/families a warm and trusting relationship. Where people have trust in each other they also respect that sometimes they will have differences (Olsen & Fuller, 2003).

Home Visits: Personal visits between families and professionals in the home or in other supportive environments are highly effective communication strategies (Powell, 1998). The key element in the home visitation strategy is the relationship-building process. It is the core of how parents and professionals behave in using this intimate context to craft and continually refine their work with children, each other, and others in the community. Perhaps the most unique aspect of the home or personal visit process is that it nurtures the strengthening of the parent and family perspective. The interactions usually happen in the home and within the parameters set by the parents and family involved. It is imperative that early childhood educators who do home visits be highly skilled in communication and relationship skills. For example, in many school-based parent involvement practices the teacher is the controlling agent of the communication even when the goal is for mutuality. In home visits, as Powell (1998) notes the central characteristic of these relationships [parent, child, teacher, family] is *mutuality*, also termed *reciprocity*.

Further, particular educational and social support goals are set by parent education or home-school programs that use the home visitation process. For example, the Parents as Teachers (PAT) program includes educational activities to enhance parent-child relations, increase parental knowledge of child development, plan and carry out needed child assessments, provide families with needed services through referrals, and other key family strengthening strategies. So it is important to know one's focus and to realize the priority of the parent and family in the process.

Particularly important in planning and having successful home or personal visits is the cultural sensitivity of the home visitor (Swick, 1993; Lynch & Hanson, 1998). Communication is essential to this understanding because within cultures verbal and nonverbal gestures, words, and other messages take on varied meanings. In The Silent Language, Hall (1981) presents "culture" as that embodiment of a group of people's common bonds, values, and daily rituals that empower their identity. Thus a priority must be to learn about the family culture in ways that highlight its strengths, increase our cultural literacy, and offer insights into our building trust with the family.

As early childhood educators, we need insight into our own culture and how it influences our perceptions of people (Swick, Da Ros, & Kovach, 2001). Our ingrained cultural perceptions about child care and early learning have a subtle and yet powerful impact on our relationships with parents and families. Sturm (1997) relates how one teacher's self-reflection on her unintended stereotyping of a mother negatively impacted the relationship:

> As our discussion group talked about these issues, we realized that unexamined values, beliefs, and patterns of interaction – learned when we were children – exert a powerful influence on our communication and care giving routines. Our sincere intentions did not prevent us from

rejecting parents' diverse values when they challenged our own cherished beliefs. We were often unable to set aside our own cultural values long enough to listen to parents. (p. 35)

CASE APPLICATION: Several parents and teachers have noted the need for a more culturally sensitive approach to communication. You have been asked to create an initial framework for addressing the important and sensitive issues related to having a more positive multicultural environment. What are your three main ideas for accomplishing this task and how would you approach implementing them? How do you hope to get the team involved in discussing and developing the final framework?

Quality home and personal visit efforts are highlighted by three additional features: goal setting, continuous planning, and ongoing staff and parent training/education (Powell, 1989).

The *goal setting process* is one of mutuality where parent/family and professionals assess, observe, identify, develop, and continually review their purposes in the home visit and parent/family-early childhood professional partnership (Wasik, Bryant, & Lyons, 1990). Goal areas emphasized in many home visit programs include: education, support, parent referrals, child assessments, family resources, home-school issues, family literacy, and many other topics.

Continuous home visit planning is critical to gaining the real value of this communication strategy (Swick, 1991). Again, parent and professionals should plan jointly, with parent, child, and family needs providing direction to the planning effort. While the plan should reflect program-specific goals, clearly the real intent is to strengthen the total family learning system.

Training, education, and more training are essential to having high quality home visit programs (Barbour & Barbour, 2001). The five basic helping-skills areas (Figure 6.9) provide one means for organizing this training/education, continuing education: observation, listening, questioning, probing, and prompting (Swick, 1993). Brief descriptors for each area are noted:

Figure 6.9
Five Basic Helping-Skills Areas

---

* Observation
* Listening

* Questioning
* Probing
* Prompting

Observation is the foundation for being an effective home visitor. With a positive and supportive perspective, the early childhood home visitor can be shaping a family empowerment effort where strengths and talents of family are interrelated with needs. The emphasis is on looking for the good in all family and also joining the family in meaningful and authentic needs assessment (Schorr, 1997). One question that may prove very enriching is: What are the cultural strengths of this parent, child, and family?

Listening is the avenue to our becoming knowledgeable and insightful about family strengths and needs. Using active-listening we need to seek the authentic meaning of parent and family messages. What are the nonverbal messages telling us about parent concerns or responses to our efforts? At the same time, we need to be reflective about our own messages. For example, what is our behavior conveying to parents during the home visit? Are we supportive in our body language and do we truly invite parent, child, and family inquiries? (McKay, Davis, & Fanning, 1995).

Questioning is the means by which home visitors can gain a full and sensitive perspective on the family. This questioning needs to be a part of true and mutually responsive parent-teacher dialogue. Facilitative questions that help parents feel more confident in their parenting are truly dialogic because they open up trust and thus future possibilities for mutual parent-teacher growth (Fruchter, Galletta, & White, 1992).

Probing is an extension of this questioning where home visitors and parents/families seek ways to constructively engage children in active and enjoyable learning and growth. It is a process where joint home visitor-parent discussion and exploration lead to new possibilities for family literacy, parent-child sharing, and expanded parent involvement in extending their own education (Olson & Fuller, 2003).

Prompting is about reminding, encouraging, and supporting each other in the learning and growth process. Home visitors may remind parents (or indeed reinforce them) to stay involved in their child's education. It is also about parents and families engaging home visitors in learning about their lives. Ultimately, these five skill areas become the home visitors' tools for establishing trusting, rewarding, and helpful relations with parents, children, and families.

In addition, home visitors need knowledge of child and family development, communication skills, home visit strategies, and skills for building a system of community resources to support families. Very importantly, ment, communication skills, home visit strategies, and skills for building a system of community resources to support families. Very importantly, home visitor attitudes establish the psychological framework for successful partnerships. Finally, Swick (1993) offers ten key guidelines for having effective home visits:

1) Carry out important advance planning, arrive on time, and establish a positive beginning to the visit.

2) Be cordial, positive, and purposeful in establishing the tone and direction of the visit.

3) Stay focused on the purpose of the visit and yet be open to parent and family inquiries.

4) Be an active, empathic listener who is responsive to parent and family questions and behavior.

5) In doing assessments of child, parent, and family situations be honest, hopeful, and helpful!

6) Show concern for family issues and be sensitive to the stressors they face. Be helpful to them in locating needed resources and supports.

7) Be proactive in understanding cultural differences in relation to family concerns and values.

8) Wherever possible (and appropriate) involve the child in the visit as well as all family who are connected to the child's well being. Children love for you to visit and thus this is prime time to gain their ownership of learning.

9) Plan visits only at times convenient and desirable for parents and family. Also, be sensitive if parents wish to have a personal visit other than their home.

10) Always end the visit on a positive note with clear plans for having follow-up contact and further visits as appropriate to the purpose of the partnership.

CASE APPLICATION: Using the 10 suggestions for having an effective home visit, design a plan for using a home visit to help parents to use natural artifacts in the home as a means to enhance young children's literacy skills. What would be your main purpose? What home learning activities in the home would you likely suggest to parents? How might you engage the parents in doing these activities while you are with them in the home visit? Finally, how do you plan to assess how the process is going as you visit the family throughout the school year?

Newsletters: One way to assure continuing contact with parents and families is the use of newsletters. In contrast to the traditional teacher developed newsletter (which still offers much value), more contemporary newsletters include parents, children, administrators, and others as editors, authors, and users. Many newsletters have become interactive where parents respond to particular topics or issues in a given newsletter. In some cases newsletters are now electronically delivered to parents and families with the needed computer resources (Couchenour & Chrisman, 2000).

Classroom developed newsletters (especially those where children and parents play a significant role) are excellent for keeping everyone informed and involved. Class projects, up-coming events, special achievements, parent topics, child highlights, teacher letter, and other items are often found throughout newsletters. Contemporary computer technology, photos, drawings, and other graphics help to enhance the quality and attractiveness of these newsletters.

Another type of communication is the newsletter calendar which includes monthly information in calendar format. Many of these calendars have a flip side to them with a menu of information for parents and children such as: a list for forthcoming class activities, special events, parent-teacher meetings, and other important items. Often a space for parent response is used to get feedback on issues parents want to see in the next issue. Some suggestions for effective newsletters are noted by Swick (1993, p. 331):

* Involve parents and children (as well as other family) in the development and distribution.

* Make them personal, attractive, readable, and interactive.

* Include ways for parents, children, and others to respond (two-way communication) to newsletter items through written returns, electronic feedback, or telephone message systems.

* Include children's work (and that of parents too) in each issue of the newsletter.

* Have a parents' corner (and one for grandparents too) where parents can share ideas, concerns, and thoughts on different issues.

* Each issue should include some family literacy activity that parents and children can do together.

* Have parents, children, and staff evaluate the newsletter periodically and integrate ideas for improvement.

Ms. Way uses the following topics for organizing her monthly parent newsletter:

Topical Outline for Monthly Parent Newsletter

* Parent Corner (a parent edits this section)
* Teacher letter (provide capsule of work achieved and planned)
* Children's work (A sample of children's accomplishments)
* Announcements of need for parent help
* Items needed for the classroom
* Child/family advocacy items
* Calendar for monthly activities

Open House and Group Programs: With an appropriate purpose and supportive family-school support context, open house and group programs can be very effective in establishing group ethos as well as meeting common needs (Barbour & Barbour, 2001). In reviewing the attributes of successful open house and group-oriented programs, Swick (1993) states:

> *The most effective open house programs* have a structure that includes an opening information and welcome segment for all parents, a more focused time for open observation and discussion in the child's classroom, and opportunities for planning for more individualized contacts with the teacher and the school. Some programs are enhanced by having a family meal or light refreshments. (p. 333)

In addition, the open house and/or other group programs offer a time and context to invite parents to share their talents, set up regular conference times, survey parents on their interests and needs, as well as develop initial times for other group meetings. Berger (2000) suggests several ways to assure that open house and group programs meet the needs of the parent-teacher and family-school-community partnership (Figure 6.10):

Figure 6.10 Ways to Assure Effective Group Programs

* Involve parents in the planning of the activities so that their concerns and issues are a major part of the program.

* Have a specific purpose for the program such as conducting an orientation on what to expect for the school year, or to introduce new curricula topics and materials.

* Use opportunities like this to involve parents in leadership development work where they take on ownership of programs and activities.

* Make sure the program is scheduled and organized in a manner that is appealing and inviting to parents. Always ask: Is this a time and day when parents and families can and will come?

* Educate and involve staff to be leaders of this family-friendly activity; they need to be front and center in all aspects of the program. This is a time where partnerships can be instigated.

* Review and evaluate programs each year and use the feedback to strengthen the activities in future years.

Group information and sharing sessions also provide a time for meeting common parent needs on various topics and issues. These sessions can involve parents in sharing information, problem-solving work, needs assessment, school improvement work, and doing things to develop and strengthen their partnership. Powell (1989, 1998) notes that parents are eager to share with each other ideas about parenting and child development, and that they like the discussion method where they can have input on the actual teaching and learning activities. Berger (2000) and Rich (1987) list topics such as the following that parents in the early childhood years note as important for discussion (Figure 6.11):

Figure 6.11
Sample Topics for Group Meeting

* Positive discipline
* Parent-Child Relations
* Brain development and early learning
* Family reading and sharing
* Health and nutrition
* Getting ready for school
* Activities for "family time"
* Safety in the Home
* Tips for Healthy Family Living

Portraits, Portfolios, Journals, and Report Forms: Early childhood educators continue to broaden their creative reach to engage parents as partners in communicating in many diverse venues. For example, some early childhood programs are using parent *portraits* of their family as one means of gaining insights and perspectives about the strengths, needs, and issues the family views important (Fishel, 1991). Portraits might include stories about the parents' childhood, special family events and experiences, child achievements, and other events that "tell the story" of the family. The focus of portraiture is on empowerment and looking for the strengths of families, thus it offers a perspective for building parent self confidence and pride in what they and their children do – which is what communication is or should be about.

The *portfolio* also presents an opportunity for building a partnership to document and communicate the strengths and needs of the child and the family (Swick, 1993). Portfolio contents will vary but the following items are common: child assessment results, family input form, key conference plans, family photographs, child work samples, developmental check-lists, teacher reports and narratives on child and family, family stories, parent-teacher partnership notes, and other items or artifacts that promote the strengthening of the parent, child, teacher, and the family-school relationship.

Interactive journals (which may be called communication logs, parent-teacher journals, or similar titles) serve to link family and school through an ongoing journal of thoughts and feelings about what is happening to each other (parent, child, teacher) throughout the school year. Swick et al. (1997) note how this process works in one project:

> Teachers use daily or weekly "communication logs" that include teacher comments on the child's performance, behavior, achievements, and other areas of work. Parents, in turn, respond by commenting on the teacher's report and adding their own observations on things the child may be doing at home. (p. 271)

The "communication logs" or interactive journals can have a very positive influence on child, parent, teacher, and other family. Swick et al (1997, p. 271) note several benefits of this interactive strategy:

* Children are effective in connecting their classroom learning to their family context.
* Parents and teachers give direct attention to specific child needs and strengths.
* Improved parent-teacher communication on a weekly basis strengthens the partnership.
* Parents pay more attention to their child's learning.
* Parent and teacher contacts are positive and facilitative of each other.
* Children are motivated to adapt and become a part of the classroom environment.
* Teachers are sensitive to parent concerns and more responsive to various family needs.
* Children's behavior improves at home and at school.

The most common *report form* used in early childhood programs is the child progress report or "grade card" as it has been traditionally known. As Berger (2000) notes, child progress report forms serve to keep parents informed on how their child is progressing with regards to expected early childhood benchmarks for a given developmental period. Swick (1993) says that the typical report form includes: child performance data in academic, social, and related behavioral areas; teacher observation reports on child behavior and functioning; and instrumental data on attendance, tardiness and related items. Most report forms now leave a space for parent feedback and signatures. In addition, many schools are making these reports available to parents in electronic email form.

Communication: A Potpourri of Ideas: The complex and dynamic lives of families during the early childhood years require a variety of ways for building strong parent-teacher communication. Several informal and/or adaptive communication means are noted.

Telephoning parents to remind them of important dates or to engage them in discussion on how their child's day went can be a valuable relationship builder.

Developing recorded telephone messages on important classroom activities that happened so busy parents can keep up with what is happening. Parents simply call a designated number and listen to the report. Some hot lines have a "leave your message" service too!

Homework Hotlines that provide parents and children with a review of the days homework and suggestions on ways to achieve the assigned tasks. Some teachers and schools connect this service with after-school homework help programs.

Electronic communication venues including email, web pages, closed-circuit television programs (Many large urban districts now have their own television stations and radio specials.)

Moles (1997) suggests additional communication modes: home-school handbooks that parents can refer to throughout the year; school-parent compacts that delineate partnership communication plans; parent liaisons who function in leadership roles to link parents and teachers in various partnership roles; use of parent resource centers for sharing books, videos, and important center or school information; family nights to simply promote healthy family relations; and special resource programs for parents enrolled in English as a Second Language programs.

Father involvement in the ongoing communication process is critical to children's healthy development and to having nurturing and positive examples of men involved in children's lives (Couchenour & Chrisman, 2000). Early childhood educators have noted several strategies for increasing father involvement (Hamner & Turner, 2001):

* Get fathers involved early in the child's life and help them establish positive involvement patterns.

* Request "father presence" at the conferences and REWARD it!

* Hold special times just for father involvement such as father lunches, father read to children times, and father networking nights.

* Be sure fathers are on your classroom or school advisory teams.

* Telephone just fathers some times to emphasize the need for their input.

* Create male mentoring programs for children who do not have fathers or access regularly to a positive male role model.

Conflict and Confrontation as Opportunities for Learning

Within parent-teacher and family-school communication it is likely that some form of conflict will occur. The challenges of parenting and teaching are so dynamic that authentic partnerships will have differences of perspective and possible resulting conflicts. Unfortunately, too often these stressful situations are seen in negative ways and the learning potential they contain is usually lost on both parents and teachers. Yet if partnerships are to be meaningful and growth-oriented, we must learn to use conflict and confrontation as learning opportunities. A beginning point is to understand the dynamics of why conflicts occur between parents and teachers, and between families and schools.

Sources of Conflict and Confrontation: Many different stressors influence the development of conflicts: lack of communication, lack of a sense of mutuality with each other, a failure to truly understand the other person's view, cultural ignorance, personality clashes, displacement of anger from another source on the teacher or the parent, and frustration about how one is being treated (McKay, Davis, & Fanning, 1995; Swick, 1991, 1993). To be sure there are other sources such as marital stress, chemical dependence, abuse, chronic poverty, illiteracy, and mental health problems. While all of these stressors are cause for concern, *we can use conflicting relationship stressors as points of growth.* Swick (1991) notes:

> All relationships experience the stress of role conflicts. Indeed, the nature of intense partnerships such as those that take place between parents and teachers require stress points as a means of feedback and stimulus for growth. For example, teachers who expect parents to be at every activity may feel stressed as some parents define their participation in more limited ways. This conflict can function as a point of dialogue between teachers and parents on what are desired and realistic expectations for each other's participation. (p. 124)

In responding to parent aggression over their frustration with a particular issue, following the guidelines for dealing with such situations is very helpful (Olsen & Fuller, 2003):

Tips for Responding to Aggressive or Irrational Parent Behaviors

---

* Listen carefully – without interruptions
* Write down the main points noted
* As they pause, ask them if something is bothering them
* Let them identify more complaints
* Ask for clarification of points as needed
* Show them the list of issues
* Ask for their ideas on solving the problems
* Be calm, speak softly
* Let them know you care

Teachers note particular stress points as parent and family trauma, family dysfunction, family-work stress, family or parent burnout, lack of support, major mental health issues, value differences so marked as to stimulate confrontation automatically, and conflicts with the teacher and/or school on procedural expectations (Becker & Epstein, 1982; Chauvkin, 1989; Swick, 1997).

Parents cite the following as very stressful: poor teacher training, negative teacher attitudes, poor working conditions (especially overcrowded classrooms), lack of support, burnout, value differences with families, and lack of time to pursue parent-teacher activities (Galinsky, 1987; Powell, 1998). Research notes that poor or ineffective parent-teacher partnerships emerge from lack of priority on this area of education, poor teacher training, lack of teacher and staff initiatives to gain parent participation, and lack of administrative support (Schaefer, 1991; Epstein, 1991).

In many situations, *parent-teacher conflicts are rooted in the cultural insensitivities* that often emerge in relationships where the partners do not really know each other or value each other (Couchenour & Chrisman, 2000). As Lightfoot (1978) noted, this cultural distortion process can create a *"Worlds Apart Syndrome"* that can become a continuing source of conflict. Three elements appear to create cultural dissonance and communication stress between parents and teachers (Swick & Graves, 1993): 1) lack of cultural understanding, 2) negative attitudes, and 3) failure to become a cultural learner. The major factor in this stress is the negative stereotypes that teachers and parents can develop of each other.

Thus, *the first and most important step for preventing and/or resolving conflicts and confrontations* is to accept and value each other's perspectives regarding concerns and issues. As Comer (1997) suggests, when teachers and parents have some common understanding, respect, and goals – they are highly effective in problem solving and in being proactive to create the best learning partnership possible.

Another effective approach is to recognize and act on the need for parent validation. Most parents need and want to be validated that they are indeed good parents. Help parents feel accepted, validated, and important in the partnership process and in their many roles as parents. They need to see themselves as growing persons, as parents who are very important in the child's life and as parents who make mistakes but who grow through this process (Swick, Da Ros, & Kovach, 2001). Teachers who fail to recognize this basic parent need for validation can do great harm by reacting only to the immediate stress caused by child misbehavior. In most cases, teacher support and encouragement can transform the immediate anxiety and anger into a more positive and growth-oriented parental perspective (File, 2001; Lawrence-Lightfoot, 2003).

Teachers have three important roles to play in building trusting and growing relations with parents during conflict and confrontation (Swick, 1997):

Building Trusting and Growing Relations with Parents

1) Develop and continually renew a trusting and nurturing relationship with parents.

2) Share information and resources with parents that are supportive of positive and empathic approaches for problem-solving.

3) Create a "we" approach to problem solving that is based on respect for parent values and concerns.

Because of the continuing nature of chronic stress, *some parents develop "difficult behaviors" and can erode teacher effectiveness* (Powell, 1998). While value differences may be at the source of the stress, Swick and Graves (1993) note that many other stressors could be at work including poverty, drugs, unemployment, a series of family crises, and other such problems. Boutte, Keepler, Tyler, and Terry (1992) reviewed several different types of "difficult parent behavior syndromes" including: the antagonistic parent, the "know it all", the complainer, the negative parent, and the very unresponsive parent. They offer several ideas for relating to these behavior syndromes and the following are some of the key strategies noted:

* Focus on the positive aspects of the situation with antagonistic parents. Try to help them see the potential for good in the

problem and offer them "tools" to make progress on particular stressors.

* Be a good listener with the "know it all" parent and realize that people who are so motivated to let you know that they are experts are also very insecure people. Help them share their ideas and talents in ways that build trust in you and that in turn helps them become more secure.

* In addition to the listening skill, with complainers try to help them redirect their efforts in positive, solution oriented ways. Model for them positive approaches to solving and preventing issues..

* Respond to negativism with positive and optimistic strategies. Use praise and establish workable plans and solutions.

Unfortunately, in some cases parents and teachers simply may face the difficult task of ending their relationship. As Nancy Jacobs (1992) indicates, there are unhappy endings where parents and teachers simply agree to part ways. Sources of conflicts that instigate such stress typically are connected to "expectations" that relate to child learning, teacher roles, and to parent and family roles (Olsen & Fuller, 2003). For example, the author was in just such a situation where a parent wanted the school to change the program to offer religious rituals of their belief system. But of course other parents had different religions and some parents had altogether different ideas about religion itself. In the end, the parents left the early childhood center with as positive an ending as was feasible. Eventually they enrolled their child in the religious school that matched their beliefs.

Swick (1993, 1997) suggests *a three-step process* to use in trying to avoid such endings: 1) reach a consensus on the problem, 2) discuss possible ways to solve the issue(s), and 3) agree to meet again after implementation of the strategies agreed upon. It is parent and teacher intent that will make the real difference. If parents are facing other major stressors they may not be able to respond to this challenge too! The value differences may just be too big to handle in the time available. Most stressors of a long term nature are not resolvable in any immediate sense. But they can be made manageable through positive and supportive teacher-parent efforts.

Dealing with Cultural Differences in Communication

In many ways, "culture is communication and communication is culture" because it is what happens in our communicative relationships that eventually comprises our cultural habits and perspectives (Galinsky, 1990). It is very important that we become "cultural learners" in our communicative relationships. Otherwise, specific parent or family behaviors or rituals may actually appear to run counter to the values or activities we are promoting in our classrooms. As Swick (1991) notes:

> When people lack a full understanding of another culture, they tend to rely on stereotypes – images that usually are very incomplete and incorrect. (p. 133)

The key role that communication should play in any relationship is for people to learn more about each other's strengths and talents.

Multicultural learning should permeate the parent-teacher and family-school partnership. If communication strategies are to achieve optimal impact on parent-teacher partnership development, multicultural learning must be a priority. Comer (1997), Powell (1998), and Swick (1993) suggest the following as multicultural learning strategies that have been effective:

* Teacher involvement in acquiring accurate and meaningful information on the values and characteristics of children and parents from different cultures.

* Parents and teachers engaging in joint activities where they have nurturing and relevant exchanges of ideas about each other's contexts and cultures.

* Parent-teacher involvement in planning classroom cultural activities that engage everyone in rewarding and enjoyable cultural learning.

* Family-school cultural festivals where families and citizens share foods, talents, ideas, and concerns in a warm and responsive manner.

* Family-school-community education programs that broaden everyone's understanding of the various cultures and groups in the community.

* Parent-teacher involvement in reviewing and refining school curricula to assure cultural content is accurate and relevant to everyone's identity.

Cultural learning needs to extend to our daily interactions and the way we see each other as learners (Swick, Boutte, & Van Scoy, 1995/96). Perceptual distortions are common where teachers have not taken time to learn about new families in the community (McKay, Davis, & Fanning, 1995). Or, past stereotypes of parents and children prevail until they are challenged through meaningful experiences that include teacher research and reflection (Swick, Da Ros, & Kovach, 2001). Review the following possibilities for continued learning experiences (Swick, Boutte, & Van Scoy, 1995/96):

* Get to know the parents and families of your children through home visits, regular conferences, and other up-close interac-

tions. Invite parents and family to share with you and the class their heritage through whatever appropriate means they choose.

* Hold regular events where parents and teachers share cultural rituals and activities with the children in a positive and nurturing manner. This might occur through "family nights" or through festivals, or in the classroom through various instructional activities.

* Enroll in courses and other professional growth opportunities to expand and enrich your cultural understanding of people.

* Make special plans to gain the cultural insights of parents on needs and concerns they feel strongly about and then design ways to respond to these insights.

* Adapt parental involvement strategies to reflect parents' needs and interests such as having a bilingual interpreter help during conferences, avoiding the scheduling of events on special heritage or religious days, and showing respect for particular cultural holidays.

* Engage parents and family in reviewing instructional materials for accuracy and import.

CASE APPLICATION: Mr. Frank, a teacher of 4 year olds, notices that the children are beginning to notice each others' differences but are also exhibiting negative attitudes toward some children. He is developing three strategies to improve the children's understanding of each other and of people from other cultures: 1) using more culturally accurate and enriching materials with the children, 2) involving parents as resource people to share information about their culture, and 3) designing service learning projects with other child development programs as a way of involving the children with children from other cultures. What are some additional strategies you might suggest?

Nonverbal Communication is the Most Powerful Form of Communication

Simply observe the mother-infant relationship in action to gain insight into the power of nonverbal communication. Without words mother and infant create a "dance" of attunement where they weave a tapestry of attachment that motivates them to become bonded for life. Contemporary research on brain development indicates that our most ingrained social and emotional behavior patterns are learned in the parent-infant and other adult-infant/toddler relationships during the early childhood years (Brazelton & Greenspan, 2000). As Satir (1988) notes:

> Each of our "fountains" is in play even in infancy. The psychological reservoir from which an infant draws self-esteem is the outcome of all the actions, reactions, and interactions between and among the persons who care for that infant. (p. 37)

Likewise, the world of parent-teacher partnerships is strongly influenced by this "silent world" of nonverbal communication. In this relationship "silence" may and often does speak louder than our words. Urie Bronfenbrenner (1979) notes that children watch closely *what we do with each other* more than they listen to what we say to each other. Clearly, our modeling of behavior is more important than almost anything else we do. Yet the nonverbal aspect of communication has been largely neglected in the education of human service professionals.

For example, Hall (1981) found that in many cases people's expectations of others was based on a limited understanding of the realities of their lives. He found that in too many cases we only listened to the words people said while ignoring their most important messages which were through gestures, facial features, and in the patterns of their actual behavior. Tragically, in several cases teachers misjudge parents, children, and families because they have not acquired an empowerment view of the lives of these people. They also may simply not understand the nonverbal communication signals of culturally different families. As McKay, Davis, & Fanning (1995) suggest, people from different cultures and even sub-units within given cultures attached different meanings to gestures, space, eye contact, and other facial features.

The physical environment: A cluttered, disorganized, or dismal classroom certainly does little to encourage communication between parents and teachers. In contrast, an attractive and appealing environment stimulates us to "open up" and engage in more dialogue (Hall, 1981). Consider Lawler's (1991) suggestions:

* Create a relaxed, pleasant environment that supports parent involvement in the communication.

* Promote an environment that fosters open communication between parent and teacher.

* Have the physical environment structured so that it speaks to your desire for ongoing communication with parents and families.

Teacher appearance: The attractive, inviting person creates an aura of positive and nurturing communication (Lawler, 1991). For example, one parent noted that when she first met her child's teacher that it was clear she cared for her "self" and that meant a lot to this parent. "I could see she took time to present her self in a positive and attractive manner, that usually means she will do the same for my child."

Teacher visual contact and gestures: In many cultures "eyes are the window to the soul" and most cultures value eye contact enough to have unwritten rules regarding who looks at whom, when, and how (Hall, 1981). For example, in some cultures children are educated "not to look directly into the eyes of an adult" when being spoken to. In other cultures the child learns that you do look directly into the eyes of the adult when being talked to. So we need to know the rules of the culture or at least be responsive to how our gestures and eye contact are impacting the communication with parents. In this regard, check out where you

sit. Do you create too much distance by sitting behind a big desk? Most parents like being closer to you; after all, you are discussing their child. Also, simple things like having refreshments available can enhance the environment.

Teacher relations with the child: In many respects, what we do with the child speak volumes to the parent even before they meet us or subsequent to our meeting them (Gelfer, 1991). What children convey to parents about their teacher(s) and what we convey to parents about their children through our telephone conversations, notes home, and other items we send home tell a great deal about our teaching, learning, and communication style.

Teacher follow through: The voice of a parent helps us see the power of our doing and not just talking about what we will do in parent communication. Jennifer says "my daughter's teacher promised to let me know how she was doing with her reading every week but it is now a month and NO WORD!" Swick (1993) offers some important points on this process:

> By taking action on parent concerns and providing them with feedback on issues they have discussed with us, a sense of trust is nurtured and developed. Positive guidance, constructive suggestions, and the proper handling of parent inquiries are nonverbal modes of communication that impact parents more than our verbal exchanges with them. (pp. 316-317)

CASE APPLICATION: List five nonverbal communication situations you have found to be very important to having effective communication with families. Why are these nonverbal situations important? How do you use these situations to strengthen your communication skills? How would you suggest others adapt these to improving parent-teacher and family-school communicative relations?

Responding to the Communication Needs of Multi-Problem Families

Families under the chronic and pervasive stress that often accompanies multiple problems and crises need special attention related to communication. In many cases the communication strategies used in regular family-school interactions are provided with more intensity, individuality, and responsiveness (Seligman & Darling, 1989). However, various multi-problem family situations call for innovative communication activities and resources.

An initial step in the communication process is to establish a framework of empowerment where the family's strengths are related to any ongoing communication (Swick & Graves, 1993). By framing the family in positive and nurturing ways, our concept of how to interact with the family is also going to be more focused on their positive attributes. When early childhood professionals view the family in deficit ways, the family is likely to mirror this projection of weakness and lack of power (Minuchin & Nichols, 1993).

A second part of this effort is to closely review one's communication style with families who differ or who may have severe stress and problems. As Boutte, Keepler, Tyler, & Terry (1992) suggest, in many cases teachers unknowingly reinforce negative stereotypes of parents or families under stress by using very rigid communication strategies. For example, Swick (1993) reported that multi-problem families he interviewed often noted that negative or cynical teacher or home visitor attitudes turned them off to early intervention programs. Thus, three questions early childhood professionals should review as they communicate and interact with multi-problem families are:

1) Am I cognizant of the kinds of stressors the family is experiencing?

2) Do I view this family from a positive, growth perspective?

3) How can I support and nurture this family toward more healthy connections to the school and community?

A third step to consider when working with families under severe stress is to review one's basic communication skills and perspectives (Couchenour & Chrisman, 2000). Four communication skills are especially relevant to our interactions with families in high stress situations:

1) Our overall communication attitude toward parents and fami-

lies (Swick & Graves, 1993). Are we open to the ideas they bring to our interactions? Do we try to learn from them? Do we treat them with respect and trust? The answers to these questions are important for any interactions we have with families but are especially important to building trust with high-risk families.

2) Active listening as it relates to our understanding the total family learning ecology. For example, is our relationship with the family based on an understanding of their strengths? Besides just knowing surface needs, are we aware of the family's perceptions of their situation(s)? Have we taken time to truly listen to how the family would like to organize resources to strengthen their lives and that of their children?

3) Engaging parents and families in empowering learning and development activities is often more powerful than simply identifying the obvious need for family change. For example, helping parents achieve needed adult educational goals may well be critical to family improvement because of the long-range economic and educational outcomes. Or, supporting teen-parents in staying in school while also receiving needed parent education and family support resources is more powerful than periodic discussions with them about their situation – although this dialogue is important and should be linked to the more concrete activities they see as having real value in their lives (Schorr, 1997).

4) Planning and arranging for long term follow-up support for families in multi-problem contexts is important to helping them make real and lasting changes. Too often our communication with families in trouble is short term, lacking in any bridges and connections to an often very uncertain future. Thus, the communication and action environment should be organized in a way that encourages parents and families to use our insights and support over whatever time period needed (Seligman & Darling, 1989).

A fourth element that can strengthen our partnerships with multi-problem families is our sensitivity to and engagement in responding effectively to cultural and personal situations of minority and high-risk families (Lynch & Hanson, 1998). The starting point in this strategy is *understanding families' cultural orientation and their position in the community in relation to achieving their goals* (Gonzalez-Mena, 1994). For example, in some cases families may feel isolated from the community's power structure and avoid particular venues that would enhance their lives. Where early childhood professionals are sensitive to these contextual situations they can encourage families to take advantage of various social and educational resources otherwise ignored by them (Pipher, 1996).

Another point of supportive intervention is *to educate families in strategies for establishing more positive problem-solving efforts.* For example, one homeless shelter for abused women with children holds ongoing workshops on empowering communication skills the mothers and children can use as they cope with the many stressors of suddenly being in a totally new situation.

Finally, *a fifth element in strengthening the communication skills of multi-problem families is in educating the helping professionals who regularly interact with them* (Swick & Graves, 1993). Too often families are treated in deficit ways and lack positive role models in the professionals who claim to be their helpers. We need to review our professional knowledge base, our personal attitudes toward others, and do an inventory on the ways we treat families who have chronic and severe problems. Our modeling of positive and nurturing relations with them can be the strongest part of our helping them to adopt proactive means to solving problems.

Ultimately, our communication with parents, children, and families is the substance of our strategies to empower them. If we hope to have a positive and meaningful relationship with parents and families we need to continually strengthen our communicative relations with them.

SUMMATIVE DISCUSSION OF KEY APPLICATION POINTS

Communication is the central element in the development and renewal of parent-teacher and family-school-community partnerships. Four important application points are shared that consistently make a difference in the lives of children and families during the early childhood years:

1) Early childhood professionals can enrich and strengthen their communicative relations with parents and families through bilingual, multicultural strategies. For example, having interpreters available during parent-teacher conferences and other family-school sharing times increases the confidence of parents in the work of teachers and schools.

2) Positive attitudes toward parents and families increase the efficacy of parent-teacher and family-school relations. For example, teachers can model appropriate problem-solving behaviors in their interactions with parents and children – thus empowering families to realize the many benefits of proactive and nurturing relations.

3) Early childhood professionals increase their communicative competence through regular professional development activities that sharpen their understanding of parent and family

situations, the special needs challenges many families face, and the role that culture plays in the lives of families.

4) Trust, respect, care, and mutuality are the values and attributes that promote healthy and successful parent-teacher and family-school-community relations. These values are nurtured through honest and open communication. As early childhood professionals we need to model these attributes in our relations with parents, children, and families.

Suggested Websites

National Parent Teacher Association: <www.pta.org/programs>

Teacher Web Site for Communication: <www.4teachers.org>

Parents Planet: <www.parents-planet.com>

Home and School Institute: <www.megaskillshsi.org/default.htm>

Teaching Strategies:

References

Amatea, E. (2009). Building culturally relevant family-school relationships. Columbus, OH: Pearson.

Barbour, C., & Barbour, N. (2001). Families, schools, and communities: Building partnerships for educating children. Columbus, OH: Merrill Prentice Hall.

Becker, H., & Epstein, J. (1982). Parent involvement: A study of teacher practices. Elementary School Journal, 83, 85-102.

Berger, E. (2000). Parents as partners in education. Columbus, OH: Merrill Prentice Hall.

Boutte, G., Keepler, D., Tyler, V., & Terry, B. (1992). Effective techniques for involving "difficult" parents. Young Children, 47, 19-22.

Brazelton, T., & Greenspan, S. (2000). The irreducible needs of children. Cambridge, MA: Perseus.

Bronfenbrenner, U. (1979). The ecology of human development. Camnbridge, MA: Harvard University Press.

Chauvkin, N. (1989). Debunking the myth about minority parents. Educational Horizons, 67 (4), 119-123.

Clark, A. (1999). Parent-teacher conferences: Suggestions for parents. Champaign, IL: University of Illinois (Clearinghouse on Elementary and Early Childhood Education. EDO-PS-99-12, ERIC Digest).

Comer, J. (1997). Waiting for a miracle: Why schools can't solve our problems – and how we can. New York: Dutton.

Couchenour, D., & Chrisman, K. (2000). Families, schools, and communities: Together for young children. New York: Delmar.

Edwards, M. (2000). *Effective parent-teacher communication*. Little Rock, AR: Center for Effective Parenting.

Epstein, J. (1991). Paths to partnership: What can we learn from federal, state, district, and school initiatives? Phi Delta Kappan, 72: 344-349.

Erikson, E. (1982). The life cycle completed. New York: W.W. Norton.

File, N. (2001). Family-professional partnerships: Practice that matches philosophy. Young Children, 56 (4), 70-74.

Fishel, F. (1991). Family mirrors: What our children's lives reveal about ourselves. Boston, MA: Houghton Mifflin.

Fruchter, N., Galletta, A., & White, J. (1992). New directions in parent involvement. Washington, DC: Academy for Educational Development.

Galinsky, E. (1987). The six stages of parenthood. Reading, MA: Addison-Wesley.

Galinsky, E. (1988). Parents and teachers/caregivers: Sources of tension, sources of support. Young Children, 45 (2), 2-3 plus 67-69.

Galinsky, E. (1990). Raising children in the 1990's: The challenges for parents, educators, and business. Young Children, 45 (2), 2-3 plus 67-69.

Garbarino, J. (1992). Children and families in the social environment. Second Edition. New York: Aldine de Gruyter.

Gargiulo, R., & Graves, S. (1991). Parental feelings: The forgotten component when working with parents of handicapped preschool children. Childhood Education, Spring, 176-178.

Gelfer, J. (1991). Teacher-parent partnerships: Enhancing communication. Childhood Education, Spring, 164-167.

Gonzalez-Mena, J. (1994). From a parent's perspective. Salem, WI: Sheffield.

Gonzalez-Mena, J. (1997). Multicultural issues in child care. Mountain View, CA: Mayfield.

Gonzalez-Mena, J. (2009). Child, family, and community: Family-centered early care and education. Fifth Edition. Columbus, OH: Pearson.

Hall, E. (1981). The silent language. Greenwich, CT: Fawcett Publishing.

Hamner, T., & Turner, P. (2001). Parenting in contemporary society. Third Edition. Boston: Allyn and Bacon.

Honig, A., & Wittmer, D. (1996). Helping children become more prosocial: Ideas for classrooms, families, schools, and communities (Part 2). Young Children, 51 (2), 62-70.

Jacobs, N. (1992). Unhappy endings. <u>Young Children</u>, 47, 23-27.

Katz, L. (1995). <u>Talks with teachers of young children: A collection</u>. Norwood, NJ: Ablex.

Koch, P., & McDonough, M. (1999). Improving parent-teacher conferences through collaborative conversations. <u>Young Children</u>, March, 11-15.

Kotre, J., & Hall, E. (1990). <u>Seasons of life</u>. Boston: Little, Brown, and Company.

Lawler, S. (1991). <u>Parent-teacher conferences in early childhood education</u>. Washington, DC: National Education Association.

Lawrence-Lightfoot, S. (2003). <u>The essential conversation: What parents and teachers can learn from each other</u>. New York: Random House.

Lightfoot, S. (1978). <u>World's apart: Relationships between families and schools</u>. New York: Basic Books.

Lynch, E., & Hanson, M. (Eds.). (1998). <u>Developing cross-cultural competence: A guide for working with children and families</u>. Baltimore, MD: Paul H. Brookes.

Marshak, D. (1997). <u>The common vision: Parenting and education for wholeness.</u> New York: Peter Lang.

McKay, M., Davis, M., & Fanning, P. (1995). <u>Messages: The communication skills book</u>. Oakland, CA: New Harbinger Publications.

Minuchin, S., & Nichols, M. (1993). <u>Family healing</u>. New York: The Free Press.

Moles, O. (1997). <u>Reaching all families: Creating famiy-friendly schools</u>. Washington, DC: U.S. Department of Education, Office of Educational Research and Improvement.

Noddings, N. (1995). (1995). Teaching themes of care. <u>Phi Delta Kappan</u>, 76 (9), 675-679.

Olsen, G., & Fuller, M. (2003). <u>Home-school relations: Working successfully with parents and families. Second Edition</u>. New York: Allyn and Bacon.

Pipher, M. (1996). <u>The shelter of each other: Rebuilding our families</u>. New York: Ballentine Books.

Powell, D. (1989). <u>Families and early childhood programs</u>. Washington, DC: National Association for the Education of Young Children.

Powell, D. (1998). Reweaving parents into the fabric of early childhood programs. <u>Young Children</u>, 53 (5), 60-67.

Rich, D. (1987). <u>Schools and families: Issues and actions</u>. Washington, DC: National Education Association.

Satir, V. (1988). The new peoplemaking. Palo Alto, CA: Science and Behavior Books.

Schaefer, E. (1991). Goals for parent and future-parent education: Research on parental beliefs and behavior. Elementary School Journal, 91 (3), 239-248.

Schorr, L. (1997). Common purpose: Strengthening families and neighborhoods to rebuild America. New York: Anchor Books/Doubleday.

Seligman, M., & Darling, R. (1989). Ordinary families, Special children: A systems approach to childhood disability. New York: Guilford.

Sturm, C. (1997). Creating parent-teacher dialogue: Intercultural communication in child care. Young Children, July, 34-38.

Swick, K. (1987). Perspectives on understanding and working with families. Champaign, IL: Stipes.

Swick, K. (1991). Teacher-parent partnerships to enhance school success in early childhood education. Washington, DC: National Education Association.

Swick, K. (1993). Strengthening parents and families during the early childhood years. Champaign, IL: Stipes.

Swick, K. (1997). A family-school approach for nurturing caring in young children. Early Childhood Education Journal, 25 (2), 151-154.

Swick, K. (2001). Nurturing decency through caring and serving during the early childhood years. Early Childhood Education Journal, 29 (2), 131-138.

Swick, K. (2003). Working with families of young children. In J. Isenberg & M. Jalongo. (Eds.). Major trends and issues in early childhood education. New York: Teachers College Press.

Swick, K. (2003a). Communication concepts for strengthening family-school-community partnerships. Early Childhood Education Journal, 30 (4), 275-280.

Swick, K. (2004). What parents seek in relations with early childhood family helpers. Early Childhood Education Journal, 31 (3), 217-220.

Swick, K. (2006). Families and educators together: Raising caring and peaceable children. Early Childhood Education Journal, 33 (4), 279-287.

Swick, K., & Graves, S. (1993). Empowering at-risk families during the early childhood years. Washington, DC: National Education Association.

Swick, K., Boutte, G., & Van Scoy, I. (1995/96). Families and schools: Building multicultural values together. Childhood Education, Winter, 75-79.

Swick, K., Grafwallner, R., Cockey, M., Roach, J., Davidson, S., Mayor, M., & Gardner, N. (1997). On board early: Building strong family-school relations. Early Childhood Education Journal, 24, 269-273.

Swick, K., Da Ros, D., & Kovach, B. (2001). Empowering parents and families through a caring inquiry approach. Early Childhood Education Journal, 29 (1), 65-71.

Swick, K., & Souto-Manning, M. (2006). Teachers' beliefs about parent and family involvement: Rethinking our family involvement paradigm. 34 (2), 187-193.

Wasik, B., Bryant, D., & Lyons, C. (1990). Home visiting: Procedures for helping families. Newbury Park, CA: Sage.

Chapter Seven

Involving Community Groups
in the Family-School Partnership

CAPSULE: Nurturing strong community support to empower parents, families, teachers, and schools is essential to providing children with a future that is healthy, viable, and successful! Community involvement can engender early childhood partnerships that support quality programs for children and families.

Chapter Seven Objectives:

1) Strengthen your understanding of what a learning community is and how it contributes to developing strong family – school partnerships.

2) Enhance your knowledge and skills in using the important elements for developing community involvement in early childhood education partnerships.

3) Explain how the "community education" construct enriches family – school – community partnerships.

4) Broaden your insight into the process of using community education to empower citizens to nurture families and schools.

5) Explain the role of partnerships in using community resources to strengthen their learning and growth.

6) Develop and organize the major elements for having strong family – school – community involvement and partnerships.

7) Strengthen your understanding of how to use advocacy to improve community support for young children and their families and early childhood helpers.

Community involvement and collaboration with families and schools during the early childhood years is essential to their healthy functioning. Without strong community partnerships, parent-teacher and family-school dynamics would be limited and not likely to achieve optimal success (Comer, 2001). The theme for this chapter is the full integration and utilization of community involvement in every aspect of the early childhood education program. Topics include: the idea of a learning community, key elements needed for having community involvement in early childhood partnerships, a brief examination of the "community education" school, community involvement in developing family-friendly work and social practices, a look at how community resources strengthen families and schools, and some suggestions for developing strong family-school-community partnerships.

The Idea of Learning Communities

Two constructs central to understanding the role of communities in early childhood family-school partnerships are: *learning* and *community* (Gonzalez-Mena & Eyer, 2001). In relation to the partnership process, *learning is about continuous growth and renewal* (Eisler, 2000).

For example, the construct of community is about relationships and the growth in these relationships toward valuing and achieving common goals, activities, and ways of living (Gonzalez-Mena & Eyer, 2001). As Sergiovanni (1996) notes:

> Communities are organized around relationships and ideas. They create social structures that bond people together in a oneness, and that bind them to a set of shared values and ideas. Communities are defined by their centers of values, sentiments, and beliefs that provide the needed conditions for creating a sense of "we" from the "I" of each individual. (p. 47)

In the context of our focus on parent-teacher and family-school-community partnerships, the defining central element is the *empowerment of parents, children, families, and citizens* toward achieving strong and healthy communities (Couchenour & Chrisman, 2000).

Learning in this partnership process is about using ideas, experiences, and our common vision of strengthening each other (Schorr, 1997). In effect, early childhood learning communities have some common values and beliefs about the purpose and functions of their partnership as noted in Figure 7.1 (Carnegie Corporation of New York, 1994; Gonzalez-Mena & Eyer, 2001):

Figure 7.1
Common Values in Early Childhood Learning Communities

* Parents and family are the primary educators of their children and need a "community of learners" to ground their efforts within and to gain needed support.

* Children deserve high-quality and enriching experiences through their relations with parents, families, early childhood centers, and the broader community and society.

* Communities need to recognize and support a "community of learners" effort to thus promote strong parents, children, families, and early childhood education programs.

* Early childhood professionals should be the instigators and nurturers of a "community of learners" effort to promote and sustain high quality environments and services for parents, children, and families.

Five elements are necessary to establish and nurture "early childhood learning communities" (Carnegie Corporation of New York, 1994; Meier, 2002):

1) Create a common vision that the community is a caring web of relationships and services that promotes strong and healthy parents, children, families, and early childhood helpers.

2) Develop the policy making structure for establishing, nurturing, and renewing policies to support the vision in having strong and healthy parents, children, families, and early childhood helpers.

3) Craft and continually review and refine an "Agenda for Children and Families during the Early Childhood Years" that addresses the critical needs identified through the policy making teams in the community of learners.

4) Actualize the agenda with the creation of "family-friendly" practices, accomplishments, and artifacts throughout the community. Publicize these achievements and use them as a launching pad for future needs.

5) Connect your early childhood learning community to policy and practice that is happening in state and federal contexts. Become advocates, supporters, and policy influencers in crafting state and federal family-supportive legislations and actions.

Critical to the growth and renewal of early childhood learning communities are several elements (Peterson, 1992; Gaudiani, 1998; Robinson & Stark, 2002):

* Faith in the core values: People must maintain belief in the central value of having strong families.

* Strategies for actualizing the learning facet of community: Our core values, faith in these values, and our ability to carry them out are interrelated with our opportunities and support for learning new ways to achieve our vision. We need access to literacy resources, dialogue with each other, and resources to strengthen our understanding of how to empower each other.

* Collaboration structures and practices: Learning communities are characterized by strong collaborative practices and structures. This element is especially important to support and enhance families during the early childhood years. All of the needed child, parent, and family services that comprise high quality family living can be actualized best through community sharing and collaboration.

* Resources to support learning communities: To build and sustain long-term early childhood learning communities, important funding, space, materials, and "human capital" resources are needed to carry out the needed strategies and refinements.

* Continuing evaluation and renewal: Strong early childhood learning communities are continuously engaged in evaluation and renewal work. Collaborative planning includes mechanisms for reviewing what is working, what is not working, why the partnership needs new resources, and other key points that comprise a "listing of indicators" which help to guide the program.

CASE APPLICATION: Using the elements noted above, articulate three ideas on how you could promote strong early childhood learning communities. Tell how these communities could then empower children and families. How would they differ from communities that often seem to neglect children and families? What suggestions do you have for continual refinement in the program?

Elements Needed for Community Involvement in Family-School Partnerships

Community involvement enhances everyone involved in the "community of learners" when there is commitment to this involvement, specific goals and objectives for focusing it, a system by which the involvement can be achieved, indicators that reflect how the process is working, and means to evaluate and improve the effort (Meier, 2002). With regards to empowering parents and families and their partnerships in early childhood education settings, each element is reviewed and discussed.

Commitment to strong community involvement: Early childhood educators have a strong belief in community involvement because they have seen the benefits to everyone: improved child care and early learning, better health care, stronger social supports, and many other outcomes (Gonzalez-Mena & Eyer, 2001). Parent-teacher and family-school partnerships in early childhood need to make visible these and other reasons for strong community involvement. We must educate citizens regarding the impacts they can have through volunteering, tutoring, fund raising, and other activities (Robinson & Stark, 2002).

Focusing community involvement through clear goals and objectives: Community and societal involvement is most effective when it is guided by clear and specific goals and values (Jehl, 2007). For example, consider the four goal-areas the Carnegie Foundation of New York's (1994) <u>Starting Points</u> report which are noted in Figure 7.2:

Figure 7.2
Carnegie Foundation of New York's Four Goal Areas

---

1) Promote responsible parenthood
2) Guarantee quality child care choices
3) Ensure good health and protection
4) Mobilize support for young children and families

These specific goal-areas provide a community with clear guidance for getting involved. Another example is found in Even Start programs where the goal is to capitalize on total community collaboration to optimize literacy opportunities and resources for young children and their families (Brizius & Foster, 1993; Judkins et al, 2008). Other early childhood programs emphasize the use of interagency teams to identify, focus, and engage various social services agencies, other family support groups, and community-wide resources (Couchenour & Chrisman, 2000).

Systematic means for achieving community involvement: Articulation of needs, resources, strategies, and **collaboration means** provide the foundation for having strong and effective early childhood community involvement (Tucker, 2000). Early childhood partnerships that have successful community involvement point to five factors that make for this success (Couchenour & Chrisman, 2000):

1) The presence and renewal of a **caring attitude** in the community toward the goals and values of nurturing strong and healthy parents, children, and families.

2) On-going needs and resources **assessment** relative to desired goals such as improved health care for children and families or having higher quality child care and early learning programs. For example, some communities have noted the value of having child care centers do self-assessments which are then used to chart desired improvements for the future. These assessments are used for achieving local and state funding and for involving community groups in providing mini-grants or scholarship funds to enhance quality care for all children (Kraemer, 1993).

3) Continuing **collaboration** among early childhood programs, family support agencies, and community groups to plan and carry out parent and family strengthening activities. This sense of collaboration involves sharing of resources, staff, materials, ideas, training, and, in some cases, funding. Successful programs note the value of frequent planning and communication, review of needs and resources, reflective and creative brainstorming, and periodic renewal of each other's commitment to the core values of the effort.

4) **Continuing education** that involves everyone in learning ways to strengthen the partnership through community and societal involvement. For example, Couchenour and Chrisman tell how the United Way developed a family-centered agenda and then engaged local United Ways in adapting it to their needs through a community education and support strategy. In other cases, communities have held family-centered programs as a means to then gain parent, family, and citizen input on particular needs and possible matching resources.

5) **Family-centered thinking** is present in the activities and strategies developed and used in the program. Citizen and professional involvement in their partnership work is centered in the following three questions:

   * What are the priority needs of families with young children as identified by parents, families, citizens and early childhood professionals?

   * What resources are being used and how are they working to the benefit of children and families?

*   In what ways can we improve our services to better meet these identified needs of families?

CASE APPLICATION: You are serving on a committee to strengthen community involvement in schools. What strategies/elements would you see as critical to gaining the needed involvement? How would you organize to implement these ideas? What indicators would you use to guide your evaluation of these strategies?

The "Community Education" School

Early childhood educators have embraced the "Community Education" concept in all aspects of functioning (Swick, 1993). This concept focuses on actualizing the "Community of Learners" philosophy through creative, innovative, and responsive strategies and practices. Parson's (1999) notes several indicators of the "Community Education" concept, all of which are very applicable to what early childhood parent and family strengthening programs need to adopt or further develop as identified in Figure 7.3:

Figure 7.3
Indicators of Community Education Practices

*   Optimal access to center services
*   Center activities and resources serve all ages
*   Decisions happen within a decision making team
*   Facilities are designed and used in multiple ways
*   The program is very connected with the community
*   Partnerships are formalized through advisory teams
*   Learning and continuing education is a vital mission
*   Innovative teaching and learning approaches are valued
*   Self-study and continuing evaluation provide the on-going education for participants

---

An important element in the "Community Education" concept in early childhood parent and family programs is the education of professionals, citizens and parents about important resources and activities for empowering them and their children (Boyer, 1991). Within this education paradigm, cultural relevance and sensitivity are important to helping each other benefit from the wisdom and knowledge of the many cultures we comprise. A few examples of how real early childhood parent-teacher and family-school-community partnerships have developed on-going education and learning practices are noted as follows. See Chapter Eight for more examples.

Parent educators learn from the parents they serve: In a family literacy program that serves families in at-risk situations, the parent educators developed a "learning day with families" to gain ideas from them on what activities and resources they saw as most needed, and to help the parents to see themselves as teachers too. To highlight this strategy they recruited a parent-leader from the previous year's program to "keynote" the day's work. It was clear that the parents were proud of a parent doing the main speech for the day. They gained real confidence as individual parent educators "recruited" them to use their expertise as a parent to mentor a younger, less experienced parent. Three things were achieved as noted by the parents and the parent educators in Figure 7.4 (Swick et al, 1998):

Figure 7.4
Major Outcomes of Parent – to – Parent Education

---

1) Parents realized that indeed they had much to contribute to the partnership and that they felt important when they were in the giving role.

2) Parent educators recognized that parents learned best when the learning was a shared and collaborative process. One parent educator said, "I plan to use more of these parent as teacher techniques in my home visits this year."

3) Parents and the parent educators realized that each person had ideas, knowledge, and perspectives that enriched the total partnership effort.

Senior citizens mentor and nurture preschool children: Boyer (1991) shares an example of how one intergenerational program enriched young children and everyone involved:

> Messiah Village, atop one of the rolling hills inMechanicsburg, Pennsylvania, is one place thatbrings the old and young together. Tuckedbeneath the chapel in the main building of thisretirement village is a Children's Family Center where 75 youngsters, ages two to five, arriveeach day for child care. Breakfast is prepared byone of the village residents known as "Grandma."Other retirees organize games, strawberry festivals, and art classes. They tell stories andhelp with meals, snacks, and song time. Children walk through the halls almost every day, greeting residents, occasionally joining them in crafts or cooking classes, in exercise sessions, or on strolls along nature trails. The generations also meet for picnics and holiday

celebrations. A Special Friends program matches a child with a retiree. Special Friends meet weekly to play games, work puzzles, read and talk. In such encounters, children learn about growing older, while older people are inspired by the freshness and energy of children. (p. 113)

Teen-parents educate the community about prenatal care: Perhaps we really do learn more about something when we are held accountable for teaching others about it. In a teen-parent education program the parent educator used this "teaching as you learn" model to assist teen-parents in doing a better job of taking care of themselves during pregnancy. She had them prepare a very comprehensive program on "prenatal care" for presentation in the community at school Parent-Teacher meetings, in shopping mall displays, and at various churches. The program was so successful that a local physician asked the teen-parents to share the program at a state medical meeting. One of the most powerful outcomes was that all eight teens improved their self-care during this important period of life and went on to have healthy babies (Schorr, 1997).

Three additional educational strategies are noted to highlight the vital part that education plays in helping families, schools, and communities to use partnerships to enhance their quality of life.

Community early childhood media literacy: A local early childhood professional association collaborated with a local television station, area early childhood centers and schools, and several community groups to promote "media literacy" related to violence in the media and its potential influence on children and adults. Two major themes in this community education campaign were to engage children and adults in more read-ing activities and less television, and for parents and family to be more involved in monitoring what children view on television and how much time they spend watching television. The association developed a literacy awareness "kit" and it was used in churches, school PTO groups, at shop-ping malls, and in various media outlets.

Health, nutrition, and physical exercise education: Early childhood teachers partnered with a local pediatric group to establish a community-wide education effort to alert parents and families to the need for better health practices, improved nutrition, and very importantly, everyone's involvement in more physical exercise. Through this collaborative effort, three activities took place:

1) Early childhood centers in the community reviewed their physical activity programs and up-graded them to assure that all children were involved in appropriate physical exercise every day.

2) Schools and early childhood centers developed nutrition as-

sessments of the food they served at breakfast and lunch and began efforts to provide children with more nutritious food.

3) Parent educators developed lesson plans on nutrition, health, and physical exercise and used these in their home visits with parents of preschool age children.

Improving child care in the community: Through support from a state child care monitoring group, local child care leaders linked up with some key community leaders to craft an agenda for involving county council in funding specific improvements for local child care centers. A three step agenda was crafted and implemented over a two year period:

1) Development of council awareness of the need for quality child care in the community.

2) Presentation of a four-part funding plan to support enhancement of local child care programs. Included: mini-grants to improve curriculum and staff training, scholarships to raise faculty pay, funding to create family empowerment centers, and funds to innovate with more infant/toddler care, which was in great demand.

3) Collaboration with the council to find ways of getting the private sector involved in developing public-private partnerships to thus truly engage the entire community in this effort.

CASE APPLICATION: Briefly give two examples of creative ways you would implement the "community of learners" philosophy in early childhood education settings and programs. In your examples show how particular groups can contribute to empowering the partnership concept in your community.

Community Involvement in Building Family-Friendly Work and Social Practices

Family-school partnerships can only achieve optimal quality and impact when the community is involved in every dimension of family-school life (Swick, 1997; The Council of Chief State School Officers, 1999). It is now well documented that parents of young children are experiencing high job stress, have difficulty finding and paying for quality child care, experience chronic stress in balancing family-work loads and issues, and need much more support in all contexts if they are to be effective family leaders (Galinsky, 1999; Thornton, 2001). In addition, many parents and family suffer from a lack of job skills, experience chronic under-employment, and when employed are often on the lowest end of the economic spectrum (Heyman, 2000). Further, parents report that too often business/industry are not cognizant or responsive to the demands families experience in contemporary society (Folbre, 2001).

234

Thus, *the involvement of business/industry and other community groups in providing more **family-friendly** support practices is essential to having workable and powerful family-school-community partnerships* (Hewlett & West, 1998). In fact, the missing link in crafting and actualizing a more viable community education concept is the wide scale integration of more family supportive business/industry practices (Parson, 1999).

With family-school support practices and strategies, parents and teachers can up-grade the quality and power of their caring and nurturance of young children. Consider the following *work practices* that help parents to be more involved in their children's development, learning, and education. See Figure 7.5:

Figure 7.5
Family-Support Practices That
Strengthen Family and Community

---

* Alternative work schedules
* Supportive parent leave policies
* Quality child care support efforts
* Parent and family strengthening programs
* Flexible family benefits
* Additional support practices
  - Work re-entry
  - Work hour bank
  - Job transfer
  - Family supports

---

* <u>Alternative work schedules</u> that allow parents to do flex-time so as to be able to attend conferences or be a part of an important happening at their child's early learning center. Or, letting parents do part-time work schedules that include benefits packages so they can, for example, stay home part of the day to care for an infant or toddler. As Folbre (2001) notes, such family work practices not only help parents to be better parents, they improve the work place environment by keeping high quality workers and thus reduce retraining costs and costs that happen when business/industry lack high-quality workers.

* <u>Parental leave policies</u> that support new mothers and new fathers to have time at home to "build the nest" for parent-child attachment and family bonding so essential to later having quality human beings. Current practices are very limited and often restricted to "unpaid leave" for parents. Most economists

now concur that the United States must change our ways on this item if we are to have a high quality workforce (Folbre, 2001). Hewlett and West (1998, p. 233) recommend *"paid, job-protected parenting leave for twenty-four weeks* – thought by many experts to be the minimally adequate period of time for a parent to bond with a new child." There are multiple ways to fund this very important need: use of existing private insurance funds, company sponsored maternity benefits packages, and government use of minimum wage scales through funds from the social security act. Parents who have had time to bond with their new child and form new family relationships are healthier and more productive workers when they return to work (Heyman, 2000).

* <u>Child care support practices</u> that provide parents with access to and use of high-quality affordable child care (Brazelton & Greenspan, 2000). Again, there are many ways to plan and fund this effort. This strategy needs to be adapted to the situations of families and employers. For example, in the case of small businesses it may be that a cooperative venture with other small businesses is ideal to establish and then provide the needed child care. Some central-city businesses have done exactly that and then provided employees who use the facility with small scholarships to further make the care affordable (Swick, 1993). In other cases it may be that on-site child care serves the purpose; or providing parents with direct payments or vouchers to use in finding their own child care placements.

Business/industry in collaboration with local, state, and federal governments can develop and field-test policies and practices that address the important elements in this issue: improved regulations for quality care, better training and improved funding for higher quality facilities and curricula (Hewlett & West, 1998).

* <u>Parent education/family strengthening programs and practices</u> that enhance the effectiveness of parents and family. Parents spend most of their day-time hours at work. Yet too often we fail to use even small pieces of this time for educational purposes. Most parents respond very positively to work-site parent education and family support efforts (Powell, 1998). Depending on the demographics of the parents and families at work, the content and structure of parenting education programs can be adapted to particular needs. Hewlett (1991, p. 208) tells of one company's very positive experience with a parenting program:

236

Sunbeam Appliance Company discovered the importance of prenatal care the hard way. Four premature babies born in 1984 to women working at the company's Coushatta, Louisiana, plant accounted for fully half of the $1 million the company paid that year in health care for 540 employees. One of the babies required so much care that medical bills exceeded the $250,000 limit in major medical coverage.

Shocked by these numbers, the company did some in-house research and discovered that pregnant women who worked at the plant (Sunbeam's labor force is 80 percent female) were waiting too long to see a doctor. So in 1986, Sunbeam started a prenatal program.

Pregnant employees were allowed to take an hour of company time every other week to attend classes in health care and nutrition taught by a specialist in prenatal nursing. In addition, the plant nurse weighed the women weekly, checked their blood pressure, and ran urine tests.

The program was highly successful with only one premature birth since its inception and that birth had no major complications. Parent education can and does have powerful benefits for participants and for their employing companies.

Flexible and enhanced family benefits packages: Most parents want to do what is right for their families (Galinsky, 1999). Companies that have explored using adaptive benefits packages where employees have choices and where the business or industry enhances the package with a matching contribution have found very positive results. For example, in many cases parents choose less vacation time but more family leave time or elect better medical insurance policies in lieu of more take home pay. Similar policies can help parents buffer the high costs of child care or in the case of having responsibility of a sick parent, they can use some company supports to negotiate those high costs (Folbre, 2001).

Additional family-friendly work practices that strengthen family-school partnerships: Business and industry can take small steps that boost parent and family power to provide children with better care and support (Parson, 1999). Swick (1993, 2004) lists the following as highly supportive of parents and families:

* Use re-entry workplace practices that help parents return to work without loss of status or salary level and that include supportive adjustment practices.

* Develop a "work hour bank" for parents (and other family where appropriate) to use in emergencies as they care for their

children, a sick family member, or for use in attending school sponsored events.

* Use "work transfer" policies that help keep families together and thus also enhance the family-school partnership continuity. Use in-house promotions where that is feasible for supporting family security.

* Develop and use family advisory councils to keep in touch with the family viewpoint on how work and family stress is being handled.

CASE APPLICATION: Using your community as a context – suggest two possibilities for building "family friendly" work/social supports for families. Explain how these practices will strengthen families. Also suggest ways communities can use the strategies you describe. For example, what are some of the challenges and how might they be resolved?

Community Resources Enhance and Strengthen the Family-School Partnership

Beneath the plethora of "hidden resources" that often go unused in most communities is the underlying reason why people fail to connect with resources that could well enhance their lives (Chen, 2002). One of the most observable problems of highly dysfunctional parents and families is their isolation from needed resources. A continuous disconnect from one's environment eventually causes harm to that person's ability to solve problems. In the world at large, the key is connections, connections, connections. The survival and success of every enterprise will be based upon stakeholder relationships, on human and electronic connections to a much broader community (Diss & Buckley, 2005).

Thus, our exploration of community resources that strengthen early childhood family-school and parent-teacher partnerships needs to be grounded in educational and social networks that facilitate people having access to and knowledge and skill in using these resources (Powell, 1998). Three sets of resources are noted as examples of "community power" in enhancing early childhood partnerships: general community resources, business/industry, and agencies/special groups.

General community resources include parks, sanitation, museums, libraries, police and fire protection, and other services and resources like community employment centers (Parson, 1999). These resources are often "taken for granted" until they are dropped because of budget cuts. Or, the services lack quality and are thus viewed as less helpful. Yet these services are the foundation upon which all community partnerships are possible. We need to see these services as vital components to early childhood family-school programs. For example, increased police skill and understanding of child and family abuse issues can lead to improved protection for families (Karr-Morse & Wiley, 1997).

Business/industry resources are only limited by the vision of people engaged in developing early childhood family-school-community partnerships (Parson, 1999). Six very important resource roles for business and industry are noted (Swick, 1993, 2004):

1) Providing early childhood centers with management expertise related to operational issues like budgeting, staff organization, and overall management guidance.

2) Adopting an early childhood center that is in need of support and validation. For example, some business leaders have provided funds, people, and psychological support to a particular center.

3) One computer technology company engaged all of their employees in mentoring at a high-risk early childhood program in a nearby rural school district. The mentoring included tutoring in reading, helping the children learn the basics of computers, and an established homework hotline.

4) Another company acquired new computers and installed them in the early childhood center, provided training, and then established matching grants to buy software when the PTO provided the needed matching funds.

5) Many early childhood centers need financial help to send teachers to professional conferences and advanced study. A company could contribute funds or help the center acquire grants to help pay for these needed resources and training.

6) Salary enhancement money is a real energizer for most programs. One company recently contributed over $50,000 in salary enhancement to a preschool center that cares for most of its employees.

Agency resources will vary depending on the size of the community and other organizational factors. However, interagency councils have proved very effective in strengthening early childhood family involvement programs. For example, in one county, the early childhood program leader uses a community-wide agency management team to achieve partnership goals not otherwise likely to be attained. Here are five agency resource areas they use to strengthen their partnerships:

* Sharing of talent to help each program achieve parenting and family education goals.

* Sharing of training for staff and parents, thus enhancing everyone's learning and skills for partnership work.

* Highlighting each other's particular strengths and resources in community-wide brochures and displays.

* Developing and distributing networking resources that help parents and families understand how to use the agency structure to their advantage.

* Service on each other's advisory teams to thus enhance the overall family-school-partnership system.

In addition, *non-profit community groups* contribute various resources and supports to early childhood parent-teacher and family-school partnerships. Success by Six is a program usually sponsored by several community non-profits and that focuses on helping children and families gain the needed power to be successful in life and school. Big Brothers/Big Sisters programs now emphasize mentoring young children, especially children who are in high-risk situations. Boys and Girls Clubs sponsor many after-school and summer enrichment programs particularly focused on early childhood education. United Way has as one of its major goals over the next ten years to support family development during the early years of life.

To gain the real value of these community resources for strengthening early childhood family-school partnerships, Covey's (1998) elements of a healthy community are noteworthy:

* Trust, honesty, and goodness prevail in people's relationships. They truly want the best for each other and for all of the children and families in the community.

* A common vision and caring about quality living conditions for families and children exists throughout the community. Yet people respect the different ways each of them goes about the business of care and love for each other.

* People aim to have economic and social justice for all families and children. They strive to have jobs, salaries, education, and other indicators of quality life for all citizens.

* Service to each other is a prevailing life style in the community. People want and value helping each other and learning from each other.

CASE APPLICATION: Using ideas noted above in the discussion about using various community resources to empower families and their helpers, develop your plan to use resources in your community to achieve family strengthening and school improvements. Share your plan with others and see what ideas they found useful. How could both of your plans achieve the enhancement of children, families, and schools?

In particular, communities must work in tandem with family and school partnerships to provide these essential resources in creative but comprehensive and inclusive ways (Brazelton & Greenspan, 2000):

* Safe, secure, and enjoyable neighborhoods: All families and children need safety, security, and enjoyment if they are to achieve their optimal growth and learning.

* Needed health and medical care: A great deal of school failure and life problems are rooted in poor health and medical care. Communities must work to provide the needed health and medical care for all children and families; it is vital to their growth and development.

* Educational and family literacy opportunities: Communities need to work with schools and early childhood partnerships to provide all kinds of literacy and educational enhancement.

* Mental health and counseling resources: Community counseling and wellness centers are essential resources for families with young children. Stress is very high in the evolution of young families and the need for counseling and therapeutic resources is high.

* Job opportunities and adequate salaries and quality working conditions: Community initiatives to advance families with solid and adequate jobs, salaries, and benefits is critical to parents being able to parent effectively.

* Violence prevention strategies and supports: Stress is very high in many families and violence is present in our societal fabric. Community involvement in educating, supporting, and promoting non-violent means of living is a key way for building stronger family-school-community partnerships.

* A community commitment to a just, multicultural society: Through many activities (e.g., international festivals) communities can join early childhood partnerships to promote justice and appreciation among all cultures and groups.

Organizing and Developing Strong Family-School-Community Partnerships

Meaningful and productive early childhood family-school-community partnerships happen as a result of vision, planning, collaboration, commitment, and an overall value system that is based on a community of learners (Couchenour & Chrisman, 2000). *First, the value of everyone in*

241

the community being involved in caring for children and families is the starting point. As Swick (1991) notes:

> Communities need to be in covenant with families and schools regarding the mission of creating learning environments where children can grow and succeed. Everyone in the community needs to see the education and well-being of children and families as their priority; schools must not be challenged to handle this role in isolation from the very sources it serves. (p. 157)

Second, a vision of how to craft and implement a family-school-community partnership is needed (Meier, 2002). This vision needs to be representative of the total community. All of the early childhood disciplines and services need representatives to assure that the vision includes all of the important child and family needs; and early childhood practitioners and citizens need to also be engaged in the visioning process (Couchenour & Chrisman, 2000).

Third, articulation of important objectives to be achieved in the partnership is essential to having some benchmarks we can use to judge our progress or needs to adapt our approaches to strengthening parents, children, and families (Parson, 1999). Objectives in three process areas can structure our work: service, support, and collaboration (Swick, 1993, 2004).

Service objectives should emphasize ways the community can indeed empower families and early childhood programs through direct and indirect services like health, medical care, immunizations, family literacy, quality child care and other very important services (Wright et al, 2007).

Support objectives might focus on ways to build a stronger "infrastructure" for families, children and the helping-professionals they serve. For example, sharing facilities where the community sponsors and houses parenting education programs is a very positive and beneficial support and service. Another example is where business/industry help to fund training programs for child care professionals who otherwise could not afford such training (Swick, 2004).

Collaboration objectives should guide the work of the family-school-community team toward establishing strong and supportive ways of achieving high quality living conditions for families. For example, planning groups need to study how they can better use and deploy their talents and resources to empower families and communities (The Council of Chief State School Officers, 1999).

Fourth, partnerships need to recognize and act on developing public policy frameworks that strengthen children, families, and early childhood professionals (Hewlett, & West, 1998). Too often community involvement is seen more in the realm of doing tasks that support short-term or very immediate needs. While this form of service is important, all citizens need to realize the power of public policy work (Schorr, 1997). To develop a safe and high quality community child care center is wonderful and powerful to the children's well being. But to also then establish public policy parameters that require quality care standards in that program is also very important. We need continuous community involvement in all aspects of public domain work that impacts children and families (Wright, Stegelin, & Hartle, 2007 Parents and family need time, knowledge, support, and validation to handle the many stressors of contemporary parenting. Community support through family-friendly policies can make a major positive impact on parents and families (Hewlett & West, 1998).

Fifth, we need a "learning paradigm" that encourages family, school, and community to continually gain new insights about child and family empowerment (Peterson, 1992). Partnerships that have a powerful impact are "learning partnerships" where everyone is involved in gaining new knowledge, skills, and perspectives for supporting families (Stronge & Reed-Victor, 2000). Communities where people study and continually review what is happening to children and families have stronger values and accompanying actions that strengthen families. As Morse (1998) notes:

> Perhaps the most important revelation about community for the late twentieth century is the interrelationship of issues and the systems that support them. Citizens and policymakers know that if solutions are to be found to society's most intractable problems, new ways of talking, deciding, and moving to action must be discovered. (p. 231)

Sixth, we need a diverse set of ideas on how to achieve partnership efforts without stereotyping one or two preferable strategies (Schorr, 1997). More is accomplished in early childhood partnerships that value and support multiple ways toward empowering children and families (Robinson & Stark, 2002). For example, in the Comer Model, parent involvement in all aspects of the school's life is required. Core beliefs in this model are: decisions are the result of everyone's work (a no-fault value), people accomplish more through collaboration, and consensus building also builds trust and shared-power in the early childhood education program (Parson, 1999). The Family-Centered early childhood model holds similar beliefs but emphasizes building strength through a variety of strategies: parent involvement through home learning, community support through media awareness, family-based leadership development, shared-learning, family literacy activities, and other activities (Diffily & Morrison, 1996).

Seventh, to achieve meaningful partnerships in early childhood education an infrastructure of staff, facilities, and training is essential

(Schorr, 1997). Without "point people" or "leadership staff" the fabric of partnership groups tends to unravel and eventually disappear (Parson, 1999). Central to all aspects of working partnerships is staff who are knowledgeable and skilled in achieving the mission of the groups engaged in the collaborative efforts. For example, it may be that a "family-school-community" leader provides the leadership and direction to the process. Or, it may be a larger staff system that is responsible for handling the different work roles (Parson, 1999).

Eighth, successful early childhood family-school-community partnerships value and use evaluation to empower their program efforts (Kraemer, 1993). As noted by Schorr (1997) three core values emerge from evaluation in relation to having successful synergy: 1) knowing what we want to accomplish and articulating that vision to all of our partners; 2) understanding how the process is working in relation to truly helping families; and 3) gaining new ideas and perspectives on how we can strengthen our partnership effort.

Advocacy as Means to Strong Partnerships

Renewing and continually pursuing our vision within the public domain is critical to the vitality and impact of early childhood family-school-community partnerships. Advocacy is one means by which we can educate, engage, and validate our community of learners as they seek to enhance families during the early childhood years. Early childhood educators can use *personal advocacy*, *public policy advocacy*, or *private-sector advocacy* to help shape the culture toward family strengthening policies and actions (Robinson & Stark, 2002). Three examples that highlight the value of each of these advocacy types are presented in Figure 7.6:

Figure 7.6
Three Examples of Advocacy in Action

---

1) <u>Forming a study group for improving the quality of child care</u>: The author used a "study group" format within a church sponsored child care setting to advocate for improved quality. It was a personal outreach activity of mine and yet this action quickly became a church interest and indeed several quality actions were taken including better training, improved salaries and benefits, and safer and more stimulating learning environment.

2) <u>Speaking out at legislative hearings on early childhood family literacy programs</u>: In Greenville, South Carolina a family-school-community team interested in maintaining funds for their state sponsored family literacy program prepared a fact sheet on the impact their program was having on families and children and presented this at a legislative hearing in the state legislature. Through their efforts and several other advocacy groups funds were maintained for this very valuable early childhood program.

3) <u>Work-family council the result of a Comer School team initiative:</u>
One school district (a Comer School) that values parent and family
participation in a variety of school sponsored activities helped to
change area business leaders thinking about several family issues
including time for parents and family to attend conferences and
other school activities. The ultimate impact was the development
by one business of a "Work-Family Planning Council" to address
parent and family concerns in positive ways. Just one result of
this planning group was the introduction of one paid leave day for
parents or grand-parents to spend at their child's school. A small
beginning but an important step toward community participation
in building family-friendly work places.

*Advocacy is a major avenue for building community capacity for
understanding and supporting children and families* (Carnegie Corporation of New York, 1994). People are amazed at what can be accomplished
when they organize in ways that are systematic, learning-focused, and

community-driven (Robinson & Stark, 2002). <u>Systematic planning</u>
promotes a long-term thought process that usually supports partnership
efforts to re-think the manner in which things are accomplished. For
example, when quality indicators are used to review a community child
care program every person involved comes away with more knowledge
about what comprises high-quality early childhood education programs
(Garbarino, 1992).

    <u>Learning-focused</u> advocacy is driven by both the desired goals and the
idea that we will learn and grow as a result of the process (Peterson, 1992).
The idea is that to achieve our goal of nurturing children and families
during the early childhood years we have to be engaged in learning not
dictating. For example, parent and citizen leadership training for early
childhood advocacy has the powerful impact of creating a cadre of educated
citizens to promote the long-term agenda of family supporet (Hewlett &
West, 1998).

    <u>Community-driven</u> advocacy is culture-changing because it inte-
grates all of the elements essential to helping us move toward new and
life enhancing values (Parson, 1999). Most importantly, it engages us in
the dialogue so essential to shaping and reshaping our common vision of
empowered families, schools, and communities (Wheatley and Kellner-
Rogers,1998).

    Important to a community-driven early childhood partnership is a
listening, empathic, and continuously renewing approach (Covey, 1998).
Through community education and engagement all of us become more
committed to an early childhood agenda for building caring and competent citizens. Regardless of the kind of advocacy we engage in, Robinson
and Stark (2002, p. 110) remind us that "it is important for all of us who

touch the lives of children to do all we can to educate the American public about the needs of children and the social and moral responsibility of our society to care for children. Our children's cries will continue to go unheard unless we stand up for them. Children can't do it themselves – they are counting on us."

An advocacy agenda must include the common elements that we know optimize the talents of children, parents, and family (Brazelton & Greenspan, 2000; Carnegie Corporation of New York, 1994; Hewlett & West, 1998; Stronge & Reed-Victor, 2000; Swick & Graves, 1993):

* Safe, secure, and enriching neighborhood/community environments.

* Family-strengthening work and community places and practices.

* Comprehensive accessible and affordable prenatal care and support.

* High-quality medical and health care and education for parents and families.

* Family-friendly work practices and policies such as family leave time, flex time, banking of hours for family needs, and creative business-school-family time for collaborative planning.

* Safe, affordable, and family-supportive housing arrangements.

* High quality child care that is affordable and available for all families in need.

* Extended-hours and summer enrichment programs that enhance learning and strengthen families.

* Early learning and education programs that link "families" from preschool to the formal school years in successful and enjoyable ways.

* Community development and planning teams that are focused on crafting and continually renewing early childhood family-school-community partnerships.

Family-school partnerships can be effective when communities support and enhance this partnership effort. A learning community implies that every citizen views the healthy functioning of families and schools as their responsibility. Community education programs aim to empower people of all ages to carry out their responsibility in empowering children and families through quality educational programs. We need strong community participation, business and industry involvement, and continuing parent-teacher advocacy to create the needed environment for promoting quality children and citizens.

SUMMATIVE DISCUSSION OF APPLICATION POINTS:

Early childhood partnerships are only as viable as the community empowerment that exists within the relationships of families – schools- and communities. A "learning community" is a place where people show their ongoing care for children and families (and their helpers) through concrete actions and through continuous learning and growth experiences. Building community education, using advocacy, and fostering strong community involvement are foundation elements but they bring to the big picture the following applications:

1) New ideas and resources to strengthen early childhood family-school programs.

2) Nurture the citizens to understand and act to help strengthen the quality of life for children and families.

3) Revitalize schools through the availability of a plethora of community resources.

4) Parents and teachers are strengthened by the support resources they receive citizens – it empowers them to care more for the children they serve as well as the families.

5) Validation occurs in all of the interacting relationships that are teaming to create a true and meaningful partnership.

References

Boyer, E. (1991). Ready to learn: A mandate for the nation. Princeton, NJ: The Carnegie Foundation for the Advancement of Teaching.

Brazelton, T., & Greenspan, S. (2000). The irreducible needs of children. Cambridge, MA: Perseus.

Brizius, J., & Foster, S. (1993). Generation to generation: Realizing the promise of family literacy. Ypsilanti, MI: High Scope Press.

Carnegie Corporation of New York. (1994). Starting points: Meeting the needs of our youngest children. New York: Carnegie Corporation of New York.

Chen, M. (2002). The virtual mentor: Business professionals go online with students. In M. Chen. (Ed.). Edutopia: Success stories for learning in the digital age. San Francisco, CA: Jossey-Bass.

Comer, J (1997). Waiting for a miracle: Why schools can't solve our problems – and how we can. New York: Dutton.

Comer, J. (2001). Schools that develop children. The American Prospect, 12 (7), 3-12.

Couchenour, D., & Chrisman, K. (2000). Families, schools, and communities: Together for young children. New York: Delmar.

Covey, S. (1998). The ideal community. In F. Hesselbein, M. Goldsmith,

R. Beckhard, & R. Schubert. (Eds.). <u>The community of the future</u>. San Francisco, CA: Jossey-Bass.

Diffily, D., & Morrison, K. (Eds.). (1996). <u>Family-friendly communication for early childhood programs</u>. Washington, DC: National Association for the Education of Young Children.

Diss, R., & Buckley, P. (2005). <u>Developing family and community involvement skills through case studies and field experiences</u>. Columbus, OH: Pearson.

Eisler, R. (2000). <u>Tomorrow's children: A blueprint for partnership education in the 21st century</u>. Boulder, CO: Westview Press.

Folbre, N. (2001). <u>The invisible heart: Economics and family values</u>. New York: The New Press.

Galinsky, E. (1999). <u>Ask the children: What America's children really think about working parents</u>. New York: William Morrow and Company.

Garbarino, J. (1992). <u>Children and families in the social environment. Second Edition</u>. New York: Aldine de Gruyter.

Gaudiani, C. (1998). Wisdom as capital in prosperous communities. In F. Hesselbein, M. Goldsmith, R. Beckhard, & R. Schubert. (Eds.). <u>The community of the future</u>. San Francisco, CA: Jossey-Bass.

Gonzalez-Mena, J., & Eyer, D. (2001). <u>Infants, toddlers, and caregivers. Fifth Edition</u>. Mountain View, CA: Mayfield.

Hewlett, S. (1991). <u>When the bough breaks: The costs of neglecting our children</u>. New York: Basic Books.

Hewlett, S., & West, C. (1998). <u>The war against parents: What can we do for America's beleaguered moms and dads</u>. Boston: Houghton Mifflin.

Heymann, J. (2000). <u>The widening gap: Why America's working families are in jeopardy and what can be done about it</u>. New York: Basic Books.

Jehl, J. (2007). <u>Connecting schools, families, and communities</u>. Baltimore, MD: The Anne Casey Foundation.

Judkins, D., et al. (2008). <u>A study of classroom literacy interventions and outcomes in Even Start</u>. Washington, DC: U.S. Department of Education

Karr-Morse, R., & Wiley, M. (1997). <u>Ghosts from the nursery: Tracing the roots of violence</u>. New York: The Atlantic Monthly Press.

Kraemer, J. (1993). <u>Building villages to raise our children: Collaboration</u>. Cambridge, MA: Harvard Family Research Project.

Meier, D. (2002). <u>In schools we trust: Creating communities of learning in an era of testing and standardization</u>. Boston: Beacon Press.

Morse, S. (1998). Five building blocks for successful communities. In F. Hesselbein, M. Goldsmith, R. Beckhard, & R. Schubert. (Eds.). <u>The community of the future</u>. San Francisco, CA: Jossey-Bass.

Nunez, R., & Collignon, K. (2000). Supporting family learning: Building a community of learners. In J. Stronge & E. Reed-Victor. (Eds.). <u>Educating homeless students: Promising practices</u>. Larchmont, NY: Eye on Education.

Parson, S. (1999). <u>Transforming schools into community learning centers</u>. Larchmont, NY: Eye on Education.

Peterson, R. (1992). <u>Life in a crowded place: Making a learning community</u>. Portsmouth, NH: Heinemann.

Powell, D. (1998). <u>Reweaving parents into the fabric of early childhood programs</u>. Washington, DC: National Association for the Education of Young Children.

Robinson, A., & Stark, D. (2002). <u>Advocates in action: Making a difference for young children</u>. Washington, DC: National Association for the Education of Young Children.

Sergiovanni, T. (1996). <u>Leadership for the schoolhouse: How is it different? Why is it important?</u> San Francisco, CA: Jossey-Bass.

Schorr, L. (1997). <u>Common purpose: Strengthening families and neighborhoods to rebuild America</u>. New York: Anchor Books Doubleday.

Stronge, J., & Reed-Victor, E. (Eds.). (2000). <u>Educating homeless students: Promising practices</u>. Larchmont, NY: Eye on Education.

Swick, K. (1991). <u>Teacher-parent partnerships to enhance school success in early childhood education</u>. Washington, DC: National Education Association.

Swick, K. (1993). <u>Strengthening parents and families during the early childhood years</u>. Champaign, IL: Stipes.

Swick, K. (1997). A family-school approach for nurturing caring in young children. <u>Early Childhood Education Journal</u>, 25 (2), 151-154.

Swick, K. (2004). <u>Empowering parents, families, schools, and communities during the early childhood years</u>. Champaign, IL: Stipes.

Swick, K., & Graves, S. (1993). <u>Empowering at-risk families during the early childhood years</u>. Washington, DC: National Education Association.

Swick, K., Grafwallner, R., Cockey, M., & Barton, P. (1998). Parents as leaders in nurturing family-school involvement. <u>Contemporary Education</u>, 70 (1), 47-50.

The Council of Chief State School Officers. (1999). <u>Early Childhood and Family Education</u>. Washington, DC: The Council.

Thornton, A. (2001). (Ed.). <u>The well-being of children and families: Research and data needs</u>. Ann Arbor, MI: The University of Michigan Press.

Tucker, P. (2000). Enhancing collaboration on behalf of homeless students: Strategies for local and state educational agencies. In J. Stronge & E. Reed-Victor. (Eds.). <u>Educating homeless students: Promising practices</u>. Larchmont, NY: Eye on Education.

Wheatley, M., & Kellner-Rogers, M. (1998). The paradox and promise of community. In F. Hesselbein, M. Goldsmith, R. Beckhard, & R. Schubert. (Eds.). <u>The community of the future</u>. San Francisco, CA: Jossey-Bass.

Wright, K., Stegelin, D., & Hartle, L. (2007). <u>Building family, school, and community partnerships</u>. Columbus, OH: Pearson.

Chapter Eight
Resources for Strengthening and Renewing Family-School-Community Involvement/Partnerships

---

CAPSULE: Parents, early childhood educators, and other family helpers renew their knowledge and skills most effectively when they use diverse resources and materials for their learning and growth needs. Continuous learning is needed to re-energize the involvement with new ideas and strategies for strengthening every aspect of the partnership process. The use of local talent in this process is particularly empowering.

Chapter Eight Objectives:

1) Strengthen your understanding of the need for family-school-community partners to renew and improve the various dimensions of their partnership.

2) Enhance your knowledge of and skills for using early childhood professional and child/family advocacy associations for renewing and strengthening the partnership in which you are engaged.

3) Strengthen your skills in using early childhood education professional journals to better inform your work with parents, families, and communities.

4) Gain insight into available local and state resources on partnership work and ideas for using them to strengthen family-school-community partnerships.

5) Strengthen your skills for more effectively using various resources to enhance and improve your effectiveness in developing and enhancing family-school-community partnerships.

Many early childhood family-community partnerships experience the loss of direction and energy because they fail to renew their commitments to each other and to ongoing learning (Eisler, 2000). As noted in the previous chapter, family involvement must be linked to a "community of learners" process. In this chapter we examine the rationale for this renewal process, explicate professional and child/family resources helpful in this effort, identify professional/technical journals as well as community/state level resources, and share two case examples of how the renewal process might work.

The Involvement / Partnership Process Needs Continual Renewal

Families, early childhood programs, and communities have at least one attribute in common: they are always in the process of changing. They achieve a sense of equilibrium and they are quickly swept up in some facet of change. Thus, as they seek to help each other through meaningful partnerships, families, schools, and communities, must continually renew and strengthen themselves as learners (Hesselbein, Goldsmith, Beckhard, & Schubert, 1998). Only if we are learning and growing can we contribute in significant ways to the partnership.

Why does the resource strengthening process work? As early childhood partners explore and use new resources such as literature from professional journals, they gain new insights relative to their purpose and functions. In addition, when all of the partners are involved in using these resources the "culture" of the partnership is transformed into a learning endeavor (Parson, 1999). These renewal efforts work because people have an opportunity to reflect, refine, and then improve the work of their partnership. For example, Garbarino and Bedard (2001) note:

> We don't know everything. We don't understand everything. Our own parenting is far from perfect. We know that, and our kids certainly know that. But if we can all cultivate mindfulness as we analyze and contemplate the imperfections of all families, all parents, all children, we will be ready to move forward – even with our imperfect understanding – as members of a caring community to relieve parents under siege, to replace blame, guilt, and the shame with acceptance, support, and compassion. (p. 211)

How does the resource strengthening process work? The resource strengthening process is most effective when partnership groups relate their needs to specific resources that can further enhance their efforts (Fetterman, Kaftarian, & Wandersman, 1996). For example, one early childhood program noted that parents were concerned about the parent-teacher conference situation. Parents had noted three areas they were concerned with:

1) Conferences were often held at times very inconvenient for them.

2) Most of the conference time was devoted to "teacher talk."

3) Very little follow-up happened after the conference was completed.

This program team could use these parent concerns to guide their gathering and use of resources to strengthen and refine their family-school-community partnership efforts. The following are just two possibilities for planning meaningful renewal activities.

1) Organize staff and parent programs that provide information, resources, and skills for enhancing the conferencing aspect of the partnership.

2) Engage parents and teachers in discussions on the various specifics of the organization and use of conferences. What are the best times for people? What do parents and teachers see as the most important elements of the conference? These and other questions can be helpful in establishing ways to renew our work with families.

Strategies for encouraging partnerships to use renewal resources: The most common complaint parents, teachers, and others involved in partnership work claim is that of being just too busy to really engage in meaningful professional and personal renewal activities (Springate & Stegelin, 1999). How do we encourage parents and teachers to engage in this work of? Five strategies are noted and briefly reviewed (Swick, Da Ros, & Kovach, 2001):

1) Build into the culture of the partnership the expectation for continued learning and growth.

2) Offer many different types of learning opportunities where parents and teachers share in joint ownership of their work.

3) Link activities to specific needs and issues the family-school-community partners are experiencing.

4) Organize resources and activities so that the partners can get easy access and have ample time and opportunity to use them.

5) Get feedback from the partners on how effective the renewal resources and activities are in relation to solving their concerns and issues.

Additional strategies include the use of electronic resources that can be easily accessed and are pertinent to the kinds of issues people face.

For example, many web sites, electronic research sites, and other media resources provide easy access through association memberships. It is important to keep these electronic sources current or they become simple tools of little value to the team. In other cases, print libraries are helpful when updated regularly and housed in a place where faculty and parents can easily use them.

Six types of delivery schemes also enhance the involvement of partners in the important work of renewal and improvement (Parson, 1999):

* Study groups: Parent-teacher study groups are effective in reviewing particular issues such as examining the relevance of homework or the most effective use of home visits. Such groups usually select a topic of need, "study" the topic, and determine a new course of action if needed. It is important to help "study groups" capture their expertise too. Local wisdom is often more powerful and relevant than ten studies conducted in a locale or context / culture that has little in common with the community (Klein & Chen, 2001). Research findings do help but in many cases they need to be interrelated with local issues, needs, and cultural rituals.

* Workshops: Parent-teacher workshops have proven especially helpful in enhancing the communication skills of parents and teachers. In addition, workshops are useful in providing new information for parents, teachers, and citizens on a variety of topics: school needs, new curriculum efforts, discipline issues, and many other issues. Workshops are most effective when guided by a specific purpose, strongly influenced by parental leadership, facilitated by people with effective communication skills, and supported with resources that are well-researched, accurate, and culturally diverse in perspectives and strategies (Couchenour & Chrisman, 2000).

* Electronic / Distance Education: A variety of distance education venues can be used to inform, engage, and renew parents and teachers. For examples:
  - Video packages on new school policies sent to each home in the district.
  - Live interactive television (closed circuit) programs that aim to inform and engage parents and/or teachers in learning about new policies or strategies for family involvement.
  - Using the school's website to inform parents and others of new program development and needs.

* Focus Groups: While the intent of focus groups is often on

research, they also offer a unique way of learning about each other's views on a variety of learning and educational issues. For example, one teacher uses annual focus groups with parents to determine the most desired forms of communication to use that specific year. She also uses the focus group to gain parent feedback on the major concerns they have for their children's school performance. These groups can also inform our selection and use of strategies and delivery systems. For example, the author found one group of parents were reticent to be home-visited because they felt too visible and enjoyed the camaraderie and closeness offered by group programs.

* Credit / Non-Credit Courses: Today's parents and teachers are interested in learning the various aspects of their involvement process. A course of study on parent and family involvement might strengthen the understanding of the partners regarding how the process can be most effective.

* Evaluation / Improvement Studies: Too often evaluation is used only to "judge" the quality of a program. But its most important contribution is in helping us be learners in continually refining how our partnership contributes to the total learning and educational process.

CASE APPLICATION: Identify and briefly discuss three strategies you would use to engage family-school-community partners in renewing their skills and perspectives for having effective and meaningful partnerships. How would you gain the "voices" of parents and citizens on their thoughts relative to program work?

Professional Associations as Sources of Strength and Renewal

There are several early childhood education professional associations that provide materials, activities, and related resources for helping families, schools, communities, teachers and parents renew and empower their skills for being effective partners. I have identified three major professional associations as examples of the types of groups and activities available to us in the field of early childhood education.

In reviewing the association information shared in Figure 8.1, relate this information to how you can enhance your skills and those of the parents and families you work with. It is also important to reflect on the various possibilities you and your partners can create through your engagement with professional groups. For example, as you learn about these associations, explore ways the materials might be synthesized or otherwise integrated into articles or newsletters for parents. Also, examine how the materials might be used to create regular abstracts for local news media outlets. Should you be a full-time student, take note that each of these associations have reduced fees for student members.

Figure 8.1
Examples of Professional Associations as
Sources of Strength and Renewal

National Association for the Education of Young Children

1509 16th St., NW, Washington, DC 20036-1426

Phone: 800-424-2460   Fax: 202-328-1846

Website: < www.naeyc.org >

Journals: Young Children, Early Childhood Research Quarterly
Journal of Early Childhood Teacher Education

Education/Training: Offers an annual conference, leadership training institutes, regional programs, specialty publications, accreditation guidelines/process, and other information on family empowerment. Excellent materials on parent-teacher and family-school-community partnership building.

Association for Childhood Education International

17904 Georgia Avenue, Suite 215, Olney, MD 20832

Phone: 301-570-2111 Fax: 301-570-2212

Website: < www.acei.org >

Journals: Childhood Education,
Journal of Research in Childhood Education

Education/Training: Provides annual conference and periodic leadership and research/development programs. Specialty publications target areas like parent and family involvement. Superb support structure and helping-system for professionals and parents/families/communities.

Southern Early Childhood Association

8500 W. Markham, Ste. 105, Little Rock, AR 72215-5930

Phone: 501-221-1648   Fax: 501-227-5297

Website: www.southernearlychildhood.org

Journal: Dimensions of Early Childhood

Education/Training: Offers an annual conference, leadership training, special training on curriculum, administration of programs, and offers excellent support resources.

Each of these early childhood professional associations have state affiliate chapters and some have local or within state / regional set-ups. They aim to foster renewal and continual learning among all people who are focused on serving and strengthening children and families. Here are five suggestions to effectively use these professional groups. Use the case application at the end of this section to sharpen your skills in using professional early childhood associations:

1) Identify important growth needs you believe would strengthen you and your partnership team. Use these needs as a guidance process for directing the partnership renewal work.

2) Inquire with the professional association on gaining overview literature so you can learn about the specifics of the group. Does the work of this group relate to your goals? What areas do you see the different associations focusing on in terms of helping you meet your professional goals?

3) Join the professional association(s) that best matches your goals. Relate your group's growth needs to the various resources available in the professional group. Also join other associations to broaden the knowledge and perspectives of the group.

4) Start a professional and parent/family/citizen library based on but not limited to the journals and materials available in the association(s).

5) Sponsor study groups that organize and use the materials and resources to solve problems and to address their skills and understanding of the partnership process.

CASE APPLICATON: Select one early childhood professional association and acquire all needed information for educating others about this group. Use the information to prepare an information orientation on this association for others in your group. Key points to emphasize in your presentation: membership information, emphases in the associations' work, journals and booklets available, electronic sources and contacts, and related materials that emphasize family-school-community partnerships.

Child and Family Advocacy Associations that Strengthen the Renewal Process

Advocacy work on behalf of children, parents, and families is renewing and supportive of our efforts to advance the quality of life for everyone in the community (Eisler, 2000). It is renewing in the sense that we gain new perspectives on how we can make a difference in the lives of children and parents while also enhancing our understanding of the needs of children and parents. Further, parents, other family, and early childhood educators agree that active engagement in empowering children's lives also educates the hearts and minds of those engaged (Pahl, 2000).

Several associations and groups offer very helpful and engaging resources that aim to increase the quality of life for children, parents, families, and early childhood professionals. A sampling of these associations and groups are noted as follows:

National Child Care Information Center
U.S. Department of Health and Human Services
Washington, DC
Website:
Resources and Activities: A part of the U.S. Department of Health and Human Services, the NCCIC offers information, links to various electronic information sources like ERIC, information on Health Child Care America, and parent and family involvement strategies.

National Coalition for Parent Involvement in Education
Website:
The NCPIE mission is to advocate the involvement of parents and families in the education of their children while also strengthening parents' in their skills to be family leaders. They represent families through their advocacy and provide activities like conferences and resources on legislative actions.

The National Association for Family Child Care
5202 Pinemont Drive
Salt Lake City, Utah 84123
Phone: 801-269-9338   Fax: 801-268-9507
Website: <www.nafcc.org>
The NAFCC seeks to improve the quality of family child care through holding periodic conferences, developing needed standards, providing resources like a newsletter, information sheets, and policy making activities. The association also is excellent in helping groups network with each other.

Council for Exceptional Children (CEC)
1110 North Glebe Road, Suite 300, Arlington, VA 22201
Phone: 703-620-3660   Fax: 703-264-9494
Website: <www.cec.sped.org>
The CEC is dedicated to meeting the needs of children with special needs and supporting professionals and families who work with children with special needs. Several parent and family materials that focus on relating to parents of children with special needs are available. Over 15 divisions of the CEC have materials and support resources for parents and professionals as they build early childhood partnerships.

National Parent Teacher Association (National PTA)
330 N Wabash Avenue, Suite 2100
Chicago, IL 60611
Phone: 312-670-6782 Fax: 312-670-6783
Website: <www.pta.org>
The National PTA seeks to support and speak on behalf of children and youth, and to assist parents and families in developing the skills needed to be effective in their various roles. They also offer many resources in their journal, publications, and support resources that do empower parents and early childhood professionals.

National Black Child Development Institute
1101 15th St., NW, Suite 900
Washington, DC 2005
Phone: 202-833-2220
Website: <www.nbcdi.org>
Provides resources and support on various projects to advance the skills of African American parents and the professionals who support them. The institute provides training, periodic workshops, research findings, and resulting publics on various aspects of the family involvement and empowerment process.

Children's Defense Fund
25 E St. NW, Washington, DC 20001
Phone: 202-628-8787
Website: <www.childrensdefense.org>
The CDF advocates for improvements in quality of life indicators for all children and families. Included in this process are conferences, research based publications, advocacy work, policy development, awareness activities, and various special activities that are related to particular child and families like health insurance and chronic poverty.

*Educational Resources Information Center on Elementary and Early Childhood Education (ERIC * EECE)*
University of Illinois
Champaign, IL 61820-7469
Website: <http://ericeece.org>
Provides comprehensive information data base on research and development on all aspects of early childhood education including data on parent and family issues and involvement efforts and strategies.

Megaskills
Phone: 202-466-3633
Website: <www.megaskills.org>
Offers many resources for parents and professionals to use in supporting children early learning of the skills they need for school and life success. Materials are updated regularly on the website.

I Am Your Child
Website: <www.iamyourchild.org>
Provides excellent videotapes of parent education information on topics such as child care, school readiness, pregnancy, and other topics. The website offers details on acquiring these videos an accompanying booklets. Very inexpensive and useful for parenting groups as well as for early childhood professional renewal work.

National Education Association (NEA)
1201 16th St., NW
Washington, DC 20036
Website: <www.nea.org>
Offers several publications on parent and family involvement and on parent-teacher and family-school relationships. Excellent library of materials on parenting and parent and family issues.

National Head Start Association
1220 King
Alexandria, VA 22314
Website: <www.headstart.org>
Provides many helpful resources that support the education and involvement of parents and families. Also has excellent training materials for use with early childhood professionals related to developing strong partnerships with the parents, families, and communities.

Parents as Teachers (PAT) National Center
Website: <www.patnc.org>
Excellent source on the training, materials, and resources that comprise the National Parents as Teacher parent education support program.

As you review the above sources of information and support on child and family advocacy keep in mind that many additional groups and associations exist. Each group provides information and perspectives that can enrich and strengthen your partnership work. In selecting the association(s) you wish to contact keep in mind your goals and needs as well as how the association might help you gain new skills and perspectives. Use the following case application to apply this process to your work.

CASE APPLICATION: In partnership with some of your colleagues or students, identify a growth activity all of you sense as a need to help be more effective in your involvement efforts. Then select one of the child and family groups noted above and contact them for needed information. Now, how does the information inform your work – how are you more able to implement your group's goals? Using the Web find an agency or group that supports your goals.

Professional and Technical Journals that Strengthen the Renewal Process

Professional and technical journals offer a plethora of resources that bring new knowledge, ideas, perspectives, and research/development frameworks to the issues in family-school-community partnerships. Figure 8.2 lists some of the more noted journals in early childhood education that address many of our parent and family involvement and collaboration renewal and growth needs:

Figure 8.2
Sample Listing of Professional/Technical Journals

---

* Early Childhood Education Journal
* Young Children
* Childhood Education
* Early Childhood Research Quarterly
* Dimensions of Early Childhood
* Child Development
* Journal of Research in Childhood Education
* Exceptional Child
* Phi Delta Kappan
* The Clearing House
* ZERO to 3
* Black Child Advocate
* Child Care Information Exchange
* Children Today
* Child Welfare
* The Single Parent

Each journal has a particular focus. For example, *ZERO to 3* clearly focuses on the first three years of life and typically uses a theme for each issue. Parent and family education and involvement and community support are topics that receive continuing attention in the journal. Other journals have their focus too. Some journals like *Childhood Education* and the *Early Childhood Education Journal* use a combination of special topics along with a general focus section to alert readers to various issues and dynamics that relate to having strong parent-teacher and family-school-community partnerships.

Some guidelines for gaining optimal value from these and other journals are noted:

* Get a copy of the journal and study it; does it have information you value?

* Select especially good quality articles and share them with your partnership team. Do people find the articles of value?

* Target your use of journal articles so that they are helping you address specific issues and needs. We tend to reuse journals that help us solve issues and attend to growth needs.

* Create a library of journal articles that are useful so that other partners can use them in future work and renewal efforts.

CASE APPLICATION: Find an early childhood or related education/social science journal not listed in Figure 8.2. Select a useful article from this journal and relate it to a partnership need you and your team are studying. What content and ideas appear to be helpful? Share this data with your colleagues or fellow parents.

Local Community and State-Level Renewal Strategies and Resources

Resources we often overlook are the talent and support groups and agencies that are a part of our local communities. For example, one early childhood program found that in planning a leadership training program for parents and staff, one of their own partnership team had many of the needed skills to do the training. Similar stories are told every day in various communities. Likewise, community support groups are often overlooked. See Figure 8.3 for a brief listing of groups and sources of help that exist in most communities.

Figure 8.3
Sample Community Sources of Renewal and Support

---

* Education and Literacy Associations

- *   Non-Profit Groups that Support Strong Parent and Family Involvement
- *   United Way of ---- Community
- *   Business/Industry Groups
- *   Teachers/Parents/Citizens
- *   Faith-based Child and Family Groups
- *   Local School Improvement Groups

These and other support groups are usually eager to engage in efforts to strengthen family involvement and to nurture family-school partnerships. Types of support range from providing funding to offering personnel to help with training or leadership development efforts. Three examples help to show the diverse ways that local community resources can be used to empower partnerships:

EXAMPLE ONE: New challenges face the Warbon Early Childhood Center where preschool children and their families have been nurtured for over thirty years. The parent-teacher team (an advisory group that typically is very influential in shaping center policies) felt the need for "rejuvenation" as their recent efforts seemed to lack the usual positive impact on children and families. Thus, they set a goal to educate each other through a community group study series where local "experts" will provide them with the most recent data on topics like team building, communication, and partnership building.

EXAMPLE TWO: Wanda Ranish, a first grade teacher in a rural area, noted how many families were not taking care of the health needs of their families and used traditional newsletters and parent meetings to try and change this situation – with some success. But to reach the really "hard to reach" group she is engaging experienced parents along with a veteran helpers in social work and medicine to educate parents and staff on this need for better health care during the early years. She hopes to conduct school-community awareness workshops and then to have parents themselves lead parent-teacher study teams to shape more effective practices.

EXAMPLE THREE: A new "Success by Six" grant/project in a mid-size urban community is educating school administrators in knowledge and skills for enhancing family-school-community partnerships, particularly during the early childhood years. Project leaders are developing "focus group teams" inclusive of school administrators, parents, early childhood educators, and other support staff in efforts to create positive family-school-community connections. Each team will use selected readings, guest speakers, and their own skills in creating an agenda they feel will help parents and families have a good start with their children's early education.

State-level renewal resources are also excellent sources of support. State Education Departments are particularly helpful in getting current information on topics, issues, policies, and "best practices" in creating and sustaining strong partnerships as well as educating personnel to carry out programs in effective ways. For example, one rural school was able to get state consultants to speak at their parent-teacher education program. Others schools have found state education agencies able to share resources, link them to other schools who have resources they need, and assist their organizing for school improvement activities.

CASE APPLICATION: Select two issues that your partnership is facing; how could local and state supports help you renew your efforts in meaningful and positive ways? How would you suggest organizing your use of these resources? In what ways do you feel these resources might strengthen your partnership?

Two Case Examples of Family-School-Community Partnership Renewal

The case examples presented show how two early childhood education programs used the partnership renewal process to strengthen their collaborative efforts and to improve the overall program for children and families. In each case, three strategies recur and form the foundation for these partnership renewal cases: 1) articulation of needs through comprehensive involvement of the partners, 2) development of clear objectives and activities that address the real needs of the effort, and 3) on-going assessment that provides feedback for improvement.

CASE EXAMPLE ONE: Ryder Elementary School is eager to regain the confidence of parents and the community. Due to administrative turnover (three principals in two years) and low teacher morale (several teachers transferred to other schools in the district or left the district), the family involvement program has deteriorated in numbers and in the quality of the partnership's efforts. Mrs. Johnson, the new principal, has formed a parent, teacher, citizen team to brainstorm what needs to be done to renew what was once a very productive family-school-community team. She charged this small team of five people to "set forth a vision of what our partnership should be like and should be seeking to accomplish."

The team's work and vision: The team (two teachers, two parents, and a local business leader) did represent the culturally diverse population and agreed to work during the summer of 2000. Five meetings were held during which the team called in over 70 people including teachers, administrators, parents, citizens, and children. Focus groups, interviews, and informal chat sessions produced three guiding elements to the ultimate vision: 1) re-develop a school infrastructure that provides continuing stability to the effort (including hiring a part-or-full time family-school-community director), 2) focus on the common desire of everyone to provide children with the highest quality of education possible, and 3) nurture parent leaders to help develop a strong and positive involvement process.

The visioning team reported their results to the principal and suggested that a day long retreat (including parents and family members) be used to create the structure needed for putting this vision to work. Mrs. Johnson worked with two teachers and a parent in establishing a Fall of 2000 "family involvement planning day." It was designed to be hands-on and to lay the foundation for a more detailed project to be presented to the parent-teacher association.

The family involvement planning day: This work day proved to be a key step in shaping the future of the school's family-school-community partnership effort. A former parent-teacher association parent leader gave the opening talk and told the group that they should emphasize some common goals that are doable and that aim to create the best learning situation for the children and their families.

Four teams were then formed (about 12 people per team) that focused on: 1) main goals of the effort, 2) needed resources, 3) desired activities, and 4) a system for getting things accomplished. The results of the day's work was noted on large chart paper which was then used to write up their overall plan of action. The plan was then organized for presentation to the Fall Parent-Teacher Association.

Family involvement PTA presentation: A teacher, parent, and the new principal presented the plan by immediately engaging parents and others in small group "needs targeting" activities. They used the results to interrelate with their work and showed how two common goals had emerged: 1) to create high quality learning experiences for all of the children, and 2) to engage parents, family, and community in joint activities to achieve goal 1.

The presentation then outlined specific ways to achieve these goals and to broaden the goals to cover even more needs outlined in various reports to the group. To start the process the principal hired a half-time director to use the work of the brainstorming team and the family involvement work day in creating a plan and system to achieve a strong partnership effort.

Director organizes action themes: Project director Mary James used all of the input gained in the early process efforts and created three action themes: 1) caring things we all can do, 2) partnership activities needed, and 3) business mentors help children succeed. Each theme provided a natural venue for engaging many parents, family, teachers, and citizens. For example, all parents can do caring activities like encouraging their child, praising their child's teacher, or helping their child's teacher with an activity. Partnership activities also are potentially very effective means to strengthen parent-teacher relations and to improve the educational program.

Renewal resources used in the process: What fueled the ideas and strategies developed by the brainstorming team, those involved in the family involvement planning day, and the director's strategic efforts. Four sets of resources helped this family-school-community partnership team renew and empower themselves:

1) Personal and professional talent in the community

2) Professional association consultants (two work-day facilitators were from the local chapter of the Association for Childhood Education International)

3) Professional and technical journals and booklets

4) Local business leaders engaged in developing the mentoring facets of the program

Very important to the success of this effort was the meaningful use of these renewal resources to address specific needs and goals set by the total team involvement system. Teaming, administrative leadership, partnership efforts, and the individual facilitation of program goals – combined to form another sources of renewal energy.

Achievements in 2000/2001 and continuation plans: Two major achievements of the school's partnership effort during the initial renewal year were the launching of the action theme activities, and the initial implementation of business mentors. Local media publications have helped to motivate others to engage in these and other emerging efforts.

Continuation plans include the offering of a graduate course on parent and family involvement for teachers and other interested people in the summer of 2002. In addition, the original brainstorming team met during the summer of 2002 to review progress, assist the new director of family-school-community partnerships, and to offer additional suggestions for furthering the goals of the project.

Action Item for YOU: Now that you have reviewed this brief description of one school's partnership renewal efforts, what suggestions would you share with them as they begin to enter year two of their programs?

1)_____

2)_____

3)_____

4)_____

5)_____

CASE EXAMPLE TWO: The previous community Head Start Center closed two years ago because the community lost confidence in what was happening at the Center. A nearby university was asked to help reinvent the Chopin Head Start Center and to assist a local Community Action group in creating the needed partnership infrastructure to sustain this program for preschool children and their families.

Professor Robert Wendlin was appointed to re-develop and to then temporarily direct the center toward healthy beginnings. Central to this process in Wendlin's mind was the formation and renewal of the family-center-community Head Start partnership team. Thus, his initial focus was on organizing this team so that it comprised representative from all parts of the community. While the Head Start project served preschool children in high-risk situations and their families, he realized that everyone in the community needed to "own" the program. Thus his early efforts included:

* Surveying members of the previous Head Start team and parents and staff of the former program as well as visiting local churches and civic groups.

* Announcing and then holding a "town meeting" on the re-development of the Head Start program. A good turnout of people helped establish that the need still existed and that "program quality" not local politics should guide the renewal process.

* Establishing an advisory team comprised of parents, staff, and citizens from all parts of the community. An executive board of members on the advisory team provided a needed structure for getting things done. This three member team had the former director (people respected her and realized she was a victim of some situations beyond her control), a very respected banker, and a mother who agreed to serve as "parent leader" until the project was fully operational.

* Planning (with the advisory team) "educational days" that emphasized the elements of high quality Head Start as well as strategies for achieving these elements. These "educational days" included consultant/facilitators, small group discussions (based on reading packets), and outcome planning sheets the groups completed to provide the program with direction. Three educational days were held: one in a conference room at a local bank, one in the town library, and one in a church that also agreed to house the new center.

Family-school-community partnership team formed: Emerging from the advisory team work and the "educational days" was the development of a formal partnership team. This team engaged in five processes to support their re-development of the Head Start effort:

1) Continuing educational involvement to enlighten themselves about quality early childhood programs and related family-community engagement strategies.

2) Conducting weekly (and in many cases twice a week) meetings to outline, plan, review, and then act on the need for a strong partnership effort in the creation of the new Head Start.

3) Researching all of the local perspectives about "What will make for a healthy and high quality program?"

4) Collation of these perspectives into an action plan that addressed all facets of the program: purpose, goals, space and facilities, staff and funding, materials and resources, recruitment, and many other elements.

5) Implementation of the plan with the goal of opening the program for children and families within the year.

Local church becomes primary sponsor and houses the program: Because the poor facility was a major cause for closing the earlier center, the local Lutheran church agreed to be the primary sponsor in terms of housing the program and offering every possible support. The university agreed to sponsor the program and be the main administrative and program management team until the community action group felt secure in taking over the project. The partnership team set about the tasks of cleaning the facility, which had been a home for the church school activities but not in use for several years, planning how the facility should be re-developed, contracting to get the facility in order, initiating all program and staff hiring activities, and conducting continuing self-review of their work.

Partnership team establishes quality indicators through various renewal and development activities: The recurring message in the partnership team's work was, " be sure to have a quality program." Thus, their early work on all aspects of the Head Start effort was to learn about and then establish guidelines for quality. The team used booklets from the National Association for the Education of Young Children, consultants from the regional education center, university faculty, visits to other centers, and their own expertise in shaping four guidelines:

1) All staff must meet appropriate educational and certification criteria for working in an early childhood education program.

2) Parents and citizens must be engaged in all aspects of the development of the Head Start center and program.

3) Facility and materials must provide a safe, secure, and enriching learning environment for the children.

4) Continuing evaluation of the program culminating in an annual evaluation report to the partnership team will provide the system for assuring refinements and improvements.

<u>Early results and continuing development efforts</u>: The Head Start program is now in operation and is operating according to the quality guidelines the team established through their renewal work. Early indications are that the community and parents as well as staff are pleased with the program's development. Continuing efforts are focusing on increasing staff to be able to serve more children and to offer current staff continuing education opportunities. The university, the partnership team, and the community action group are crafting a transition plan for the action group to take over during the next year.

Action Item for YOU: What would you do differently than the Head Start partnership team? Why? How would you do the renewal and re-development process? What strengths of their effort would you keep and why? What areas of concern do you have and why?

_____

_____

_____

_____

SUMMATIVE DISCUSSION OF APPLICATION POINTS:

Family-school-community partnerships are only as effective as their engagement in renewal and growth activities. As shown in this chapter, the renewal process is most effective when it is guided by systematic and intentional needs assessment and collaborative learning and sharing by the partners. During the early childhood years this effort is critical because child and family needs are constantly changing and in many cases highly stressful. Thus, the partnership team must have insight into the process and how they can use it for promoting the well-being of everyone involved.

Important to having successful partnership renewal and growth efforts are the following application points:

* Develop a plan that is grounded in clear and important needs as adopted by the team.

* Use a variety of professional and community resources to assist you and the team in your continuing education efforts.
* Target local community resources that can be easily deployed and add local credibility and "ownership" to the process.
* Use parent leadership strategies that help parents and family in becoming the guiding forces in the partnership work.
* Review the renewal process regularly and refine it so that you and the team are gaining the needed support.

References

Couchenour, D., & Chrisman, K. (2000). <u>Families, schools, and communities: Together for young children</u>. New York: Delmar.

Eisler, R. (2000). <u>Tomorrow's children: A blueprint for partnership education in the 21st century</u>. Boulder, CO: Westview Press.

Fetterman, D., Kaftarian, S., & Wandersman, A. (1996). <u>Empowerment evaluation: Knowledge and tools for self-assessment and accountability</u>. Thousand Oaks, CA: Sage.

Garbarino, J., & Bedard, C. (2001). <u>Parents under siege</u>. New York: The Free Press.

Hesselbein, F., Goldsmith, M., Beckhard, R., & Schubert, R. (1998). <u>The community of the future</u>. San Francisco, CA: Jossey-Bass.

Klein, M., & Chen, D. (2001). <u>Working with children from diverse backgrounds</u>. New York: Delmar.

Pahl, R. (2000). <u>On friendship</u>. Malden, MA: Blackwell Publishers.

Parson, S. (1999). <u>Transforming schools into community learning centers</u>. Larchmont, NY: Eye on Education.

Springate, K., & Stegelin, D. (1999). <u>Building school and community partnerships through parent involvement</u>. Columbus, OH: Merrill / Prentice Hall.

Swick, K., Da Ros, D., & Kovach, B. (2001). Empowering parents and family through a caring inquiry approach. <u>Early Childhood Education Journal</u>, 29 (1), 65-71.